LIVING
DOCTRINES
of the
NEW
TESTAMENT

H. D. McDONALD
D.D.(Lond.), Ph.D.(Lond.)

LONDON
PICKERING & INGLIS LTD.
1971

DEDICATED to HER of the INNER and THOSE
of the OUTER CIRCLE

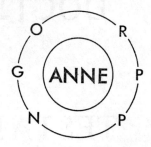

PICKERING & INGLIS LTD.

29 LUDGATE HILL, LONDON, E.C.4
26 BOTHWELL STREET, GLASGOW, C.2

ISBN 0 7208 0201 6
Cat. No. 01/1206

Printed in Great Britain by
Northumberland Press Limited, Gateshead

CONTENTS

3

FOREWORD

It is with pleasure that I accept the invitation to write a short foreword to Dr. McDonald's latest book. True, a good book does not need a foreword like this (just as a bad book does not deserve one), and an experienced author and theologian like Dr. McDonald has already secured a discriminating public who eagerly welcome something fresh from his pen. But since the structure of *Living Doctrines of the New Testament* is largely exegetical, it may be thought appropriate for it to be introduced and commended by one whose main business in life is the teaching and practice of New Testament exegesis. To treat the doctrines of the Bible in general, or of the New Testament in particular, on one uniform level in the older systematic way tends to obscure the individuality of the writers in thought, language and other respects. Dr. McDonald's way is much more fruitful: he examines the contributions of separate authors (like Paul or the writer to the Hebrews) or of groups of authors who in considerable measure share a common viewpoint (like the Synoptic Evangelists) and expounds the leading doctrines presented in the various documents or groups of documents. In this way he covers the whole range of Biblical theology, and covers it in context. Having read these pages with personal enjoyment and profit, I am happy to commend them both to readers who have already learned to appreciate Dr. McDonald's work and to those who here come to know him as an author for the first time.

F. F. BRUCE

There are many ways of writing a New Testament theology, and each has its own number of advocates. Some, for example, regard the chronological, and others, the thematic approach as the most satisfactory. And in the fulfilment of their self-chosen method have put many students of the New Testament in their debt. For what is of supreme importance is, after all, not the method by which the New Testament is approached but the message which the New Testament contains.

For our own part we have decided to take the New Testament material just as it has been brought together for us. This procedure will, we hope, be of most help to the general reader and the beginner student for whom the present volume is specially written. At the same time, we have not been unmindful of the needs of the preacher and the teacher. We have sought to provide material which may be useful to them in their important work as servants of the Word of God. Yet while following the sacred literature as it has come down to us, we have singled out in the larger groups of writings, the Four Gospels and the Epistles of Paul, certain themes for more general treatment. In this way it will be easier for the reader to grasp what the Synoptic Gospels or the Apostle Paul teaches regarding a particular topic. It seems proper, too, to mention, that in discussing the doctrine of the Person of Christ we have drawn in a limited measure on our JESUS-HUMAN and DIVINE.

A special word of thanks is due to the Rev. George Carey, B.D., M.Th., Lecturer in Christian Doctrine at St. John's College, Nottingham, for undertaking, in the midst of his teaching programme and preparation of a Doctoral thesis, the responsibility of correcting the proofs. In so doing he has relieved the author of a burdensome task. Our gratitude must also be recorded to Professor F. F. Bruce who gave time, out of his busy literary and teaching schedule, to read the manuscript and write a Foreword. His words of commendation are greatly appreciated.

H. D. McDonald

'I have become somewhat impatient of those who regard "ortho-dox" as a term of abuse, as if no thinking man could profess the same faith as his fathers.'

Nathanael Micklem, *What is the Faith?* p. 17.

'...this intellectual love of Christian truth, which should be found especially in the *teachers* of the church, is inseparable from a personal experience of Christian truth.'

H. Martensen, *Christian Dogmatics*, p. 2.

'The truth of the Christian faith is the truth of a faith, or way of life which shows itself true by authenticating itself for those who live it ... There is more to faith than assent to propositions; but to allow there is more is not to disallow that assent to proposi-tions has its place in faith.'

Donald Mackinnon, *Borderlands of Theology*, p. 82.

'Our understanding of the possibility of knowledge of God can only carry us up to a penultimate, never to an ultimate, point, for it belongs to the very nature of the object we are concerned to know that we are unable to make our knowing of it comprehensible as *our* action, or therefore as a possibility of *ours* ... This is to say, it is through the gift of His Spirit to us and by the presence and power of the Spirit, that we are enabled to share in the know-ledge of God accessible to us in Jesus Christ.'

T. F. Torrance, *Theological Science*, p. 52.

'Theology is not a complex system constructed for their own enter-tainment by scholars in the quiet retreat of their ivory towers. It must have a significance for the unquiet times; but it can achieve its proper relevance only in obedient attentiveness, not to the times first of all, but to the Word.'

G. C. Berkoüwer, *Faith and Justification*, p. 9.

'If we do not approach the Bible from the standpoint of the church, we do so from the standpoint of some world view. There is no third possibility such as neutrality without presuppositions.'

Ernst Kinder, in *Kerygma and History*, ed. and transl.
Braaten and Harrisville, pp. 66, 67.

THE
FOUR
GOSPELS

1

God

THE SYNOPTIC GOSPELS

The gospel records make clear that, in line with the whole Old Testament, Jesus never sought to prove the existence of God. He never argued for His reality. For Jesus God was not even a presupposition for faith whose actuality would give rationality to world order and sanction to moral duty. To Jesus God was immediately real. Yet what He did say about God makes evident that He was heir to the 'ethical monotheism' of the Old Testament, although even then such ideas were enriched by His own living awareness of God's being. Thus from one point of view, the teaching of Jesus about God was all square with that Israelitish religion within which He was born. From another point of view, however, there was something compellingly original about the attitude of Jesus to God; there was a naturalness of relationship, an openness of being, a consciousness of unbroken communion, which justifies the interpretation that Jesus did not aim to define God. He rather set Himself to intensify the idea of God and to illuminate His reality. The central fact, then, of the gospel records, is that Jesus lived out God in the actualities of human experience; and clearly demonstrated God's existence and being by reference to His own activity. Had Jesus sought to prove that God is, by pointing away from Himself, He would have contradicted the significance of His own person and presence. The important thing about

Jesus was precisely Himself, as Irenaeus reminded the Marcionites. In bringing Himself He brought what was new. When, therefore, the question is asked, 'What did Jesus teach about God?' we find little data for theological system-making in His teaching.

Indeed to ask, 'What did Jesus teach about God?' may well be an improper question, in that it may suggest that the historical position He occupied was that of a sort of instructor in divinity. But He was nothing of the sort. Jesus did not lecture 'on God': He gave witness to Him. What he said about God was born out of His own experience of filial relationship with the Divine Father. His words about God were prophetic testimony stemming from His openness to God. They were not therefore single pieces which can be constructed into a rounded artistic theological mosaic. They are rather outflashings of His own God-centred personality. What then is of consequence in the New Testament is Jesus's attitude to God. And it is only by penetrating to the inner reality of Christ's filial awareness of God that His understanding of God can be finally determined and assessed.

It is for this reason that the question, 'What did Jesus teach about God?' becomes at the same time the least important and the most momentous of all that can be asked. For, on the one hand, it can presuppose an answer which drains out the very essence from the Christian gospel, or, on the other hand, it can lead right to the very centre of the New Testament faith. It can do the first by leaving the impression that Christ is to be conceived as the first Christian and that Christian faith is to believe with Him in God thus making Him merely the pattern believer. This is the thesis much alive today but in a form different from that of the 'old liberalism' of which Harnack was the most eloquent exponent. According to Harnack the gospel, as Jesus proclaimed it, has to do with the Father only and not with the Son. Essential New Testament faith, then, as he saw it, was to believe in the all-inclusive Fatherhood of God made known

as such in the teaching of Jesus. While much present-day
theology has changed the figure, its fundamental characterization of what the gospel is has not much changed. If God
cannot now be presented by the symbol 'Father' He can be
regarded meaningfully, we are assured, as 'the Ground of all
being'. In this way, it is said, the teaching of Jesus about
God can be given relevance in modern terms and to modern
minds. Jesus was necessarily bound, in the religious context
of His day, to the use of the symbol 'Father' to make effective
for the people of His time, the understanding of their
ultimate human concern. Such terms as He used must not
be taken in any factual sense and certainly not as final. It
is enough if we can get hold of what He was trying to say
to the people of His day—the ideas about man which can
be distilled out of His use of the mythology of the religious
language then in vogue—and present them to men of our
day in language appropriate to our times. In this way we
can retain what we can of the profounder insights of Jesus
into our human conditions and concerns. We cannot enter
here into the eccentricities which this way of reading the
data of Jesus' teaching about God will produce. But we must
insist, however, that Christian faith is not finally a believing
about life with Jesus but a believing in God through Him.
Thus is it that to pose the question, 'What did Jesus believe
about God?' can presuppose an answer which avoids the
crucial issues of a Christology by reducing the historical
person of Jesus to that of a teacher of profound psychological
insights or that of a prophet of deeper ethical penetrations.
But to approach the teaching of Jesus in the gospels with
such presuppositions would itself fail to do justice to the
place of Christ in Christian faith.

For, and this is the other side of the matter, to consider
the teaching of Jesus about God is to be led into the very
heart of the gospel. Can we indeed believe in God as He
believed in Him? He spoke of God as His 'Father' and of
Himself as 'Son', but whom amongst us would be so

audacious? We have no consciousness of unbroken sonship. We are not aware of any filial communion. Jesus accepted the ethical monotheism of the Old Testament. But what does that imply? Surely this: if we were really to believe as He believed it would affect us as it did Him. *Monotheism*— the belief in one God—was no mere intellectual affirmation to Him. It held for Him a warm conviction which found expression in the prayer of the Garden, 'Father not my will but thine be done'. The most self-assured among us will hesitate to speak in terms so intimate. But He was heir of the *ethical* monotheism of Israel. And He confessed to an ethical relationship with God which showed that for Him there was no strain in that relationship or stain on the ethical nature of it. To believe in God as Jesus believed in Him one would need be as He, holy, harmless and undefiled. Who amongst us would dare to proclaim that he shares this faith of Christ? Who is there who can say with honesty of mind and holiness of heart that he believes in God as Jesus believed in Him? To believe in God as Christ believed in Him is not the gospel; it is rather to show the overwhelming need of the gospel.

Inevitably, however, Jesus let fall words which do give some understanding of how He conceived of God. And these ideas can be given fairly summary form. First is the fact that He saw God as world creator. There was no dualism in the teaching of Jesus. He recognized more vividly and profoundly than any other the power of 'the evil one', but He did not attribute the world's origin to him. For Jesus this is God's world; God clothed the grass of the fields. In a significant passage Jesus lifted up His heart to the Father as 'the Lord of heaven and earth'.[1] In the thought of Jesus this world which God made was not now out of touch with Him. Yet He was no pantheist for He did not regard the world as an emanation of deity. God was still distinct from the world. On the other hand Jesus was no deist. God's providential government was over all; not a sparrow can fall to the ground without His knowledge; and the fowls are fed by Him and His loving care is extended to the least of earthly creatures.[2]

Inevitably, Jesus regarded God as moral being. True, He did not speak frequently of God in such precise terms although He did allude to the divine holiness. For Him the one who is uniquely Father is yet 'Holy Father'.[3] And He contrasts the evil of man with the righteousness of God.[4] What, however, is only incidently expressed in words is everywhere revealed in the attitude of Jesus. His profounder conception of sin springs from His deeper realization of God's holiness. Jesus quite clearly thought of the holiness of God in a manner different from the Pharisees and Scribes. For them, God's holiness put Him at a distance from men; with Jesus, the very holiness of God involved His concern for men. More particularly, the holiness of God was shown to be ethical rather than ritual; it is a quality or side of the divine nature which makes it incumbent on men to 'hallow' His name. It is that attribute of God which defines His character in relation to human sin and shame. It is that fact about God which makes it impossible to trace the origin of evil up to Him.

It is this reality of the divine nature which makes Him the moral ideal for men. God's perfection is the standard by which all is to be judged: 'Be ye therefore perfect as your Father which is in heaven is perfect'.[5] The general goodness of God consequent upon His righteousness is emphasized by Jesus. He is kind to the evil and the unthankful. All men alike share His benefits.[6] The total of the unsought and unbought benefits which come to everyone derive from that deeper ethical 'goodness' of the divine nature so that Jesus can declare that there is none good but one, God alone.[7]

But the most characteristic name for God in the teaching of Jesus is that in which He speaks of God in terms of personal Father. All other references to the divine nature are more or less incidental; but this is frequent and focal. The revelation of Jesus was in a special sense limited to an unveiling of the Fatherhood of God. This was the one inspiring and ruling thought throughout His life and ministry. The saints and prophets of the Old Testament regarded God mainly as the lawgiver, the judge, the king; and these Jesus did not discard. Rather He took up the ideas which these epithets made familiar into His own usage of the term Father. This does not mean that the description of God as Father was new and strange. If scarce in the Old Testament in reference to God it was not quite unknown. Isaiah, for example, assured the exile people of God's fatherly concern;[8] and the Psalmist likens God's pity for His people to that of a human father for his children.[9] The correlative term 'son' is also used but more frequently in reference to God's dealings with Israel.[10] The two terms are brought together as indicative of God's intimate personal relation with Solomon as Israel's chosen king in 2 Samuel 7 : 14.

The Old Testament use of the title 'Father' for God betokened for Israel the special providential care of God. As father He would watch over them for His own special purpose.[11] In general, however, the idea of fatherhood connoted for the Old Testament people of God position and authority rather than that of warm intimacy and relationship. Thus the aspect of sovereignty and lordship was given prominence. For the great prophets God was sovereign over all nature and nations; over all history and all homes. He rules over all; and the earth is the Lord's and the fulness thereof. He is the Creator of all,[12] and He is the Creator of Israel.[13] Because He is Creator, He is King exercising Fatherly rule over all He has made. The faithlessness of Judah and Israel is a denial of the fact that they are under one father who has created them.[14] In broad terms, then, the Old Testament conceived of God as *de jure* King over the whole created universe; and as *de facto* King over those who acknowledged His sovereignty. And in the context of the Old Testament the idea of fatherhood tended to merge into that of king-

16

ship. It was indeed frequently under the designation of King that the authority and rule involved in that of Father for Israel was usually stated.[15]

It is of special significance to note, however, that Jesus made little reference to the designation King when speaking of God, clearly preferring the more restricted and intimate one of Father. The Jews had tended to read God's kingship in terms of legal power and to overlook its more spiritual aspect. It was this legal conception of God which had shaped and strangled Pharisaic piety. For this reason, maybe, Jesus avoided it, although He did make use of that of 'kingdom'. But for Jesus the kingdom was God's fatherly rule; God's gracious sovereignty in the hearts of those who responded to it in the spirit of filial reverence and moral obedience. By avoiding the term King and using instead that of kingdom in the sense of God's fatherly rule Jesus was evidently emphasizing in another way what He intended by the concept Father. Father clearly suggested for Him something of an acknowledged relationship.

In the Old Testament two general contexts for the idea of the Fatherhood of God are found. God is Father because He is Creator. A number of Old Testament passages speak of God's creativity and of His faithfulness to all He has made. Then, too, God is Father because He is King. Here His Fatherhood, as was noted, involves the sonship of the nation of Israel, and in a particular way the individual believing Israelite who owns in life the kingship of God. There was, therefore, a spiritual relationship based on redemption out of Egypt in which the idea of the divine Fatherhood acquired a deeper and profounder intimacy. It is just here we have a foreshadowing of the New Testament understanding of the Fatherhood of God in relation to the new Israel redeemed not with corruptible things but with the precious blood of Christ as a Lamb without blemish and without spot.[16]

With this in mind we find in the teaching of Jesus the

same general references; but a new dimension added. Jesus spoke to the disciples of God as their Father,[17] and He spoke of the Father who cares for the sparrows and the grass.[18] But the distinctive thing in His teaching was the way He spoke of God as *His* Father. The Fatherhood of God has then evidently a different meaning and message in these three contexts. And these can be specified as follows:

(i) God is the Father of all men by virtue of an ethical relationship. God cannot be untrue to Himself. The goodness of God cannot be cancelled out by the folly of man, for the gifts and callings of God are without repentance. It is as Father that God sends His rain upon the evil and the good. Thus God is the Father of all men in so far as He is the source of all the blessings in which they share. In this sense the father in the story of the prodigal son was father still. But he became father in a new way when he took the returning son to himself and said, 'this my son was dead and is alive again'. God is Father of all men because He has made man in His own image. Thus in some sense man is kindred to God and capable of realizing that spiritual sonship which is conditioned upon the recognition of His Fatherly-rule in the individual heart and life. God is Father because He is one with man in the bundle of life as man's provider. In this sense the Fatherhood of God is unbroken. But, still, the idea of the universal Fatherhood of God does not carry with it the correlative of the unbroken sonship of man. Most suggestive, however, is the way Jesus refrained from designating as sonship this kinship of nature which all men have with God. Nevertheless, by giving supremacy to the divine love in the character and activity of God, Jesus made effective for the individual and for society the moral foundations upon which the good of both can be built. In specifying loving regard as the regulative principle of all God's functions in relation to men, Jesus set forth for human imitation the regulative principle by which human society can best en-

18

hance the value of each and secure the rights of all. We must beware, however, of suggesting that this natural relationship of God to man in terms of the Divine Fatherhood is itself sufficient to make effective a universal brotherhood of man. The simple thesis that the proclamation of the Fatherhood of God is bound to generate and propagate the brotherhood of man, has been too often belied throughout history. It has in fact been demonstrated frequently enough, what the teaching of Jesus underscored, that the Christian idea of God as heavenly Father loses its creative force if cut loose from faith in Christ as the unique Son of God, and from the renewed experience of sonship which is bound up with that faith.

(ii) This brings us to say that God is the Father of believing men by virtue of a redemptive relationship. It was always in discoursing with His disciples that Jesus spoke of God as Father. The basic assumption of the Sermon on the Mount was just this; because you are the Father's children you are to glorify Him by letting your light shine so that others may come to the same relationship with God. It is to the little flock that the kingdom is given because of the Father's pleasure.[19] In truth in no single passage in the sources does Jesus speak explicitly of God as the Father of all men. The whole drift of His teaching was to emphasize that it was in virtue of His own unique awareness of filial relationship with God as His Father that He called men to Himself so that they might come to know the secret of sonship which He Himself mediated through His own person and in His own work. Jesus nowhere taught a redeeming Fatherhood of God of all men: indeed His blunt words to the cavilling Jews, 'Ye are of your father the devil'[20] may be taken as an explicit repudiation of any such easy-going doctrine. He firmly based the right relation between man and God in the context of the divine lordship of God in the life of man. Thus the filial relationship which Jesus proclaimed was spiritual and ethical: and the later New Testament writers

19

were only unfolding His message when they specified the divine Fatherhood as based on a redemptive relationship with God.[21]

Yet it is in the context of God's all-embracing Fatherhood that His special redemptive relation to those who believe gets its meaning and measure. God's Fatherhood is His universal benevolence in which all men have a share. At the same time the fact of the divine generosity does not do full justice to all that is meant by speaking of God as Father. For there is a further factor presupposed, namely a relationship of Fatherhood which God sustains only with personal, moral beings. Matthew 6:26 shows this deeper distinction; there Jesus stresses that it is *your* Father, not *theirs*, who cares for the birds. Thus does God's Fatherhood involve the necessity for a personal and ethical relationship, as well as that of a universal generosity. Such an awareness of the divine Fatherhood can, however, have significance only where the correlative of sonship has been realized. 'God's essential self-imparting goodness and man's creation in God's moral image are the two fundamental elements of God's Fatherhood, and they unite to give it the note of universality. God's universal Fatherhood is grounded both in what He is and in what He has made man to be. He must be the Father of all men, because He is perfect in love,[22] and love is at once the sum of His inherent moral perfections, the motive of creation, and the basis of man's kinship to Him.' It is indeed this Fatherhood in love which is the cause and the characteristic of God's seeking and saving grace. He would have men restored to the enjoyment of that filial position which their sin has forfeited. It is thus in the sonship of the unique Son that the special Fatherhood of God is displayed and discovered.

(iii) God is the Father of Jesus by virtue of an essential relationship. When Jesus called God His Father, and when He spoke of Himself as Son, the titles had a force and distinctiveness which made the relationship unique. It is significant

20

that Jesus never put Himself together with His disciples in referring to God as Father. He taught them indeed to pray 'Our Father', but that prayer was for them. This special kind of Father-Son relationship is clearly demonstrated in the Synoptic gospels,[23] and definitely in the Johannine-like passage of Matthew 11:25-27 where, as the Son, Jesus claims a knowledge of the Father which none else but He possessed and can impart. This one sentence would be itself sufficient to show that Jesus is both to God and to man what no other has been or could be. In two broad ways a son may be said to reveal a father. He may be so essentially and entirely like him that it may be said, to see him is to see his father; or, he may reveal his father by giving to him reverence, love and trust and thus making it manifest that he is such a father who is worthy of such. In both these ways Jesus exhibited His relationship to His Father. And while the first may be more characteristic of the Fourth gospel and the second of the Synoptics, the distinction is by no means clear-cut. For in the first three gospels as well as in the fourth the two ideas overlap. Throughout all His teaching in whatever context He used the concept Father, Jesus seemed to give to it a warmth and tenderness which brought His message about God into marked contrast with the Judaism of His day. No prophet of Israel even had gone so far as to state in so many words that God is good to the unrighteous as well as to the righteous. It was by declaring God to be Father, and in particular as being *His* Father, that He shocked and shook the religion of His time. In order to bring out the freshness and fulness of His teaching on the divine fatherhood, the Evangelists combined the Aramaic and Greek. God is the Abba, Father. It was in truth the idea of the Fatherhood of God in relation to Jesus which most deeply impressed the apostolic writers and witnesses. In the fact of it they read something of the absoluteness and uniqueness of Jesus. And they say in its reality the means whereby their own awareness of the divine Fatherhood might be realized and their own assurance of divine Sonship could be secured.

THE FOURTH GOSPEL

Like the Synoptics, the Fourth Gospel's most characteristic word for God is Father. But here special emphasis is
placed upon that unique Father-Son relationship which exists
between God and Jesus. It is a relationship which goes back
beyond creation and history.[24] And it is as a consequence
of this eternal love-relationship that Jesus is given 'in the
days of His flesh' special privilege, power and authority.[25]
It is out of this sense of double awareness of what He was
by nature and who He was as executive of the divine purpose of redemption that Jesus becomes for man the
actualization of the knowledge of God. Thus to know Him
is to know the Father,[26] and to see Him is to see the
Father.[27] But to remain in unbelief is to remain in darkness
and to know neither Him nor the Father who sent Him.[28]
Those who believe and keep His words are in the Father's
love.[29]

But in addition to designating God as Father, John has a
few additional adjectives which have a special significance
for an understanding of the teaching of the gospels about
God.

God is spirit.[30] It is certainly correct to omit the indefinite
article here, for it is not the personality of God but His
nature which the declaration seeks to emphasize. God is not
localized; He is everywhere. His nature is spiritual. Such a
God is, therefore, to be approached in a manner consonant
with the sort of Being that He is. Throughout John's Gospels,
as we have observed, special place is given to the divine
Fatherhood and it is in connection with the statement that
God is spirit that this thought of His Fatherhood must be
read. The Father is the one whose nature is Spirit. Thus
when we find the term Father used in the fourth Gospel in
an absolute sense, it corresponds in general with the Synoptic

title of 'the Father in heaven', or, 'the heavenly Father'. Because God is 'spirit' Jesus can declare that no man hath seen the Father except the Son.[31] Only One who is of the same spiritual nature can behold Him. Here is a statement by Christ Himself of a community of nature with God. He alone who is truly God can naturally see God. Christ is then the revelation within human history of the One who is in nature spirit.

God is one.[32] The ethical monotheism which underlies the Synoptic gospels pervades that of the fourth Gospel. Yet Christ's assertion of oneness with the Father—'I and the Father are one'; one in essence not one person—means that this monotheism has to be reconsidered. The Gospel of John, which is in a sense an elaboration of Christ's declaration in Matthew 11:25-27 (Lk.10:21-22), makes clear that while the Christian understanding of God is monotheistic it is not that of a static monad. There is variety in the divine nature. Jesus speaks of the Spirit who proceedeth from the Father thereby establishing a relation between the two. In John's Gospel, then, while the oneness of God is asserted, the distinctions of beings are implied.

God is love.[33] This was a startlingly new relevation; the idea of the divine love, we have noted, underlay the Synoptic doctrine of the Fatherhood of God. Here in John's Gospel it is brought out into a declaration of the very nature of God. God is love. The love of God was not a thought clear to the saints of the Old Testament. Christianity practically created the word *agapē*. And it was in the revelation of Christ that the love of God was made manifest. John does not say that God loves us because Christ came to us. It is rather the reverse. Christ came—was sent—because God loved. Love is the foundation of all His relationships. His love for the Son is grounded in the identity of nature. The Father loved the Son before the foundation of the world. Love is the inspiration of God's saving work. God sent the Son that through Him the world might be saved. The 'little gospel' as Luther calls John 3:16 epitomizes the whole teaching of the New Testament. There was never a love so sovereign as this—*God* so loved; there was never a love so strong as this—He *so* loved; there was never a love so sacrificial as this—that *He gave His only begotten Son*; there was never a love so sweeping as this—*the world* He loved; there was never a love so selective as this—*whosoever* believeth; there was never a love so saving as this—*should not perish*; there was never a love so secure as this—but *have everlasting life*. God is absolute love; this surely is the message of John. The world is built on the shoulders of love. The last word about God is not that He is omnipotent, omniscient, omnipresent; but that He is love. It is His love which gives grace to His omnipotence, goodness to His omniscience and glory to His omnipresence. His love is as great as His power and knows neither measure nor end.

Throughout the four gospels, then, we are taught about God's self-affirming character in terms of holiness; and His self-imparting character in terms of love. And in the end we are aware of God as 'holy-love'.

SCRIPTURE REFERENCES

1. Mt. 11:25
2. Cf. Mt. 6:30 (cf. Lk. 12:28); Mt. 10:29 (cf. Lk. 12:6)
3. Jn. 17:11; cf. Mk. 8:38
4. Mt. 7:11; cf. Lk. 11:13
5. Mt. 5:48
6. Mt. 5:45
7. Mk. 10:18; cf. Mt. 19:17; Lk. 18:19
8. Is. 63:16
9. Ps. 103:13
10. Deut. 1:31; 8:5; cf. Is. 1:2; Jer. 3:19; 31:9; Hos. 1:10; etc.
11. E.g. Hos. 11:1; etc.
12. Cf. Gen. 1:1; Is. 42:5
13. Cf. Is. 43:1, 15
14. Mal. 2:10
15. Cf. Ps. 5:2; 24:10; etc.
16. Cf. 1 Pet. 1:19

17. Cf. Mt. 5:16, 45, 48; 6:1, 4, 6; etc.
18. Mt. 6:26, 30
19. Lk. 12:32
20. Jn. 8:44
21. Cf. e.g. Jn. 1:12; Rom. 8:14-17; 1 Jn. 3:1-2; etc., etc.
22. Mt. 5:48
23. Cf. e.g. Mk. 1:11; 9:7; etc.
24. Jn. 17:24
25. Cf. e.g. Jn. 3:35; 5:20
26. Jn. 14:7
27. Jn. 14:9
28. Jn. 16:3
29. Jn. 14:23
30. Jn. 4:24
31. Jn. 6:46
32. Jn. 5:44; 17:3
33. Jn. 3:16; etc.

2

Jesus Christ

THE SYNOPTIC GOSPELS

We are attempting in this chapter the impossible task of presenting a picture of the Person of Christ as it can be drawn from the Gospels. In doing so we declare our acceptance of the authenticity of the sources and of the figure of Jesus which they embody. Clearly in one chapter all that can be attempted is to give the barest outline, but enough, we hope, to show Him for whom He is as the Lord Jesus Christ.

1 Jesus—the Real Man

No one can read the story of the Gospels and come away with the impression that there was anything unreal about its dominant character. The Figure of Jesus as it is presented to us in the records and interpreted to us in the rest of the New Testament is that of One who was no unearthly angelic visitant, no demigod in human shape. It was as man Jesus came and lived and died. It was as man He came back from the secret gloom of the sepulchre after three days. However unique and unaccountable He was, He was no phantom being. However more than man He was, He was not less. He was quite literally and truly a man.

(a) The Evident Man

We can approach the evidence for the human reality of

26

the man Jesus from the point of view of the 'outercourt' of His natural life and the 'holy place' of His moral and spiritual personality. The 'holy of holies' of His ultimate being will engage us later.

There is no doubt that Jesus had a body no less real than that of other men. He took upon Himself our nature with all its limitations, its feelings and its openness to suffering and pain. He came into human life in the human way of natural birth after the lapse of the requisite time.[1] He grew as other boys do, to maturity and manhood.[2] He partook of food.[3] He knew what it was to be hungry.[4] He was under the necessary limitations of space as are ordinary men and thus had to make His way laboriously from place to place.[5] He was under all the conditions of our human way.

When we pass further into the inner court and closer to the holy place we are assured that He was still human in all that here pertains to manhood. He possessed those human elements of soul which distinguish man from the animals and which make him more than a different type of somatic creature. He revealed those properties of mind, emotion and will, characteristic of the human individual. He showed that He possessed the normal mental processes by asking questions to gain information.[6] He showed surprise, and took evident delight in ordinary things. He had a will of His own[7] and throughout the days of His flesh there were occasions when He had to steel Himself with purpose against temptations and to set His face as a flint to the fulfilment of His vocation. What are called the virtues of the will are particularly exemplified by the steadfastness and persistence with which He continued loyal to His calling despite the contrary suggestions of His friends,[8] and the constant hostility of His enemies.[9]

He displayed throughout, the emotions common to all men; the love of family and friends, and even, perhaps, of country;[10] as well as the more particular form of emotive[11] and the more general form of complacent love.[12] He could express the anger of moral indignation.[13] With sorrow He was not unfamiliar.[14] He knew what it was to 'wail' (*klaiō*) by reason of disappointment[15] and to 'weep' (*dakruō*) by reason of sympathy,[16] while again and again we read of the compassion which flowed from His noble heart.[17] His temptations, too, were real and endured in all their intensity in His manhood. A true psychological reading of the gospel narratives will, then, secure the one important fact that Jesus possessed those human realities of mind and heart which are fundamental requisites of an actual personality.

But we must press into the inner court, the holy place of His moral and spiritual life. More particularly do we become aware within this vantage-point of what we may call Jesus's religious relation with God. He certainly knew God in an intimate and personal way. It has been rightly remarked that Jesus was not one of the many seekers after God, not even if we call Him one of the successful. He bore witness to God. His understanding of God is a prophetic testimony born out of His inner experience. His knowledge of God was the natural outflow of His intercourse with God. He felt Himself to be in possession of God; to be in His presence always. He never had any doubts about God, for God's presence was for Him a living and felt certainty.

It was out of this living and felt certainty of God's reality and presence sprang His faith, prayer, joy and obedience with reference to God, and His service and patience with reference to man. His trust in God was real and whole-hearted. He was not nervous and timid amid life's uncertainties, for to Him everything was in the Father's hands.[18] It was this burning certainty which accounts for that unconcern which characterized His ministry. His strong courage and His serene restfulness of spirit grew out of His absolute confidence and trust in God. Jesus belonged to God first and then to man, in that proper order. It is for this reason that He sought the place of solitude before His times of service. He waits that He may be alone. He knows He needs God, though He shares His life. He is sure of God all the day through and all the way along; but He must talk to Him, He must get together with God. Has He not taught us that man needs no spectators, no congregation, no priests when he prays?[19] Thus He prays.[20] His praying is no parade; it meant something. He prayed because He had need to pray; that He might find refuge under the shadow of the Almighty wings; that He might renew His innermost being in the strength of God and find nerve for the ordeals of living in His reverent trust in His Father.

Bound up in His life for and trust in God was that joy in God with which all His words and works are permeated. They breathe the spirit of assured joyfulness. It was in this attitude of faith, prayer and joy He rendered His full obedience to the will of God. Thus was the religious relation to God at once both natural and spiritual; the same that is required of all men, but which none but He has met.

When we turn to the manward reference of Jesus's religious relation to God we find them all there; candour, compassion, patience and humility, and all else beside, which spring out of a man's faith in, and communion with and obedience to God. All that it takes to be a man is found in this Man. In this One called Jesus we encounter a human reality.

(b) *The Sinless Man*

Jesus fulfilling all righteousness and resisting all temptation—Jesus the man, at every point and at every moment of His earthly life under the Spirit, is presented in the New Testament and confessed by the Church as the one perfect Man that the world has ever seen and known. That authentic human life differed from the rest of mankind by not entertaining that which makes the rest of us less than human. He alone lived within our human sinful race a human sinless life. The Synoptic Gospels do not seek to 'prove' His sinlessness, but then they betray no attempt to gild the lily. They

29

tell the story without affectation; just as He was among men. The fact is the historic records make no explicit claim to moral purity on the part of Jesus. But neither do they set themselves to prove His innocence or to eulogize Him. They give the account of His life as He lived it; and that is enough.

Yet as we follow the record we note how He stood the test of intimacy and enmity. His very presence was a rebuke, a cause of shame in others.[21] The question of Mark 10:18 cannot be taken as 'a veiled confession of moral delinquency'. In very truth the adult life of Jesus, as depicted in the Gospels, was pure from the traces of sin which means that in His case there was no derangement of nature or native sickness of soul, as with us from our beginning.[22] The verdict of all is that we find no fault in Him at all.[23]

The man Jesus as portrayed for us in the gospel records is, then, the truly normal man—the one sinless man. The remarkable fact is that it is the reality of Jesus's sinlessness which has produced throughout the history of the Church, not a claim to perfection, but the sense of imperfection in His followers. For, the sinful human mind is no Jupiter-head from which this sinless human figure could have emerged. In every way His life is what human life was meant to be. He loved God with His whole mind and heart and soul and strength. He fulfilled all the requirements of the blessed life, making actual those beatitudes which He taught to His disciples.[24] He took a towel and demonstrated that He had taken the position of lowly service. The poem of love in 1 Corinthians 13 can be taken as a vivid portrait of His life of perfect love. The consecrated life of which Romans 13 is an outline found incarnate reality in Him. There is no glory to equal that of the sinless life of Jesus; the real Jesus of the Galilean road.

(c) *The Son of Man*

In an earlier period the title Son of Man was taken without

further ado to refer to the human nature of Christ in contrast with that of Son of God, which specified His divine nature. The term 'man' in the title gave easy justification for this ready equation. There are certainly a few instances in which the use of the title does indicate reflection on Jesus's part on His human nature. For example, in Mark 2:27,28 Jesus may be identifying Himself with the children of men and vindicating their rights as men, while at the same time indicating His supremacy above them. So, too, it may be in the passage in which He contrasts Himself with the austere preacher of the wilderness with the words, 'the Son of Man came eating and drinking'.[25] Is He here suggesting His sympathy with all natural and simple enjoyments of human life? There are those who on the strength of such passages, still prefer to understand the title 'Son of Man' as expressive of His deep connection with humanity.

There is no doubt that He is the Brother of all men, and the Man of men. Yet when examination is made of all the passages in which the title occurs it will be found that those which can have this undoubted reference are comparatively few. Thus the title which holds the term 'man' will present Him to us as more than man.

It is well known that Jesus's most frequent designation of Himself was as the Son of Man. He seems to have preferred this name above all others. Other names He might acknowledge, or at least not repudiate, but this one alone was His favourite. It occurs seventy times in the first three Gospels, and is found as early as Mark 2:10. Although it becomes more frequent in its use towards the end of the Gospels, it is clear that it was on the lips of Jesus from the beginning of His ministry. After the great confession of Peter it appeared to gain a profounder significance with a wider public. Yet Jesus never defined the title nor did He indicate where He found it. It occurs frequently in the Old Testament.[26] By general consent it is believed that Daniel 7:13 is the source of the title. There we have the vision of one like unto a Son of Man who receives a kingdom. The title occurs, too, in both the Similitudes of Enoch and Esdras—if the passages are indeed pre-Christian. Special interest is taken by scholars in the first of these references in which the figure of the Son of Man who is of old and wears the aspect of a celestial being, is definite and personified. It cannot be said for certain, however, that Jesus drew upon this circle of ideas in taking the title to Himself. The truth is, perhaps, that Jesus derived it partly from the Old Testament and partly from His own messianic consciousness.

What Jesus was asserting in so designating Himself was that He was in the world to fulfil a divine mission in connection with the messianic kingdom. He seems to have preferred the title to that of 'Messiah', possibly for the reason that it stood furthest from the Jewish prostitution of the messianic office into a military dictatorship of a this-worldly pomp. It may be conceded that the title acquired a more definite messianic connotation as Jesus became more and more able to unfold to His disciples His messianic calling and intention. It is, at any rate, significant to observe that the more He disclosed His Messiahship so the more frequently He used the title Son of Man. The first open admission of His messianic vocation is definitely associated with the term.[27]

A consideration of the passages in which the term is found shows that it combines the two ideas of suffering and glory. There are several references where the thought of suffering is uppermost.[28] Passages which show the Son of Man in the context of triumph and glory are no less numerous.[29] Seen, then, according to the distribution of its use and the contexts in which it occurs, it becomes certain that Jesus took the title as stating His openness to and oneness with mankind, as real and representative Man. But with this there goes into the term the thought of His uniqueness in humanity, by reason of His appointment to future glory and transcendent sway. This primary significance was enriched, especially towards the closing days of Jesus's ministry, with the added thought of suffering. Humanity and apocalyptic triumph in the future thus combine to make the term Son of Man one of supreme interest and importance. Jesus called Himself Son of Man against the background of Daniel 7 : 13 which has reference to a kingdom; and it was as founder of the Kingdom of God that He came like unto a son of man. 'The Son of Man must suffer . . . when the Son of Man comes in His glory.' Here are united the ideas of suffering and sovereignty. The humiliation is offset by the exaltation. The King comes to the throne by way of the Cross. Humility and majesty meet and blend in the character and experience of this Son of Man.

2   Christ—the True Messiah

(a) The Fulfiller of the Messianic Promise

The religious atmosphere of the early days of Christ's life was charged with expectation for the Coming One. There were those, like Simeon, waiting for the consolation of Israel. John the Baptist was puzzled by Christ's apparent failure to make open proclamation of His messiahship; and in prison he mused whether He were indeed the Christ. He thus sent word by his disciples to get a straight answer from Jesus if He was 'he that should come', or if there were not another.[30] Already John had announced that the Coming One was mightier than he.[31] After Christ had ridden into Jerusalem as its King that cometh,[32] the people joined in chorus which showed that the idea of a Coming One was a popular notion.[33] By taking to Himself the prophecy of Isaiah 61 : 1,2, Jesus was declaring that as the 'sent one' He was 'the coming one'.[34]

(b) The Bearer of the Messianic Title

(i) The title 'the Christ' related to the messianic kingdom.

The term 'Christ' is the Greek equivalent for the Hebrew 'Messiah', and by its use Jesus is presented as fulfiller of the messianic hopes of the Old Testament prophets and of the Jewish people. In English the word is rendered 'Anointed'. With the exception of His birth name 'Jesus', no other has rooted itself so firmly in the thought of the world as that of 'Christ'. On a number of occasions Jesus referred to Himself as the Christ. Matthew has nine references, Mark five, and Luke nine. On twenty-four occasions others designate Him as such in the Synoptics—some of these are, of course, parallel accounts.

In the Old Testament the king was referred to as the Lord's anointed,[35] in virtue of the pouring upon Him of the sacred oil which was a symbol of the Spirit of God. Out of the failure of the kings, reinforced by the prophetic word, grew the expectation of the coming ideal King who would fulfil the hopes of Israel. It is this Ideal Figure who is pictured in Isaiah 11:1-5. In the Second Psalm the title 'Messiah' (Anointed) is attached to this expected One, and as more and more the hope of the appearance of the Coming Deliverer grew in Israel the more the simple title 'The Messiah' was referred to Him. So it was that in the heyday of the Baptist's ministry 'all men mused in their hearts concerning John, whether he were the Christ'.[36] It need cause no surprise that Jesus should rebuke the devils for proclaiming abroad the fact that He was the Christ. This was possibly because of the Jewish colourful notion of their coming King as a warrior with pomp and power; and for the further reason that He would have the discovery made at first-hand by those who would follow. At the same time there were vital moments when Jesus declared His identity with the expected Messiah. We have noted above how Jesus took to Himself the words of Isaiah 61:1,2. The word 'anointed' in the passage He read as being fulfilled in Him must have suggested the 'Anointed One'. In Matthew 11:3 the question of the Baptist can hardly leave any doubt who was the personage intended or what was the force of our Lord's reply. In the crisis of Caesarea Philippi, Jesus drew from His disciples the acknowledgement that He was the Christ, and He manifestly rejoiced in their testimony. Having secured the confession of His messiahship, those disciples were now to learn from Him what manner of Messiah He was.[37] At the trial He was asked the direct question about the reality of His messianic claims. And being put on solemn oath by the priests He declared that He was.[38] Jesus was crucified because He confessed His messiahship.

(ii) The title 'The Beloved' related to the messianic King. In such passages as Matthew 3:17; 17:5 and Mark 1:11 the *Agapetos* would appear to be a separate title. Christ is to the Father 'the Beloved'. The designation seems to have been a current messianic one which united the two statements of Psalm 2:7, 'Thou art my Son, this day have I begotten thee', and Isaiah 42:1, 'Behold my Servant, whom I uphold; mine elect in whom my soul delighteth'. The title 'Beloved' in its turn appears practically synonymous with that of 'Chosen' or 'Elect' One of Jehovah.[39]

3 Son—the Divine Lord

In this place we are to say something to indicate that the gospel records present us with a figure of Christ which cannot be explained in human terms however glowing may be the adjectives used to describe Him. It was at Caesarea Philippi that Jesus Himself raised the question regarding Himself. Having listened to the various ideas of the crowd He pressed for a statement of what the disciples themselves had discovered about Him. He employed the title Son of Man in the question. But have they seen anything of the hidden glory of the Man of Galilee? Have they discovered anything of the majesty which shone through the humanity? It was Peter who voiced the confession, 'Thou are the Christ' (Luke), 'the Son of the living God' (Matthew). It has been main-

35

tained that the added words of Matthew are a mere expansion probably inserted to offset the term 'Son of Man'. The suggestion is improbable. Matthew's words express the simple yet profound truth about Jesus. The contrast, if one must be sought, is reality with what follows, 'Blessed art thou, Simon, son of John, for flesh and blood hath not revealed this unto you, but my Father in Heaven'. The use of the term 'my Father' in Christ's words instead of 'God' suggests that the divine disclosure that had been made by Peter had reference to the fact of the paternal and filial relationship between God and Jesus. The verb used for 'hath revealed' is reminiscent of Matthew 11:28 where the unique knowledge by the Father of the Son and the Son of the Father, as well as the exclusive work of the One to reveal the Other, are declared. In Peter's declaration we have a concrete example of the revelation of the unique Sonship of Jesus. The contrast, therefore, is between Simon, son of John, who knew himself to have a human father, and 'the Son of the living God' as Jesus immediately refers to God as 'my Father' since He knew no human one.[40] Jesus openly accepted Peter's acknowledgement of His Messiahship and Himself asserted a unique Father-Son relationship between God and Himself. He regarded Himself as having a rightful place on the divine side of reality.

This fact can be given clarity by reference to something of Jesus's own self-testimony and some of Jesus's own accepted titles.

(a) *His Self-testimony*

No reader of the Gospels can escape the conclusion that Christ knew Himself to be uniquely related to God from the beginning. He spoke in the most intimate manner of God as His Father and in the most personal way of God as '*my* Father'. It was by reason of His unique Sonship that He was qualified by nature and attested by the Spirit for the fulfilling of His office of Messiah. As Messiah He is called to act in the very closest relationship with God. He is God's absolute representative. Such a purpose and such a position presupposes a deep and profound oneness of nature that only One who is in the highest sense Son could truly fulfil. When we remember how strict and exact Jesus was in His utterances, and how He placed limits upon Himself in keeping with His incarnate state[41] then we see how utterly certain He was in the enduring consciousness of His filial relationship with God. Some of His direct claims put Him without question on God's side. Throughout the records Jesus is found making assertions which do not come as exaggerated, unreal and absurd. He calls men to service and sacrifice 'for His sake'; a claim that is enhanced and becomes credible when it is recalled that in the Old Testament the prophet and the psalmist reinforce their messages with the words 'for the Lord's sake'. By deliberately substituting 'for my sake' Jesus was clearly putting Himself in God's place. His words have about them the quiet certainty of a divine authority. He will build His Church and no opposition will frustrate His purpose.[42] To confess His name is to be blessed of Him and to be accepted of His Father in heaven.[43] He identified the word and will of God with His own.[44] He asserted in His own name as authoritative a new commandment.[45] His use of the expression, 'Verily I say unto you', was a deliberate substitution for the prophetic 'Thus saith the Lord'. In the famous passage Matthew 11:27 (Lk.10:22), He lays claim to a relationship of an intimate knowledge of God which none shared with Him. He grew as a true human, as we have seen, in knowledge and wisdom; at the same time He revealed a more than human insight into man's inner being.[46] And with this knowledge which was unique went a power which was divine. His miracles, for example, were profoundly 'natural' to Him. He acted divinely in His own name, so that His miracles were, so to speak, forthflashings of His total being. They were so much His own that His was a

power He could communicate to others.[47] The miracles of
Jesus were part of the fact of Jesus. They demonstrate the
reality of blessings from the throne of God upon men, and
they proclaim the saving deeds of the gospel. He showed
that He possessed the Godlike power to forgive sins.[48] He
asserted His authority over the temple,[49] and the Sabbath,[50]
and over the kingdom of Satan.[51] Behind everything in the
Gospels there is a divine Person, who came to fulfil a unique
vocation. The teaching He gave, the deeds He wrought, the
commands He made, the authority He wielded, the knowledge He possessed, the position in which He placed Himself,
all proclaim His deity.

(b) His Titles

In addition to those already alluded to there is a word to be
added about two other titles in particular.

Lord. Like the term Christ, that of Lord can be seen to
become more and more charged with deep religious meaning. The Greek word *Kurios*, either with or without the
article, occurs over 240 times in the Gospels. This large
number is obscured, however, by the fact that many English
equivalents are used, for example, 'master', 'Sir', 'owner' and
the like. The fundamental idea of the term is a description
of power or authority over a person or things. It implies
ownership, and as such is used as a title of courtesy or
reverence. In many places it is addressed to Jesus in this
way or is used as a name for Him. Of the Synopticists it is
applied most frequently by Luke (18 times), and carries a
heightened sense of reverence for Him amounting to worship.
Within the Gospels it becomes evident that the term *Kurios*
which began as a title of respect for a teacher deepened into
a realization that He was more.[52] To the Jewish Christian,
Jesus was 'Messiah'; to the Hellenistic Christian Jew, He
was 'The Christ'; to the Gentile Christian, He was 'The
Lord'. And all three are combined in the familiar name 'The

Lord Jesus Christ'.

Son of God. Only on a few occasions does Jesus designate Himself Son of God in the Synoptic Gospels. Thirty-two times, however, is He called such by others, Himself sometimes adopting the title or accepting it in a manner as appropriate to Himself. But He spoke of God as His Father with a force which reveals a sense of profound and unique relationship to God.[53] Deeper, however, than the mere mathematical occurrences of the term relating to His Sonship is the basic fact that His work for men is made to rest throughout the New Testament upon the special and personal relationship between Him as Son, and God as Father. Thus, when in the Synoptics the title is applied to Him it is intended to convey the existence of a deep kinship between God and Christ.

The term Son of God was, of course, well known in Jewish circles. In the Old Testament it is applied to angels,[54] to magistrates,[55] to the Hebrew nation,[56] to the Theocratic King.[57] In the New Testament it is applied to the first man.[58]

All these examples show that the undergirding idea is that of a special nearness to God; of special privileges and endowments conferred by Him. In the reference to Jewish kings we have more probably the source of the title as referred to Christ. The application of the title to the nation culminated in that of the kings; while in turn the application of it to the kings found its fulfilment in Him who summed up in Himself the regal idea in Israel. Basic, however, as is this politico-messianic idea, it does not give the ultimate sense of the term as applied to Christ. All the passages where the title is found point to the personal qualities of Him who bears the title and to the unique relationship to God whose Son He is said to be. The official or messianic sense of the term describes not essential nature but office. As Heir or Representative of God, the Messiah could truly bear the title Son of God without reflection on His name. Yet although the term has a messianic flavour, it is not as a synonym for Messiah that the term Son of God is used in the Gospels. When the demoniacs applied it to Jesus it may well be in a messianic sense, and the same may be true of the trial passage before the high priest.[59] But in those passages in which Jesus speaks of Himself as 'the Son' and calls God 'His Father', the official messianic idea is entirely absent. He is not, that is to say, called Son of God because He is Messiah; He is Messiah because He is Son of God. Even explanations in terms of an ethical relationship between Jesus and God are not sufficient to exhaust the full significance of the designation Son of God. Passages such as 'O my Father, if it be possible . . .',[60] and 'Father into thy hands . . .'[61] may be taken as expressive of this personal ethical relationship. And the profound words of Matthew 11:27 may be read as the climax of this ethico-religious sentiment.

The ethical relationship demands a deeper and profounder one. Thus the title Son of God is no official designation of office or no pattern sonship for discipleship; for He never was other than Son. Jesus unfailingly spoke of God as 'my Father' and 'your Father', but never as 'our Father'. Thus the ethical union implies a metaphysical one—a union of nature. To say that Jesus was in ethical relation with God is really to say that He was in essential relation to Him. The consciousness of His own sinlessness gives Him the right to use the title without stain or strain, and thus to set Him apart from others. Between Jesus and God, indeed, all things are common. It is the filial consciousness not the messianic consciousness which is the basic fact of our Christian faith and gospel.

THE FOURTH GOSPEL

The doctrine of Christ's Person in the Fourth Gospel is firmly based in the Synoptic presentation. John has not another Christ which is not another. It is indeed his declared purpose to prove that Jesus is Christ, the Messiah.[62] And throughout, this fact is everywhere made clear.[63] He performs the messianic deeds in fullest measure, in healing, in raising the dead, in meeting human needs, and in every way fitting the highest messianic hopes. But He shows that His reign is not limited to the people of Israel. It is for this reason that the term 'world' in the sense of His unrestricted sway is given constant reference in John.[64] The Jewish horizons have disappeared; and Jesus is set forth as the world's Saviour. Thus in the Fourth Gospel all that He is as Messiah, He is for all the world.

The dozen or so references to the title Son of Man in the Fourth Gospel are in general harmony with its usage in the Synoptics. There is the same double aspect of suffering and sovereignty.[65] Throughout the gospel the title reflects a theology, which not only presupposes, but also amplifies the messianic significance of the designation for the personality of the incarnate Lord. John gives special emphasis to the pre-existence of the Son of Man.[66] Of particular importance is the way John preserves those Son of Man sayings of Christ in which His saving purpose in the world,[67] and His decisive significance for man's destiny, are stated.[68]

Although we shall be dealing with the book of Revelation in later chapters it may be noted here that surprisingly the title Son of Man, as such, does not figure in it. On two occasions the exalted Christ is presented as one like the, or, a Son of Man.[69] Since Revelation is concerned with the triumphant reign of the resurrected Jesus it is natural that the particulars surrounding His unveiling should have the appropriate symbols. Thus He appears amid the golden candlesticks, the churches in whose midst He walks as Lord, as possessing the robes and radiance of divine majesty. In the later passage the Lamb who stood on Mount Zion appears like unto the Son of Man with the crown of glory upon His head and the sharp sickle in His hand. He is thus set forth as the decisive One in the harvesting of mankind.

Only once in Revelation is He referred to as Son of God,[70] but throughout the book there is the felt presence of Him who is the Son of God in the humility of grace and the Son of Man in the triumph of glory.

It is only possible in the space remaining to suggest three important considerations which must be well noted in assessing John's doctrine of Christ. First to be observed is that in the Fourth Gospel Christ's humanity is stated with a new starkness. No one reading John's account is left with the impression of a spiritual being parading among men in some sort of unreal body. John is at pains to show that the Word came to be 'flesh', literally and authentically, a human person. Thus we find the one who was 'in the beginning with God' taking His place in our human situations. He walks our common way,[71] is wearied by extended journeying,[72] weeps (*dakruō*) at Lazarus's grave.[73] And all the human qualities and characteristics we have seen as true of Him in the Synoptics are in John's account. Jesus felt the indignities and the inhumanities attending a mock trial and a public execution.[74] The fact that His death was not a temporary loss of consciousness, nor a swoon, nor make-believe, but a real death is attested in the most unconscious and unaffected manner by one who could not have been conversant with the essential principles of human anatomy.[75] All of these facts add up to underscore that for John the Christ of whom he wrote was a real figure and no fake at all.

The second fact in John's gospel is that Christ's Sonship is stated with a new intimacy. In the Fourth Gospel the presentation of the Sonship of Christ has a larger place than in the Synoptics. But the essential facts are the same except that there is a new note of tenderness in the way He speaks of the Father. He regarded Himself as having been the object of the Father's love before ever the world was. He brought His Sonship with Him from heaven.[76] In the depths of His own consciousness there was the continued prescience of His divine origin. For Him it was natural to regard the proper ending of His life on earth, when His work is done, as a return to the glory which was His in a prior existence.[77] Thus Jesus called for faith in Himself as the Son of God,[78] and manifestly accepted the declaration of it.[79] The new thought, however, in John is the description of the Son as 'only begotten'. The word used in 1 : 14; 3 : 16,18 for 'only begotten', *monogenes*, underlies the fact that His Sonship is unique. Stress is given to the personal Being of the Son as such. Christ is the One only Son, the One to whom the title belongs as an absolute right. Others are sons by adoption and grace; but He was never other than Son. In the Septuagint the word *monogenes* is used to translate the Hebrew word for 'only' (*jachid*, of Judges 11 : 34); and the only begotten one is the only loved one (cf. Gen.22 : 2,12,16 where the Septuagint has *agapetos*, 'beloved' for 'only'; cf. Mk. 12 : 6).

The third fact in John's gospel is that Christ's Deity is stated with a new clarity. The Fourth Gospel puts Christ squarely within the realm of Deity in many ways. Peculiar to John is the designation of Jesus as the *Logos* or 'Word' of God. Thus Christ is the incarnate speech of God. It should be stressed that the Prologue in which the *Logos* idea comes is an integral part of John's gospel; thus, although the term does not occur in the body of the writing, its significance is maintained throughout. More particularly does the *Logos* concept reappear under the categories of Truth, Light and Life. The designation 'Truth' describes the *Logos* in its nature. The connotation of the term is 'reality', and for the apostle, it is only in the person of Christ, the incarnate *Logos*, that men can take hold of the Divine reality. The word 'Light' may be said to describe the *Logos* in its source. He came as the Light into the world; He came from Him who is Light Unapproachable except through Him. The designation 'Life' describes the *Logos* in its action. Christ, as the incarnate Word, communicates to those who receive Him, who believe in Him, eternal life. In his Prologue John states

43

the unbegun life, the absolute Deity, and the personal existence of the Word. And he then goes on to say that 'He who
was God'—'became flesh': 'He who was with God'—'dwelt
among us': 'He who was in the beginning'—'became', 'came
to be in time'.[80] By Him the worlds were made, and to His
own world He came. In Him as the Word made flesh, the
eternal self-revealing God was incarnate.

By His constant use of the phrase 'I Am', Jesus was in an
oblique way identifying Himself with the 'Jehovah Great I
Am' of Exodus 3:14. The declarations themselves relate
broadly to what Jesus can claim to be in Himself,[81] and to
be and do for others.[82]

In the most direct and yet unaffected way Jesus puts Himself and allows others to put Him, without equivocation, on
God's side. By the declaration of a unique Sonship with God
as His Father, He made an assertion of equality with God
which those who heard it understood it to be.[83] This equality
with God He steadfastly maintained.[84] The honour due to
God He regarded as due to Himself.[85] There is in John's
Gospel a veritable substantial identity between Himself and
the Father which did not begin with His becoming flesh.[86]
He co-existed with the Father prior to the days of Abraham.[87]
He descended from above,[88] because He was 'from above'.[89]
As the Only Begotten Son He alone has declared God.[90]
Thus to see Him is to see the Father,[91] for He can declare
that 'I and the Father are one'.[92] Throughout the Gospel the
Son's equality of nature with the Father is surely stated.
The whole Gospel depicts Him as sharing a community of
life with the Father before the ages. There is no thought of
His Sonship beginning within time—there is no adoptionist,
no achievement Christology here.

SCRIPTURE REFERENCES

1. Mt. 1:25; 2:1; Lk. 2:7
2. Lk. 2:40

3. Lk. 7:34-36; 14:1; 15:2; 24:41, 43
4. Mt. 21:18; Lk. 4:2
5. Lk. 8:1; etc.
6. Mk. 9:21; Lk. 2:46f.
7. Mt. 26:39
8. Mt. 16:22
9. Mt. 12:14; Mk. 11:18
10. Mt. 23:37
11. Mk. 10:21
12. Mk. 14:6f.
13. Mk. 3:5; 10:14; Lk. 11:46
14. Mt. 26: 37, 38
15. Lk. 19:41
16. Cf. Jn. 11:35
17. Mt. 9:36; 14:14; 15:32; 20:34; Mk. 1:41; 6:34; 8:2; etc.
18. Mt. 10:29
19. Mt. 6:6
20. Mk. 1:35
21. Cf. Mt. 3:14; 27:19; Lk. 5:8; 23:47
22. Cf. Lk. 1:35; etc.
23. Lk. 20:4, 14
24. Mt. 6:3-12; cf. Lk. 6:20-23
25. Mt. 11:19
26. Cf. Ps. 8:4; 80:17; it appears 90 times in Ezekiel where it refers to the prophet himself.
27. Mt. 16:13, 21f.; Mk. 8: 27, 31f.; cf. Lk. 9:18, 22f.
28. Cf. Mk. 8:31 (Lk. 9:22); Mk. 9:9 (Mt. 17:9); Mk. 9:12 (Mt. 17:12); Mk. 9:31 (Mt. 17:22); Mk. 10:33 (Mt. 20:18; Lk. 18:31); etc.
29. Mk. 8:38 (Lk. 9:36); Mk. 13:26 (Mt. 25:31; Lk. 21:27); Mk. 14:62 (Mt. 26:64); etc.
30. Mt. 11:3 (Lk. 7:19)
31. Mt. 3:11
32. Mt. 21:5
33. Cf. Mt. 21:9
34. Lk. 4:18f.
35. Cf. Ps. 18:50
36. Lk. 3:15
37. Mt. 16:21
38. Mt. 26:63f.
39. Cf. Mt. 12:18; Lk. 23:35
40. Cf. Mt. 1:16-25; Lk. 1:26-38; cf. Mt. 11:28; Lk. 10:22
41. Cf. Mt. 5:34, 37; 12:36; 20:23; 24:36
42. Mt. 16:28
43. Mt. 10:32, 33; Lk. 12:8, 9
44. Mt. 7:21-29; 12:49, 50; Lk. 6:46-49; 11:28
45. Mt. 5:43f.; Lk. 6:37f.
46. Cf. Mk. 10:21; Lk. 7:37f.; Mt. 12:25; Mk. 2:8

47. Cf. Mt. 10:8; Mk. 6:7; etc.
48. Mk. 2:5-10; Lk. 7:48
49. Mt. 12:6
50. Mt. 12:8
51. Mt. 12:24f.
52. Cf. Lk. 5:8; etc.
53. Cf. Mt. 21:38; 22:2f.
54. Job 38:7; cf. 1:6; 2:1
55. Ps. 82:6, 7
56. Cf. Ex. 4:22f.
57. Cf. 2 Sam. 7:17; Ps. 89:27
58. Lk. 3:38
59. Mt. 26:63; cf. v. 68
60. Mt. 26:39
61. Lk. 23:46
62. Jn. 20:31
63. Cf. Jn. 1:49; 7:31: etc.
64. Jn. 1:9, 10, 29; 3:16, 17, 19; 4:42; 6:14; etc.
65. Cf. Jn. 1:51; 3:14; 6:62; 8:28; 13:31
66. Jn. 3:13; cf. 8:58; 17:5
67. Jn. 3:14
68. Jn. 5:25; 6:27, 53
69. Rev. 1:13; 14:14
70. Rev. 2:18
71. Jn. 1:36; 6:19; etc.
72. Jn. 4:6
73. Jn. 11:35
74. Jn. 19:28, 33
75. Jn. 19:34
76. Jn. 6:38, 46, 62; 8:23, 42
77. Jn. 14:12, 28; 16:10
78. Jn. 10:35
79. Cf. Jn. 11:27
80. Jn. 1:1, 14
81. Cf. Jn. 11:25; 14:6; etc.
82. Cf. Jn. 6:32f.; 10:11; etc.
83. Jn. 5:18
84. Jn. 10:30
85. Jn. 5:22, 23
86. Jn. 3:3; 6:33-42
87. Jn. 8:58
88. Jn. 3:21, 31
89. Jn. 8:23
90. Jn. 1:18
91. Jn. 14:9; cf. 12:45
92. Jn. 10:30; cf. 17:11, 21

46

3

The Holy Spirit

THE SYNOPTIC GOSPELS

In approaching the subject of the Holy Spirit in the Synoptic Gospels two facts must be kept in mind. The first is that
the Spirit's presence must be read against the background
of the Old Testament allusions to the activity of the Spirit
of God; and the second is that the reality of the Spirit's
presence has only infrequent mention in the three Gospels.

It is almost a surprise to discover that the Old Testament
never uses the phrase 'the Holy Spirit' as such. In a couple of
passages there is the association of the adjective 'holy' with
'Spirit', but in each case it is still further qualified with the
use of the possessive pronoun, 'thy'[1] and 'his'.[2] The broad
fact is that the Spirit and the Word are often quite closely
related in the Scriptures of the Old dispensation. And in this
connection they suggest the Divine Breath and the Divine
Voice. So the Spirit is the communicated life of God through
His 'word'.[3] As such God's Spirit is related to the divine
activity of creation, both of the world[4] and of man in
particular.[5]

In widest sweep the Old Testament can be designated the
age of the manifestation of God as Creator—the creator of
the world as the sphere of His purpose and the creator of a
nation as the vehicle of His grace. During the days of the
historic Jesus comes the manifestation of God as Redeemer.
If the first can be designated the time of the revelation of

the Father as Creator, and the second as that of the revelation of the Son as Redeemer, then the present age is preeminently that of the Spirit as Sanctifier. For Pentecost was certainly the beginning of something new. From the specifically Christian point of view, the presence of the Spirit is the new factor in world history and Christian experience, for up till then the Spirit 'was not yet given'[6] in such manner. This broad characterization, however, must not be taken to mean that there are three successive manifestations of a single Being —first as Father, then as Son and now as Spirit. For however much the Old Testament can be read as the activity of God as Creator-Father, one is aware throughout of the presence of a divine plurality—of, as well, a Divine Word and a Divine Spirit.[7] At the same time it would be a mis-reading of the Old Testament account to try and deduce from it a full trinitarian doctrine. It is indeed hardly correct to say that Christianity inherited its trinitarianism from Judaism. It is only in the light of the New Testament that this proper understanding of the Old Testament allusions can be made out.

It is, of course, beyond our purpose to go into any details concerning the eighty-eight Old Testament references to the Spirit. But in general it may be said that the Spirit's activity throughout was only occasional, temporary, and restricted. The Spirit of the Lord came upon certain men for particular service.[8] It is not clearly stated that the Spirit took possession of the nation as a whole to constitute it into one body like the New Testament Church, although it does appear that the Spirit did act upon the nation.[9] It is just here we have the contrast between the Spirit in the Old Testament and in the New. In the New Testament the Spirit has come to indwell the people of God, so as to make them His temple and to unite them into the one body in Christ. Yet there are, even in the Old Testament, activities of the Spirit which make for a more personal reading of the Spirit's presence.[10] Wickedness grieves the Spirit of God,[11] and it is the Spirit which 'strives' with man on behalf of God.[12] By possessing such 'personal' characteristics of mind, will and affections, the Spirit, like man, by whose activity man was created, may be regarded as an image of God's own proper being.[13]

There are, however, two significant relationships into which the Spirit is brought in the Old Testament which are important for an understanding of what the Synoptic Gospels have to say on the subject. There is the role of the Spirit in the new covenant,[14] and upon the Mediator of that covenant.[15] It is this fact which provides the point of contact between the two Testaments. The Old Testament has the promise of the outpouring of the Spirit in connection with the establishment of the Messianic kingdom,[16] while the New Testament has that promise in realization.[17]

If the absence of the phrase 'the Holy Spirit' in the Old Testament is surprising, then no less so is the lack of reference to the same Spirit in the Synoptic Gospels. Reasons have been advanced to account for this phenomenon. Some have suggested that Jesus spoke little about the Spirit because of His desire not to make open confession of His Messiahship. The fact that there are any such references at all are then dealt with, and their number drastically reduced on the supposition that some of the Synoptic sayings are a reading back by the Church, which had experienced the Spirit, of its own developed doctrine, into the teaching of Jesus. In this way certain passages about the Spirit in the Synoptic Gospels are written off as community productions. But this easy method of dealing with the subject will not do. For in allowing that not all the Spirit sayings can be disposed of in this way, the question still remains why should any be attributed to Jesus? If indeed the early Church wanted to find actual authority for its faith in the teaching of Jesus why did it stop where it did? Why not represent Jesus as instructing His disciples concerning all aspects of the Spirit's relation to His people? The truth of the matter is that the Spirit's sayings are of such a character that they find their self-authentication in their context with the Gospel story. They arise out of credible historical situations and can sometimes be seen to illustrate Jesus's swiftness of repartee and profound insight.

The atmosphere of the Gospels is one of spiritual power. One is aware throughout of currents of divine energy. The events recorded are the result of divine action: and yet no attempt has been made to give an altogether post-Pentecostal account of the phenomena. The coming of John the Baptist and the happenings surrounding the birth of Jesus accord with the Old Testament view of the Spirit. There is a ring of authenticity about the account. The testimony of John the Baptist,[18] the song of Elisabeth,[19] the prophecy of Zacharias,[20] the inspiration of Simeon,[21] are all connected with the work of the Holy Spirit and yet in terms akin to that of the Old Covenant, and not after the fashion of men who had shared in the fulness of the Pentecostal blessing. The Gospel writers, it seems clear, were seeking to guard against any colouring of the facts, as they had received them, by the fuller understanding of the Church concerning the Spirit. When it is remembered that the Gospels were written after the epistles which are saturated with allusions to the Spirit, this fact is all the more impressive. Here is the true reason for the sparseness of reference to the Holy Spirit. Its writers were being faithful to the accounts they had received; they deliberately refrained from polishing up the story with their own comments.

In developing the Synoptic doctrine of the Spirit it will make for clarity to deal with the subject under two broad divisions; first, the Spirit in the life of Jesus and, secondly, the Spirit in the teaching of Jesus.

1 The Spirit in the life of Jesus

It seems clear that Jesus experienced an indwelling of the Spirit for the perfecting of His life as man and an enduement of the Spirit for the fulfilment of His life as Messiah.

The effects of the Spirit were, that is to say, both personal and ministerial. It is declared in John 3:34 that the Spirit was given to Him 'without measure'. True enough the words 'unto Him' do not occur in the original Greek, but the arguments that they should be presupposed are overwhelming. All that was necessary for Him by virtue of His human nature to possess was imparted to Him without lack by the Holy Spirit.

It is evident that the indwelling and overshadowing went together with the development of Jesus's manhood, and were the cause of that development. Jesus needed the gift of the Holy Spirit to enable His human nature, in increasing measure, to be His instrument in the working out of His holy design. All that He needed was bountifully supplied. Born of the Holy Spirit,[22] He grew in spirit (*pneumati*).[23] The Spirit who secured that His human flesh, derived from Mary should not become the basis of sin's operation, made certain also His progress in spiritual and mental development and His advance in holiness and knowledge. The Holy Spirit not only endowed the human nature of Christ with all necessary equipment, but He also caused these to be exercised, gradually, into full activity. During the days of His flesh, Jesus was under the constant and penetrating operation of the Spirit. It was as a man under the Spirit that Jesus carried out His duties in the carpenter's shop in Nazareth, and there submitted to the rule of His earthly home. He was prepared of the Spirit for the time of His showing forth and sending forth to fulfil His messianic office. In and by the Spirit He fulfilled all righteousness and resisted all temptation;[24] and in the power of the Spirit He returned into Galilee.[25]

At the baptism He was consecrated for His office by the Spirit's descent in the form of a dove; the inner strengthening and equipping for the task He needed. The outward symbol was not for His sake, but that human eyes might behold the evidence of His official calling and human lips might declare what they had seen and heard. Now developed to manhood under the Spirit, He goes forth freshly anointed to His messianic work. Coming into Galilee in the power of the Spirit, in that power He will remain and under that power He will work out a life of obedient service. For the Spirit that descended upon Him at the baptism 'abode on Him'.[26]

It is important, therefore, to note our Lord's own declaration in the synagogue of Nazareth, when He took to Himself the words of Isaiah 61 : 1 'the Spirit of the Lord is upon Me', anointing Him to preach and to fulfil the messianic work of this prophetic passage.[27] Jesus carried out every function of the messianic office in the power of the Spirit. And since the Holy Spirit is the divine executive of the mighty acts of God it need not be thought strange that Jesus should have lived and fulfilled His divine mission through His power. He cast out Satan by the Spirit of God;[28] and even if the parallel passage in Luke has 'by the finger of God',[29] this does not lessen the fact. For it is in the enduement of God's power that He acts and in the might of the Spirit of God He invades the territory of the devil and delivers those held in bondage and captivity. The casting out of evil spirits is indeed throughout the Gospels a signal demonstration of the possession by Jesus of another Spirit. And it was in the *dynamis* of this other Spirit, the Holy Spirit, that Jesus performed all His mighty works. Thus 'filled with the Spirit' as a permanent condition, for that precisely is what the adjective used by Luke is intended to convey,[30] Jesus lived His life for God. The Spirit remained with Him throughout His days in the flesh controlling His mind, will and actions so that He learned from God, acted for God, and was taught of God unto the fulness of the stature of a perfect man. It is, then, in the Holy Spirit He will rejoice at the success of those He has empowered in His name to overthrow the kingdom of Satan.[31] So John the Baptist had signified the meaning of the presence of the Greater than he—but dimly and unclearly. He is the One who will baptize with the 'holy Spirit',[32] and 'with fire'.[33] John spoke better than he perhaps knew. For he had not the Christian experience to give specific content to his words. Maybe all he could have intended by the declaration was what he understood by reference to its Old Testament antecedents. This, however, he did see, that the One who had come had some unique function which marked Him off from all who had gone before. For Him, in Him, and by Him, God was to act in a special way by His Spirit. John knows himself to be but a worker for God and makes no claim for himself to possess the Spirit or to bestow the Spirit. But John's prophetic insight is seen in the fact that he recognized the Mightier than he as having in Himself the right to baptize with the Holy Spirit. And this right He has because He was Himself supremely the Man under the Spirit.

2   The Spirit in the teaching of Jesus

Only six of the eight passages call for comment here, as reference has been made above to the other two. The most difficult one of all is the statement about blasphemy against the Holy Ghost.[34] In the estimate of Jesus the most heinous sin of all is to belittle the Holy Spirit. Yet Jesus is not intending a contrast between Himself and the Spirit as if it were but a venial sin to blaspheme the Son of Man. Rather the point is that in saying of Him that He works by Satan's power and has an unclean spirit is the very essence of blasphemy against the Holy Spirit. To call good, evil, and the Final Good, final evil, is the sin of sins. This is a state in which all appreciation of and desire for good is forfeited. To say that Jesus has an 'unclean spirit' and to fail to recognize that in Him the Spirit of God is present, is to carry obtuseness to its unpardonable heights. An unclean spirit is a spirit which can have no communion with God; and can only be excluded from God's presence as it must exclude those who are possessed thereby. But the Holy Spirit is specifically 'of God'; the Holy Spirit is God's very presence among men. To repudiate that presence for what it is and the blessing it brings is to enter the eternal darkness. To fail to see that it is by the Spirit of God that Jesus works, is to fail to see that the kingdom of God has come among men.[35] To withstand so signal and unambiguous a display of Divine Power, and to do so with deliberate and settled intent, is to put one's self outside the kingdom. For that finally is the spirit which killed Jesus rather than acknowledge His reign; and that is the unpardonable sin.

In one place Jesus promises the Spirit's aid to His disciples to give them needed speech in the time of coming stress.[36] Reference is also made by Jesus to the inspiration by David by the Holy Spirit,[37] although strangely enough Luke does not mention the action of the Spirit in connection with Psalm 110.[38] Yet in chapter 11 : 13 Luke has, for Matthew's 'good things' which the Father gives to those that ask Him,[39] the assurance that the heavenly Father will give the Holy Spirit to them that ask Him. And what better thing can any man receive of God than the Spirit of God, the Spirit of adoption by which we are able to call God Father. The risen Jesus assured the disciple band that 'the promise of my Father upon them' would be fulfilled.[40] The Holy Spirit is not specifically mentioned in the passage, but the implication that reference is to the coming of the Spirit at Pentecost is inescapable. Then will they be clothed with power from on high. Indeed, Christ's last word to them, whether we follow Matthew's account or Luke's has reference to the power upon them and through them of the Holy Spirit. For in the great commission they were charged to go and make disciples of all nations, and baptize in the name of the Father, Son and Holy Spirit.[41] This trinitarian formula must make it clear that the disciples had learned much about the Spirit from our Lord's own teaching, especially as this is recorded by John in Christ's Upper Room discourses.

In general, then, in the Synoptic Gospels the Holy Spirit

is regarded as a special divine power working in Jesus for the fulfilment of His messianic mission; and a power from on high promised to His disciples for their part in the accomplishment of God's purposes of redemption. At the same time it needs to be observed that while the action of the Spirit in the life and work of Christ is evident throughout; it is not, so to speak, obtruded. For the Spirit's action in Him did not lessen His own perfect humanity: there is no suppression by the Spirit of His full humanness, but rather an intensification of it. There is throughout the naturalness of the human behind and within the supernaturalness of the divine.

THE FOURTH GOSPEL

The late date of the Fourth Gospel as distinguished from that of the Synoptics has led some writers to suggest that what John has to say about the Spirit derives from Church tradition rather than from the authentic teachings of Christ. The point is made that John had outlived the period of eschatological tension within the Church; the expected end had not come, and the hope of the consummation died out. The death of Paul had turned the Church's thought to emphasize the presence of the Spirit in the community of believers. The passing of so great an apostle as Paul was a shock to the Church; but the hope flickered that maybe in a short time under the guidance of the Holy Spirit there would be a return of the Messianic King. John survived to witness the dashing of even this hope. So to meet the new situation, it is argued, he took hold of the Pauline doctrine of the Spirit and reinterpreted the eschatology of the Gospels as a present experience of the Spirit. This is, of course, a rather hasty statement of how some modern writers would have us understand John's data. The truth in it derives from the fact that in the Fourth Gospel it is difficult, always, to distinguish between the specific teaching of Jesus and the reflection of the apostle. So fully had the apostle assimilated his Lord's message, so much a part of his own thought had it become, that we cannot on every single occasion say for sure that any specific passage is a saying of Jesus or a comment of the apostle. For our part, however, this is no serious matter; for we believe that it was the same Spirit who spoke in Jesus that gave John his thought and guided him in his recording. But, on the other hand, care must be taken against divorcing all that John has to say from the authentic history of the New Testament story. One of the main features of the Fourth Gospel is precisely this, that, although it is called the 'spiritual' Gospel, it is firmly grounded in history. John will not allow his message to be unhinged from its factual basis; he will not have Christianity turned into a theosophy without any historical anchorage. All through he shows us the Word become flesh moving among men as a living actuality and speaking the divine message and fulfilling the divine purpose. In the light of the underlying historicity of the Fourth Gospel there is no reason to deny that what John has to say about the Spirit, and what he attributes specifically to Christ, is not the actual teaching of Christ. No one reading what is recorded about the Spirit in chapters 14 to 16 of the Gospel can fail to realize the naturalness of the context and fittingness of the occasion. Of course, John wrote in the full light of Pentecost and where he comments it will be natural that this fact will find expression. Yet it is not John's intention to adopt the role of an interpreter. He will not make Jesus say what he would have Him say, even if, as we believe, what John has to say is itself 'of the Spirit'. When the data of the Gospel on the teaching of the Spirit are examined they betray an evident historicity. For what he has to say about the Spirit, outside the specific teaching of chapters 14 to 16, is almost pre-Pentecostal in tone, and accords well with the Synoptic presentation. But there is an advance in emphasis. For in the Fourth Gospel the divine Otherness and the Personal activities of the Spirit come to prominence.

What John states on the subject of the Spirit can be brought out under the headings of the wider idea of the Gospel and the specific teaching of Christ in the Upper Room discourses.

(i) It is significant that John links up his Gospel with the Synoptics by reference to the Spirit's descent upon Jesus at the baptism.[42] It would almost seem that the writer wishes to underscore the declaration of the Baptist that the One upon whom the Spirit descended and abode is He who baptizes with the Holy Spirit. Quite evidently his intent is to relate the experience of the Spirit with the Person of Christ. The experience of the Spirit is the result of Christ's action. The coming of the Spirit authenticated Him as Son of God,[43] and it was for this reason that John wrote, to establish faith in Jesus that He is Son of God.[44] Such belief assures 'life' through His name; and such 'life' is of the Spirit.[45] He who is Lamb of God is, then, the Baptizer with the Spirit; what He does for us He would make real in us.

One of the most important references to the Spirit, as well as one of the most difficult, comes in chapter 3. To enter the kingdom one must need be born from above (*anōthen*), of water and of the Spirit. Most would take the reference to 'water' here to be to baptism; and we see no convincing reason to deny a certain allusion. It is therefore important to observe that according to John the early ministry of our Lord turned upon the idea of cleansing. His first public act in Jerusalem was to sweep clean the house of God of the money-changers. He will make a new temple for the worshippers: but the story of Nicodemus and the women by the well tell us that He will make new worshippers for the temple: those who will worship God in Spirit and Truth. But associated with the dominant theme of cleansing in the early chapters of John's gospel goes the idea of 'water'.[46] For Nicodemus it is the water of birth,[47] for the woman by the well it is the water of bounty.[48] The water of which Jesus

57

spoke must not be taken then, either as literal or as figurative, but as symbolic. The idea was, so to speak, 'in the air' at the time, for John's baptism was symbolic; and at the time of Jesus's speaking to Nicodemus John was baptizing at Aenon.[49] At the feast to which Jesus had come water played a vital part in the ritual; no sacrifice could be offered without the priest first washing. All of which was a shadow of the true. The kingdom of God was at hand, present in the presence of Jesus. But His kingdom could be entered only by a new birth, an inward change. The way of that new birth is by cleansing through the inward action of His Spirit. Jesus had cleansed the temple; that was a sign of His work. He entered in and cast out. Now He will come to as many as receive Him and His incoming will mean cleansing. This is the washing of regeneration and the renewing of the Holy Ghost of which the New Testament speaks. This is what is symbolized in the idea of water of which baptism may be taken as the outward seal. But significantly the symbolism of water is not carried through;[50] it is the Spirit that remains. It is the Spirit that is the reality, the source of the life-giving experience. Thus the idea of water becomes merged into that of the Spirit, and the emphasis throughout is on the blessed effects of the Spirit's indwelling.[51] The Spirit is, then, associated with Christ's gift of life under the symbolism of water. So the Spirit becomes the indwelling reality of Christ. This is what Christ declared by His act of breathing upon His disciples His resurrection gift.[52] The truth now dramatically expressed is that it is the Spirit who gives life. A further gift of the Spirit will come to the Church at Pentecost as endue-ment for service. But Christ's symbolic act of breathing upon them the Spirit, as expressive of life[53] will tell them that if any man has not the Spirit of Christ, he is no Christian.[54]

(ii) The specific teaching of Christ in the Upper Room discourses is pivotal in John's Gospel. Point is specifically made of the Divine Otherness of the Spirit. He is described as 'Another', but not as one different. He is Someone distinct

from the Son. But the Spirit is associated with the redemptive mission of the Son in such a way as to make it clear
that the Spirit belongs to the same realm. Only God can do
God's work with the adequacy needed to complete the
Divine act of redemption; and it belongs to the Spirit to do
precisely this. It is the Spirit who deals with man on behalf
of God, convicting of sin, of righteousness and of judgement.[55] Dealing with personal beings makes the Spirit not
less than personal. Throughout the Discourses, therefore, the
personal nature of the Spirit is given sharp statement. Indeed
Jesus had to disrupt the laws of grammar to make clear the
fact. Masculine pronouns are sometimes associated with a
neuter noun to get the truth across. It is when 'He' the Spirit
of truth comes, 'He' shall teach. The names by which the
Spirit is called and the activities which they connote are all
personal. He is the Teacher, the one who guides, the one
who witnesses, the Advocate who comes alongside the people
of God to aid in times of need. The Discourses present the
Holy Spirit as Christ's Deputy. When Christ has gone, the
Spirit will come to take His place.[56] By Him the Son will
be glorified,[57] for He will be Christ's true witness.[58] His
presence will no longer be that of a veiled and undeclared
visitant, whose subtle benefactions are for the most part
anonymous. He will come to the people of God in an open
manner, as Pentecost records that He did, to be the Son's
Other Self until the consummation of all things. Thus will
the presence of the Spirit guarantee divine truth,[59] inspire
waning memory,[60] strengthen apostolic testimony,[61] assure
spiritual fellowship[62] and bring real conviction.[63]

SCRIPTURE REFERENCES

1. Ps. 51:11
2. Is. 63:10
3. Cf. Ps. 33:6; 104:30; 139:7
4. Cf. Ps. 139:7; Wis. 1:7
5. Cf. Gen. 1:27; 2:7; Job 27:3; 33:4

6. Jn. 7:39
7. Cf. Gen. 3:7; Is. 6:3, 8; see Gen. 22:11, 16, etc.; Prov. 8; Is. 9:6; 48:16; 61:1; etc.
8. Cf. e.g. Ex. 31:3; 1 Chr. 12:18; Ju. 3:10; 6:34; 11:29; 14:6; 15:14; etc.
9. Cf. Neh. 9:20, 30; Is. 63:10-14; Zech. 4:6; Hag. 2:5
10. Cf. Job 33:4; Ps. 51:11; Is. 11:2; 40:13; 48:16; Ezek. 3:12, 14; etc.
11. Is. 63:10
12. Gen. 6:3; Neh. 9:30
13. Cf. Wis. 2:23
14. Cf. Is. 44:3; 59:21; Jer. 33; Ezek. 36:26, 27; 37:14; Joel 2:28-29
15. Cf. Is. 11:2; 42:1; 61:1
16. Cf. Ezek. 39:29; Joel 2:28, 29; Zech. 12:10
17. Cf. e.g. Lk. 4:16f.; Ac. 2:16f.
18. Cf. Lk. 1:15
19. Lk. 1:41f.
20. Lk. 1:67f.
21. Lk. 2:25f.
22. Mt. 1:18, 20; Lk. 1:35
23. Cf. Lk. 2:40
24. Mt. 4:1; Mk. 1:12; Lk. 4:1
25. Lk. 4:14
26. Jn. 1:32; cf. Lk. 4:1
27. Lk. 4:17
28. Mt. 12:28
29. Lk. 11:20
30. Lk. 4:1
31. Lk. 10:21
32. Mk. 1:18
33. Mt. 3:11; Lk. 3:16
34. Mt. 12:21f.; Mk. 3:28f; Lk. 12:10
35. Mt. 12:28
36. Mt. 10:20; Mk. 13:11; Lk. 12:12; Cf. 21:15
37. Mk. 12:36
38. Cf. Lk. 20:41
39. Mt. 7:11
40. Lk. 24:49
41. Mt. 28:19
42. Jn. 1:32f.
43. Jn. 1:34
44. Jn. 20:31; cf. v. 28
45. Cf. Jn. 3:5, cf. 6:63
46. Cf. 2:3f.; 3:5f.; 4:1f., 14f.; 5:3f.
47. Jn. 3:5f.
48. Jn. 4:14f.
49. Jn. 3:23
50. Jn. 3:5, 8

51. Jn. 4:14; cf. 4:23, 24; 7:37f.; etc.
52. Jn. 20:22
53. Cf. Gen. 2:7
54. Rom. 8:9, NEB
55. Jn. 16:9-11
56. Jn. 14:16, 26; etc.
57. Jn. 16:14
58. Jn. 14:26
59. Jn. 14:17; 16:12, 13
60. Jn. 14:26; 16:14
61. Jn. 15:26, 27
62. Jn. 16:22f.; see ch. 17
63. Jn. 16:8-11

4

Man

THE SYNOPTIC GOSPELS

There is no formal doctrine of man in the Synoptic gospels. Jesus did not generalize about manhood or speak abstractly about humanity. He was interested in man as man. He was concerned with the human individual in his concrete situation. There is, therefore, no systematic anthropology in His teaching, high-sounding and hollow. Jesus met men in their need, encountered them in their common ways and their everyday activities. It was by His attitudes and activities that Jesus revealed His understanding about man.

The question 'What is man?' cannot be escaped. Man may ignore the question of God, but he cannot evade that which involves his own nature and destiny. It may indeed be that in asking the question about himself he may ultimately be brought face to face with the question about God. It is the view of man which is today central in the conflict. The answer returned to the enquiry must inevitably shape the sort of way human life should be lived and human individuals should be treated. The significant thing in all the creative philosophies and the dominant political systems of the past and the present is the view of man contained therein. Is man a stage in a long process of evolution or is he a cog in a relentlessly moving machine? Is he a being, all body and only body, impelled and compelled to action by stimuli from his environment or is he the slave of some primitive, passionate and intensely selfish urge which lurks in the jungle of his unconscious? If Darwin is right then man is an advanced animal only and sin is but the residue of animal instincts brought over and not yet outgrown. If Marx is right then man is in the grip of social and economic forces and the only way to make him better is to destroy all class distinctions by the forceful changing of his conditions. If Behaviourism is right then man has no moral responsibilities; and while he may be frustrated he can never be guilty. If Freud is right then man can be explained in terms of sexuality and sin be regarded as obstructed desire. Conscience is nothing other than an artificial barrier invented to hold in check instincts which would be otherwise impossible in society. Of first importance, then, is it for those for whom Jesus is final authority to grasp what He would have us understand about man.

Quite evidently He considered man to be of supreme value. Both in His acts and attitudes He showed that man is a creature of worth. Jesus say beyond the externals of life, the distinctions of class, the disparities of conditions, the shame of corruption, to the infinite value of human life. It was first through Jesus Christ that the worth of every human being became manifest. Here indeed is one of the most distinctive contributions of Christianity to civilization. When Kant, the philosopher of a later day, declared that man should never be used as a means to an end, since he is an end in himself, he was but re-echoing the estimate of Jesus regarding man. Jesus discovered the ordinary individual, and gave significance to the single man. This was the new stress in His teaching and way.

In Israel, even in the Israel of His own time, the individual tended to be lost in the community because of the strength of the desire and hope for the continuity of the nation. The value of the single person was often obscured; and the scribes and Pharisees spoke slightingly of the 'people of the land', the common folk who were wont to hear Jesus gladly.[1]

63

These were judged accursed not knowing the law.[2] Beyond Israel the individual man counted for very little and was of no worth in and of himself. It was the very absence of the certainty that life had any final meaning and permanent value which was the canker at the very heart of heathenism. For Jesus man was not a mere creature of passing time, a bearer of borrowed values, a worthless thing whose failures bring no regrets and whose death brings no sorrows. Karl Marx sums up well the teaching of Jesus about man even if he then goes on to repudiate it. In Christianity, he declares, it is taught that not one man alone, but each man has significance on his own account as a sovereign being. Man as uncultured and unsocial, man in his casual manner of being, man as he walks and stands, every man, has value. Such Marx pronounces to be the postulate, the dream and the illusion of Christianity. But Marx did not read the facts aright, did not diagnose the case aright, and did not proclaim the truth aright in his own analysis of the human individual. He who knew what was in man and had no need that others tell Him, is the best qualified to speak about man. And anyone who will think through the estimate given by Jesus to man will want, in the light of history and his own experience, to add his testimony that His witness is true.

In His teaching Jesus gave clear expression to His regard for man as a creature of value. In a series of comparisons He emphasized the pricelessness of the single individual. He contrasts man with the most cherished institutions of His day. There was no custom so firmly established and so fiercely defended at the time of Jesus than that of Sabbath keeping. That which had been designed for man's good had become his master and its purpose lost and its pleasure gone. Christ sought to shake man free from the shackles of custom and to teach him that no institution has the worth of the human life for which it was instituted. The Sabbath was made for man and not man for the Sabbath.[3] All customs are dangerous and deadly if they are not subordinate to the spirit of man.[4]

Jesus declared man's value to far outweigh the whole created universe. He is of more value than the sheep of the fields and the birds of the air.[5] The material universe is nothing when compared with the spiritual possibilities of one life.[6] The parables also indicate the same high view of man by Jesus. However 'lost' man is, it is clear that he is not unloved and unsought. The story of the Prodigal son accentuates this estimate of man. The heart of the father is stirred to its profoundest depths at the return of the lad. Such is the worth which, Jesus teaches, God puts on even a moral outcast. The significance of the parable of the lost coin is just this: while lost its value could not be fully realized. In His attitude, Christ showed the same high regard for men. A sinful woman was not cast aside. He made friends of tax gatherers and sinners. He openly took the side of the downcast and outcast; and He made it His special concern to care for those for whom no one else cared. His miracles, as acted parables, likewise illustrate the same view of man: for Him man has supreme value.

In the teaching of Jesus, too, man has immortal nature. Jesus did not conceive of man merely as a part of nature. He saw him as a spiritual being. And it was this aspect of man upon which Jesus laid special emphasis. True wealth is, therefore, in His teaching, that of the soul. To have treasure in heaven is to have that which abides.[7] It profits nothing to gain the whole world and to lose one's soul.[8] Life is more than meat, and the body than clothing.[9] Consequently a man's life does not consist in the plentifulness of possessions.[10] This does not mean that Jesus decried the body as did some of the Greek philosophers when they spoke of it as the prison-house of the soul. For Jesus the body has a place in the structure of human life; so much so, indeed, that for His coming on the stage of history the Son of God had a body prepared for Him.[11] It is for this reason that Jesus attended so often to man's bodily needs. In His

declaration that man cannot live by bread alone but by every
word of God, He put the truth about human life in right
perspective. To live under the word of God is the first
necessity; yet, clearly, He suggests that while man cannot
live by bread alone, he cannot live without it. Jesus, therefore, sees man as a duality of body and soul, of flesh and spirit.
Yet it is hardly right to say that He was setting forth a
minute analysis of man's psychological nature. His concern
was rather to stress that while man lives his life in the world
he is not fulfilling the high purpose of his being who lives
only for the world.[12]

In this sense His own life among men demonstrates His
own valuation of man. It has been said that Jesus's willingness to share the life of a peasant, is the best 'race-asset' that
men possess. His presence in humanity itself gives an
incalculable sense of dignity and worth to humankind. Of
all teachers He spoke less in sonorous generalities about
mankind yet 'stood stoutly for the human'. He made man's
cause His very own and man's well-being His first concern.
The presence of Jesus among men has given a new dignity
to man's otherness from the system of things.

According to the teaching of Jesus man has tremendous
possibilities. It is open to man to lose and forfeit the very
things which give to human life its value and meaning. It
is possible to cut one's self off from one's high destiny. To
such an utter moral perversion Jesus was referring in what
He had to say about the sin against the Holy Spirit. On the
other hand, one can attain to true life under God and to
regain the consciousness of a lost sonship.

In the view of Jesus man has broken relationships. There
is a rift in the relationship between God and man. This
comes out in the teaching of Jesus upon the necessity for
man to trustfully obey God while making it clear that this is
an ideal which can be reached only when that relationship
is restored. Only as men become sons of God can they trustfully obey. Jesus was conscious that His own Sonship was

66

unbroken.[13] This fact but emphasizes that the rest of men are estranged from God and as such are aliens and foreigners. Jesus, however, refused to remain within the realm of unstrained and unstained Sonship, whilst all other sonship but His own was broken by human sin. He, therefore, came in His Sonship to unite man to God; to give that Spirit whereby he might cry, 'Abba, Father'.

On the other hand Jesus made it plain that the relationship between man and man was snapped. Man's broken sonship with God has brought about a broken brotherhood between men. This means that in the thinking and teaching of Jesus man's broken brotherhood is restored in his renewed sonship. Fellowship is rediscovered in discipleship. Thus the vital test of sonship is brotherliness.

Yet if Jesus throughout His whole ministry, in precept and by practice, showed man to be something of worth, He did not on that account leave us with an optimistic picture of him as a creature able on his own to become a superbeing. Jesus was no comfortable idealist to whom man's goodness was ineradicable and man's progress inevitable. Nor was He a pessimist to whom every man was dirt and all life a hell. Jesus was a realist who saw life as it is, with its value, its immortality, its broken relationships and its eternal possibilities. Man needed healing, but it was His assurance that healing could be found. He knew man entirely and understood man fully, and He has told us the truth about man. What He has said, history has not falsified and experience has confirmed. He who knew man most, loved them best and died for them finally. He is *par excellence* the True Man, the Ideal of manhood, the Goal of humanity. He is the Friend of Man because He is man's Saviour restoring to man that sonship with God in His own unique Sonship which authenticates again the image of God in him.

THE FOURTH GOSPEL

In the Fourth Gospel three characteristic Johannine emphasises unite to re-inforce the Synoptic picture of man. There is to begin with the stark manner in which John, who throughout stresses the eternal divineness of the Son of God, portrays the humanness of the Word made flesh. We are made aware of His sheer manness. He is presented as a Man among men, as the real man, the full man. He does all that becometh a man: as man He could be wearied with journeying and surprised by joy. Again and again we find Him referred to as man—what people saw was 'a man that is called Jesus'.[14] Thus Pilate could present Him to the people with his not uncynical but wholly accurate exclamation, 'Behold the man!'[15]

It is in the very humanness of Jesus that the dignity of every man is to be measured. The nature of man is such that He who existed before the world was in the glory and the love of God the Father, did not despise our human state. The Word was made flesh and took up His abode amongst us. By this uniting of Himself with man He has made it clear for always that being human is no mean condition.

The second feature emphasized in John's Gospel which has a bearing on a Christian doctrine of man concerns Christ's knowledge of man's inner motives. Without the need of prolonged psycho-analysis He knew what was in man.[16] The woman by the well reclaimed by Christ's penetrating word went away to testify to Him as the man who told her all things she ever did.[17] He knew the murmurings of His disciples,[18] and the dark intent of Judas.[19] 'Man is a great deep', observed Augustine, but Jesus could plumb the depths. He had something wherewith He could draw out what lay in the deep well of man's being. Dr. Johnson, so often cogent in his remarks, contended that we form many friendships by mistake, imagining people to be different from what they really are. But Jesus made no such errors of

68

judgement. In spite, however, of His thorough knowledge of man He did not give man the impression that he was either a chip of deity or a by-product of animality—he is neither an angel nor an ape. Jesus saw man as man; and seeing through to his inner nature He addressed him as responsible and as capable of hearing the divine word. Knowing what was in men, He loved them fully, sympathized with them truly, and commanded them divinely. Of all teachers of men Jesus alone understood man. He alone, among those who claim to be humanity's benefactors, had and has a genuine 'enthusiasm for humanity'.

But His was no enthusiasm for humanity as a general thing, for the other striking fact about Jesus as the Fourth Gospel reveals Him is His interest in the individual. A broad division of John's Gospel would show chapters one to twelve as the manifestation of Christ's grace to the world and chapters thirteen to eighteen the manifestation of His glory to the disciples. But the significant fact is that although John has so much to say about 'the world', yet the first section is almost a series of personal interviews between Jesus and single individuals. There is the encounter with Nicodemus in chapter three, the woman by the well and the nobleman of Capernaum in chapter four, the infirm man at Betheseda in chapter five, the man born blind in chapter nine, Mary and Martha in chapters eleven and twelve. Thus did Christ find the single individual, discovered the man in the mass, and made the person count for something in himself and before God.

SCRIPTURE REFERENCES

1. Mk. 12:37
2. Jn. 7:49
3. Mk. 2:27; cf. Mt. 12:10f.; etc.
4. Cf. Mt. 12:1-21; Mk. 2:23-28
5. Mt. 10:31; Lk. 14:5
6. Cf. Mk. 8:36, 37

7. Mt. 6:20
8. Mt. 16:26
9. Mt. 6:25
10. Lk. 12:15
11. Cf. Heb. 10:5, 10
12. Cf. Mt. 10:28, 29; 16:26; 26:41; Mk. 8:36; Lk. 16:22
13. Cf. Mt. 11:27
14. Jn. 9:11
15. Jn. 19:5
16. Jn. 2:25
17. Jn. 4:29
18. Jn. 6:61
19. Jn. 13:11

5

Sin

Although Jesus gave high value to man He did not on that account give him any reason for boasting. None more than He underscored the terrible reality of the darker side of human nature. It has been said that the subject of sin formed but a small element in the thought of Jesus. But this is too baldly and too badly stated. The fact of the matter is that Jesus did not construe a theory of sin in general; least of all of its origin. He presupposed its reality as a fact without need of demonstration. He showed its evil nature by indicating the penalties attached to it. Jesus was more interested in the personality of sinners than in the philosophy of sin: and He consistently revealed sin's nature by reference to its manifestations.

Sin is not given a simple definition in the teaching of Jesus. To say that its essential nature is pride, or sexuality, or selfishness, or dishonour, would not be to characterize it. The many terms familiar to Jesus through the Old Testament were all true for Him. Sin is iniquity, transgression, failure, trespass, error, unrighteousness, lawlessness: it is all these, and more. Sin is sheer, downright evil. In the last reckoning sin is hostility to the declared will of God. It was in relation to God that Jesus brought out the exceeding sinfulness of sin. Sin is not man's misfortune, it is his fault.

Four broad facts emerge in the synoptic gospels concerning the teaching of Jesus regarding sin.

The first is sin's universality. Jesus certainly saw all men as sinful in the sight of God; all as blind, lost, and unrighteous. The whole tenor of his attitude and action among men show that He held sin to be universally present in the actual world. He set forth on His public ministry with a call to repentance, and He declared that the repentance of even one sinner brought joy to the angels of God.[1] Jesus viewed all men as debtors in God's sight; all as unprofitable servants. The best of parents are described as sinners.[2] Even when He spoke of the 'righteous'[3] as being outside the scope of His ministry, He was not suggesting that there were those who stood clean before God. He was simply referring to a class of people who in their own estimate were righteous. His words cannot be taken as an exception to the truth that He treated all men as in some sense sinful. There is, of course, no quantitative calculation of sin in the teaching of Jesus. The Pharisees regarded the woman of the city as more of a sinner than the common herd; it is for this reason that they were shocked that Jesus allowed her to touch Him.[4] The Jews supposed that the Galileans on whom the tower of Siloam fell were sinners above the rest, but Jesus would have none of it.[5] He was content to point to the path that men were taking, rather than with speculating upon the position they had reached. Yet He did teach, at the same time, that there was a point of no return. This terrible reality is brought out in the remarkable passage concerning 'blasphemy against the Holy Ghost'.[6] Here is the 'eternal sin', the essence of which is allowing oneself to become so blind and obtuse as to fail to see God at work. It is the cutting of oneself off from the grace of God; the getting of oneself into a position in which good is called evil and evil good. In such a state the verdict can only be 'myself am sin'. No way is left open into such a life for the Spirit of God; the soul has lost its sensitiveness, forfeited its power to repent, and

72

slipped into a place where even the forgiveness of God cannot reach.

The second emphasis in the teaching of Jesus is sin's inwardness. Jesus consistently pictured sin as having its seat in the human heart. The individual heart is the laboratory in which the poison of evil is distilled by each man for himself. Out of the heart proceeds all manner of evil things.[7] The outside of the cup of life may appear clean but within it is unclean.[8] The outward covering of the sepulchre may be decorated well, but within it contains all manner of evil.[9] Jesus therefore traces sin right down to the inner being of man. The tree of life is there poisoned at the roots and the whole of life's outgrowth is afflicted by its deadly influence.

The third feature which finds a central place in the teaching of Jesus is the guilt of sin. The fact of sin's inwardness by an act of man's will carries with it the conclusion that man is responsible for what he is and is not. The place and power of the Devil have a prominent emphasis in the teaching of Jesus, but this fact is not allowed to detract from the responsibility of the individual.[10] The connection made between sin and repentance underscores the fact of sin's guilt. And evil is to be resisted.[11] The guilt of sin is sharpened when it is brought into relation to God and recognized as evil in His sight.[12] In the presence of Jesus, seen for what He is as the holy one of God, man finds himself revealed as sinfully guilty.[13] The teaching of Jesus gave stress to the social effects of sin. Its baneful influence is not limited to the life and character of those immediately guilty but extends beyond to a circle without. No man sinneth to himself. It is for this reason that Jesus spoke strongly against those who of set purpose set out to drag down the weak and innocent.[14] And He uttered strong words of condemnation against those who made themselves out to be holier than they really were. This was the point of His parable of the Pharisee and Publican. He denounced the hypocrites, the play-actors, who made a show of goodness. The sin of make-believe was one to which the Pharisees were specially addicted, and to it He drew attention unsparingly.[15]

The fourth and most significant aspect of Jesus's teaching about sin was that it was forgivable. The Pharisees were not over generous in this regard. They held out little hope for the common people. Indeed Jewish theology generally had failed to grasp the profound significance of the message inherent in her own position as a nation specially chosen of God and declared by her prophets, that God's purposes of mercy extended beyond her borders. In most of the passages in the Synoptic gospels where the word sin occurs it is connected with the idea of forgiveness.[16] In the teaching of Jesus sin is such that the Heavenly Father must deal with it in forgiveness;[17] and salvation from sin is accomplished in the name of Jesus.[18] And the prayer of the children of God's kingdom to their heavenly Father must ever be, 'forgive us our trespasses, and deliver us from the Evil One'.

THE FOURTH GOSPEL

John asserts the universality of sin under the term 'world' which he uses some sixty-seven times in his gospel and twenty-one in his epistles. In the vast number of occurrences it has a moral sense in contrast to the physical sense of the actual material world. For John the 'world' is the natural order and, specifically, man as alienated from God. It is the world as lost and which the Son of God came to save. For John the whole world lieth in the Evil One.[19] This is the teaching of the fourth gospel. The 'world' is the devil's kingdom; and the realm in which men are by virtue of their natural birth. This is the world which knows not God and is in bondage to Satan and cannot receive the spirit of truth.[20] But Christ's kingdom is not of this world. It is 'from above' and is entered by spiritual birth.[21]

The contrast, therefore, between the two spheres is clear and sharp. There is the kingdom as a spiritual reality for which is needed a spiritual birth. That which is born of the flesh is flesh, and that which is born of the Spirit is spirit. This new kingdom-life is possessed here and now. Over against the kingdom as a spiritual reality there is the world as the realm of evil. Those who are 'in the flesh' belong to this sphere. In this state man is in bondage and blindness. Sin is an enslaving power,[22] and a perverting principle.[23] Yet for John sin is more than sinful acts. John distinguishes between sin and sins. Sin is the inward principle; sins the outward acts. Sin is the root; sins the fruit.

For the most part John represents sin under the figure of darkness, in contrast with which Christ comes as Light of life. Darkness suggests ignorance. Thus Christ comes with His offer of heavenly wisdom.[24] He is the Truth. Darkness means loss of direction. Men of this 'world' walk in darkness and do not know where they are going.[25] For those who would take to the right road Christ declared Himself as the Way. Further darkness means death; and for such Christ is the Life.

In parallel with the kingdom and the world there is also the contrast between spirit and flesh. In a sense the 'kingdom' suggests collectivity while 'spirit' is individual; so, too, is it with the terms 'world' and 'flesh'. The contrast between the two rests on the concept of two orders of existence, that of nature and that of spirit. By our natural birth we are brought with the realm of independent and personal activity. But if we are to attain a destiny in the sphere of God's rule we must come to possess eternal life in Christ.

There are two other points in the teaching of the fourth gospel concerning sin which are thrown into the very sharpest contrast. John states sin to be a satanic fact, but he also regards it as a voluntary act.

John has much to say about the devil, of Satan. Satan is clearly represented as causing man's moral fall,[26] and as being God's foe from the beginning.[27] In seeking the death of Jesus the Jews were acting in the spirit of the devil; from him emanates that evil which corrupts, binds and destroys. Sin is in the fourth gospel alliance with Satan. It operates in the world and through the flesh.

Yet John never allows us to think that sin is anything other than self-caused. It is that for which man is individually responsible. It is primarily a turning away from the light; a perversion of the will. Nowhere in the teaching of Jesus, and least of all in the gospel of John where the causative agency of Satan is most accentuated, is sin viewed as the action of Satan on a passive instrument. It is something wilful on the part of man for which he is guilty. It is a violation by man of his true nature and his forfeiture of his divine destiny.

Sin, persisted in, becomes our master.[28] The supreme revelation of sin is seen in the attitude taken up to Christ: 'If ye believe not that I am He ye shall die in your sins'.[29] It is His presence in the world which manifests most fully human evil; if He had not come sin's essential sinfulness would have remained hidden.[30] It is significant that Jesus in His last great discourse with His disciples, which took place in Jerusalem, the centre of hostility to His claims, should specify unbelief as the decisive sin.[31] It was the manifestations of the manifold evidences of God's love and mercy in the life and work of Jesus, which left men without excuse in the presence of the divine judgement. It was in truth this very manifestation of God, designed by Him as the eternal remedy against sin,[32] which, in its development and actions, affords further opportunities to sin and sin's consequences.[33]

SCRIPTURE REFERENCES

1. Lk. 15:7
2. Mt. 7:11; Lk. 11:13
3. Mt. 9:13; Mk. 2:17; Lk. 5:32

4. Cf. Lk. 7:37-39
5. Cf. Lk. 13:1f.
6. Mt. 12:31f.; Mk. 3:29; Lk. 12:10
7. Cf. Mt. 15:19; cf. Mt. 9:4; 13:15; Mk. 3:5; Lk. 1:51
8. Mt. 23:26
9. Mt. 23:29
10. Cf. Mt. 5:39; 9:4; 18:21
11. Mt. 5:39
12. Lk. 15:21; 16:15
13. Lk. 5:8
14. Cf. Mt. 18:6; Mk. 9:42; Lk. 17:2
15. Mt. 23:5-7; Mk. 12:38f.; Lk. 11:43; 20:45; cf. Mt. 6:1-6; 5:20
16. Cf. Mt. 1:21; 3:6; 9:2, 5, 6; 12:31; 26:28; see parallels in Mk. and Lk.; and in passages peculiar to them the same observation holds.
17. Mt. 6:15
18. Mt. 1:21; see chapter 7 'Salvation'.
19. 1 Jn. 5:19
20. Cf. 14:30; 17:17, 25
21. Cf. Jn. 3; etc.
22. Jn. 8:34
23. Jn. 8:21
24. Jn. 3:19, 21
25. Jn. 12:35, 46
26. Jn. 8:44
27. Jn. 8:44
28. Jn. 8:34
29. Jn. 8:24
30. Jn. 15:22
31. Jn. 16:8f.
32. Jn. 1:29
33. Jn. 9:41

6

Grace

THE SYNOPTIC GOSPELS

Christianity, it has been said, practically created the New Testament concept of love (*agapē*), but it had the verb 'to love' (*agapaō*) ready to hand. But there was no corresponding Greek verb for grace (*charis*) in existence. The word *charis* itself was indeed in vogue, but it had virtually to be reborn for use in the gospel of God. By the new message of Christ it was filled out with a profounder and richer content. Yet there was in vogue the verb *chairō*, meaning to give delight. Here possibly we have the beginning of the stages in the religious function of the term. In classical Greek literature the word *charis* had reference to that which gives delight or joy. Hence its original idea is that of charm and winsomeness. From this, it would seem, *charis* took on a subjective connotation with the notion of kindly or courteous predominating. The man who had *charis* exhibited a gracious disposition, and so the word became equivalent for favour or goodwill. But a favour is an expression of goodwill revealing a certain attitude on the part of the giver. Thus the favour can be taken as the concrete token of the bestower's kindness. A favour bestowed should be gratefully received; therefore *charis* denoted, not only the sense of gratitude felt by the recipient of the favour, but also the actual expression of the gratitude. In the Greek translation of the Old Testament, the Septuagint, the term grace is confined to the first

78

sense of the term, that of charm and winsomeness. In the New Testament all these ideas are present, but *charis* finds, especially in the writings of the apostle Paul, new content becoming almost an equivalent for salvation.

The term is absent from the Old Testament and significantly the apostle never quotes any Old Testament passage for his own special use of the concept. Yet while the Old Testament has not the word as such, it has its own 'grace-words'. Of these the nearest in approach to the New Testament term *charis* is the Hebrew word *hēn* which carries the idea of undeserved favour. This word is translated as 'grace' some thirty-eight times, and as 'favour' twenty-six.[1] When we turn to the Synoptic gospels we are immediately struck by the absence of the word from the teaching of Jesus. On four occasions only did Jesus use it with the ordinary sense of 'thanks'.[2] The word does not occur at all in Matthew and Mark. Luke has it on four other occasions three of which have the sense of 'favour'.[3] Two important conclusions are to be drawn from these facts. The first is the significant one that it shows that the early Church was not in the habit of reading back into the teaching of Jesus ideas which it wished to make secure. The word 'grace' came to have a supreme place in the doctrine of the Church, yet it is not placed in His mouth so as to have the stamp of His authority. There are those who are all too ready to assert that ideas which they regard as too 'advanced' for His time, as being the later reflection of the Church put into a saying of Christ. The absence of this word should cause them to ponder for it would seem to suggest that the New Testament writers were more careful to preserve the actual teaching of Jesus rather than what they desired Him to have said. The other conclusion to be drawn is this; there is a sense in which Jesus could not have used the term to convey what, for example, the apostle Paul put into it. His own life and death and resurrection were the very facts which were to give to the word its real meaning.

There is, however, one remaining instance of the word in Luke which may possibly lead us on to its peculiar significance in the New Testament epistles. Luke 4:22 has in the original text two possible renderings, according to whether the emphasis is put on the manner in which Jesus spoke or the matter of which He spoke. The people in the synagogue at Nazareth wondered at the gracious words which proceeded out of His mouth (AV, RSV, Phillips). The manner of His speaking must have been specially winsome; there was an attractiveness about His every action on the occasion. But not only did the people marvel at the gracious manner of Jesus's speaking; they marvelled, too 'at the words of grace' (RV, NEB). Luke would have us understand that there was more in his mind when he wrote these words than their mere aesthetic impression. In Acts 14:3, Luke uses the phrase 'the word of his grace' as an equivalent for the gospel, and he records Paul's statement 'the gospel of the grace of God' in chapter 20:24. It need not be doubted therefore that the expression 'the words of grace' in Luke 4:22 could have this full objective sense, especially in view of Luke's companionship with the apostle.

The context strengthens this objective reference. The passage read by our Lord from Isaiah proclaimed a coming acceptable year of the Lord. Here our Lord asserts its fulfilment; indeed He makes the references more gracious still by omitting the reference to the divine vengeance in the original passage.[4] Luke's object, then, was not simply to record the fascinating effect of what Jesus was saying, but to indicate at the same time that His 'grace' went beyond the frontiers of Israel. He had come as the Lord's anointed to do a work of grace for men in need. There was in Christ's reading of Isaiah a real hint of a gospel of grace for all. Luke, of course, would not have us deny the subjective reference of the words. He, of all the Synoptic writers, was strongly impressed by the gracious manner of Christ's bearing; but he would make us aware of the gracious matter of Christ's teaching. His words, then, were 'words of grace about grace'.

While, however, the word grace was not on our Lord's lips, the reality of grace was expressed in His life, teaching and work. There is then the deepening of the meaning of the concept in the story of the gospel. This fact emerges in a number of ways, making it clear that the message of the Synoptic gospels is in full harmony with that of the apostle Paul, that it is by grace man is saved through faith. And if of faith then it is not of works.

There is, first, Christ's acceptance of His mission. He came to fulfil His Father's purpose and will. The constant recurrence of the phrase, 'I am come', accentuates this divine undertaking by God the Son on man's behalf.[5] God sent His Son, and the Son has come to seek and to save that which is lost. This consciousness of a mission to accomplish was for Him the purpose of His life and the burden of His work. The initiative lay with God. This is grace!

The reality of grace is focused, further, in the attitude of Jesus during the whole course of His ministry. He sought out the needy and the sinful. He made it evident by the compassion that He showed and the care that He evinced, that God was not only waiting to be gracious, He was going to the utmost lengths to find men. So it was that Jesus broke through class barriers and conventional taboos. It has been pointed out that just here comes the radical difference between Judaism and the gospel of Christ. Judaism taught clearly enough that God was gracious to the repentant sinner, but it left the first step with the sinner. The distinctive thing about Jesus was that He took the deliberate move on God's behalf to meet man's dire need. If it is suggested that man is helpless, then it is no less suggested that God is not. Jesus met men in their human situation and at the point of their sin and shame. This is grace!

The reader of the Synoptic gospels comes upon certain passages, the logical drift of which is that salvation is a matter of grace. The Kingdom parables of Matthew 13, for example, throw out several such illuminating suggestions. In the case of 'The Sower' the seed sown is the same whether it falls on stony, thorny or good ground. The difference is in the nature of the soil. But in the end it is 'God who gives the increase'. The workings of grace may be small to begin with, as the parable of the 'Mustard Seed' teaches, but it can grow. Each parable has something to say about the Kingdom of God; and the accent should be allowed to fall upon the two words *of God*. In the end only those who ask of God can receive the blessings of the Kingdom. It is a matter of grace.[6]

In addition there are passages which enshrine in their context, as clearly as does the apostle Paul in direct statement, the doctrine of grace. There is the conversation between Christ and His disciples following the departure of the rich young ruler. Jesus had made it clear that this eager enquirer had not and could not gain entrance to the new realm of God by his obedience to the Torah, or law. The law had, in fact, found him out and ruled him out. Riches were no passport to the kingdom. The perplexed disciples, who had been encouraged in the belief that prosperity was a reward for goodness, asked in amazement, 'Who then can be saved?' Jesus replied, 'With men it is impossible, but not with God, for with God all things are possible'.[7] Nothing a man is or has can win him a place in the divine realm. The ultimate ability to enter life is from God alone. In this passage Jesus is announcing the gospel of grace in contrast with that of works and law. Indeed at this point some critical writers have introduced the very word 'grace' so as to uncover the inner meaning of what Jesus was saying.

The same is true of the passage in which Jesus deals with the sons of Zebedee. They wanted to secure a place of privilege in God's kingdom only to be reminded that the kingdom was not for the great and mighty, but for those humble enough to be there.[8] At the end of Matthew 19, Peter raised the question of what the disciples were to have by way of reward for their leaving of all and following Jesus.

It is made clear to them that God is under no obligation to any man; and that those who suppose themselves to be first may find themselves last. Jesus then follows in Matthew 20:1-6 with the parable of the Labourers in the Vineyard. The teaching of it is that the kingdom is not got by anything given up. It is folly to seek to bargain with God. The final principle of His dealing with men is His own generosity. It is the Householder himself who went out and sought the idle. He did not owe them anything; they had no rights over him. He gave them a place in his vineyard out of sheer goodwill. It was a boon unsought and unbought. This is grace!

The parable of the Pharisee and the publican accentuates the truth that it is the man humble enough to look to God for mercy who is justified. Here is contrasted the self-expressed morality of the Pharisee with the self-confessed misery of the publican. And the former counted for nought in the presence of God. It was the man who could not look up to God who was the man upon whom God looked. That man was accepted. This is grace!

In the symbolism of the last supper, perhaps, more than anywhere else is the doctrine of grace best set forth. Jesus was conscious of some unique purpose in His vocation. He was aware of a special value in His ultimate death. Thus at the end He faced the cross, not merely as One loyal to some ideal, but as One whose death was to bring about a new and a better age. He was giving His life as ransom for many. The cup of the last supper was the cup of a new covenant. He was serving by the giving up of His life and that death was redemptive. The cross was essential as the means and the medium of God's redemption. This was no idea hit upon by the later Church. It was part of Christ's own interpretation of His impending cross. The message of the cross did not originate with the Christian movement, but with the Christians' Master. This means that right from the very first the life and work of Christ were read in the category of 'grace', which was authenticated and vindicated by His rising from the dead.

Two broad basic facts are, then, evident from the Synoptic gospels. On the one hand, the fact that the saving initiative is with God; and on the other hand, that any plea to human merit is inadequate. These two facts together are what is meant by 'the grace of God'.

THE FOURTH GOSPEL

While the term 'grace' is only three times present in John's gospel the truth of grace is everywhere presupposed. The three instances occur in the prologue.[9] In 1:14 the Word made flesh is declared to be 'full of grace and truth'. The phrase echoes the Old Testament frequent combination of 'mercy and truth' as a description of the character of God.[10] But, of course, the term 'grace' is much fuller and richer than that of mercy'. In 1:16 the inexhaustible nature of grace comes out in the phrase 'grace for grace'. From the 'fulness' of the Incarnate Logos 'grace' is constantly outpoured for 'as many as receive him'. In 1:17 John brings the law which came by Moses into contrast with the grace and truth which 'came to be' by Jesus Christ. This contrast becomes in the writings of the apostle Paul an antithesis. There, as we shall see, whatever is of 'the law' is not of 'the gospel of the grace of God'.

Apart, however, from these three references it can be said that the grace-concept underlies the whole gospel of John. As in the Synoptics there is reference to the Son being sent by the Father;[11] and of His coming.[12] As the One who has come for man's salvation Christ has to be 'received'.[13] It is those who believe who have eternal life: indeed the term 'believe' occurs some ninety times in the gospel thus making it clear that salvation is by faith not of works. In 4:10 there is reference to the 'gift' (*dōrea*) of God. Other instances of the use of the word[14] suggests that it specifies some definite gift

of the very highest and best order, such as those comprehended in the most objective sense of the term 'grace'. Those
who come to Christ are drawn of the Father.[15] The true sons
of God are those who are born 'from above' (*anōthen*).[16] That
which is born of the flesh remains flesh. The sons of God are
those who believe in Him and in this faith are reborn: their
birth depends 'not on the course of nature nor on any impulse
or plan of man, but on God'.[17] 'He that speaketh for himself
seeketh his own glory':[18] here is the repudiation of works.
'Without me ye can do nothing':[19] here is the principle of
grace.

SCRIPTURE REFERENCES

1. Cf. e.g. for 'grace', Gen. 6:8; 19:19; Ex. 33:12; etc.; for 'favour', Gen. 18:3; 30:17; Ex. 3:21; 11:3; etc.
2. Lk. 6:32; 33, 34; 17:9
3. Lk. 1:28, 30; 2:52
4. Cf. Is. 61:2; Lk. 4:19
5. Cf. e.g. Mt. 9:13; Mk. 9:37; 10:45; 12:6
6. Cf. Mt. 7:8, 11; Lk. 11:13
7. Cf. Mk. 10:13-31
8. Mk. 10:35-40
9. Jn. 1:14, 16, 17
10. Cf. Exod. 34:6; Ps. 25:10; 85:10; etc.
11. Cf. Jn. 3:17; 6:29, 57; 7:29; 8:42; etc.
12. Cf. Jn. 5:43; 12:47; etc.
13. Jn. 1:12
14. Cf. Ac. 11:38; Rom. 5:15, 17; 2 Cor. 9:15
15. Jn. 6:44, 65
16. Jn. 3:3
17. Jn. 1:13, Phillips
18. Jn. 6:18
19. Jn. 15:5

7

Salvation

THE SYNOPTIC GOSPELS

Only once in the synoptic gospels is Christ called Saviour.[1]
But the title once given is significant of all that as divine Person He had to come to do. He had, Himself, first, and after
Him the writers of the New Testament, used the term 'to
save' as a comprehensive one to describe His mission. And
He was heralded on to the stage of history with the angelic
announcement that He was to be called Jesus as the one who
should save His people from their sins.[2] The presence and purpose of Jesus in the world had then a declared saving significance. He impressed His contemporaries, both friend and foe
alike, with this aspect of His mission. There were those in His
day who sought and found His saving grace. The sneer at the
cross from those who rejected His way, that 'He saved others,
Himself He cannot save' is its own testimony to how deeply
the meaning of His mission and message had impressed itself on men. What they meant as a harsh criticism turned out
to be a high compliment.

Of course, the idea of salvation in the gospels has an enriched content; nevertheless it is against its Old Testament
background that its meaning is best understood. The basic
thought of the principal words there used for salvation is *to
be roomy*, or *to be broad*. Salvation is, therefore, an enlargement.[3] But in a more definite sense salvation in the Old Testament has reference to God's act of deliverance whether for

the nation[4] or individuals within it.[5] In broad terms it signifies the rescue of the people of God from the restrictions im-
posed by their enemies. Yet God's acts of deliverance had
their moral and spiritual conditions. It is the righteous who
are assured of God as their rock and their salvation. Thus
whenever the people of Israel turned from the path of righteousness and abandoned themselves to wickedness, deliverance could only come to them by a change of heart. Ultimately
therefore, their salvation included forgiveness of their sins on
condition of repentance. Their external blessings, victory
over their enemies, restoration from exile, and the like, were
consequently related to their spiritual and moral condition:
and God's favour was promised to all who sought God with
a penitent heart. It remains, however, that the dominant idea
of the Old Testament is of God saving His people from
trouble and distress.[6] This was indeed the connotation of the
word uppermost in the mind of the Jewish people when Jesus
began His ministry. There was, therefore, an easy equation
in the popular mind between 'to save' and 'to heal'.[7] And
His disciples in distress upon the stormy lake appeal to Jesus
to save them.[8] But there are passages in which the term 'save'
is used as something real apart from a physical cure or deliverance.[9] Of special interest here is the story of the rich
young ruler.[10] As he turned away sorrowful, unable to set
himself loose from his great possessions, the disciples, who
readily took such as evidence of the blessing of God, asked in
perplexity, 'Who then can be saved?' This passage makes
it clear that to inherit eternal life, to enter the kingdom of
God, and to be saved, are three ways of saying the same
thing. It was evidently part of the programme of Jesus to
take up the idea of salvation, which the prophecies of the
Messianic age had announced as more spiritual and universal,
and to show that in His own person and ministry men were
seeing 'the salvation of God'. The important advance then in
the New Testament is in its insistence that salvation is something less physical and environmental. God who in past days

delivered good men from suffering was also ready to deliver bad men from sin. Thus our Lord announced it as His special mission to seek and to save them that are lost, like a Shepherd rescuing the wandering sheep;[11] and like a Physician whose duty and delight is to heal.[12] What attracted the disciples to Him was not His noble ethic, but the conviction that He would 'save' them for the new age. He would prepare them for life in the 'coming era' and lead them into the kingdom of God. The disciples came to understand the salvation which Jesus brought to them, and offered to all, as a life of perfect blessedness to be realized in its fulness hereafter. It was such a fellowship with God which would guarantee peace in the present world, and life for evermore in the world to come.[13] The term salvation is then a comprehensive one comprising within it all that Christ came to do for man.

The 'why' of salvation is based upon a fact about man and a fact about God. There is the fact of man's need. For Jesus, as we have seen, sin was real; yet He did not talk of sin so much as draw attention to sins. He spoke of its inwardness and guilt. It was not, however, the evidently 'sinful' for whom this salvation was necessary. It was in fact axiomatic with Jesus that all men needed the salvation of God. And that need is shown in the words by which He characterized men as 'lost', 'dead', 'weary', 'heavy laden', and so forth. It is also shown in the severity of His ethic. There is really no account of sin to match the demands made upon men in the Sermon on the Mount. The Sermon on the Mount is not the gospel; it shows rather the overwhelming need of the gospel. Thus for Christ, the righteous, or those who considered themselves to be so, were as much in need of salvation as the 'sinners'. For salvation was something more than morality touched with emotion; something more than ritual performed with punctiliousness. Salvation is for the synagogue as much as for the slum; needed equally by the people in the pew as by the people in the pub. And the great thing about the gospel records is that the love of God is not restricted to any one

88

class; it is a love which would save the evil man from his sin and the good man from his goodness.

There is, then, the other fact about the 'why' of salvation, the fact about God. The ground of salvation is the undeserved favour of the all-loving God who has taken the initiative on man's behalf. Nothing indeed is more compelling and challenging in the teaching of Jesus than His insistence that salvation flows from the illimitable goodness of God. The Jews thought otherwise. To them God was the exacting judge whose favour had to be won by meritorious acts. They thus performed their wearying and wearing round of rituals, fastings, Sabbath observances, almsgivings. Jesus showed God to be a God who cared; and His own presence was demonstration of the lengths that God would go to to recover His lost children. The gospels make it clear that the need of man was anticipated in the love of God. God had not to wait for a nod from man before He took the initiative.

To the divine offer of salvation there must be the human response. From the divine point of view the gospel of salvation is at the same time a call and a command. It is an invitation. Men are invited to 'come', they are 'bidden to the wedding feast', they are called 'to follow'. Yet it is an imperative. It comes as a command to repent and to believe the gospel. There is no one so urgent as God. There is no sense of an easy-going salvation; no cheap ticket to heaven. There is no idea of living as one likes and hoping to pick up salvation easily and cheaply at the end. Jesus had something to say about taking to the 'narrow way', 'entering by the straight gate', of being prepared to 'lose one's life', and 'of forsaking all' and the like. Yet those who accept all that salvation involves will be 'rich towards God' and 'have treasures in heaven'.[14]

The primary synoptic condition is repentance. This is a moral act, a decision of the mind (*metanoia*). Sin is something deeper than the outward act, so repentance is more than an outward act. It is an inward decision to turn from sin to

89

God; it is a life-shaking and soul-shattering inward revolt. The change is not that of the intellect only, but of the whole nature. It is an altered view of God which carries with it a heartfelt sorrow for wrong done, and a confession of it with a decisive turning to God and righteousness. Repentance is, then, what the word literally signifies, a 'change of mind', but not just the attainment of a new idea, the gaining of a new concept. It is the acceptance by the whole man of what the changed view of both God and sin involves. It is a turning around from the way of loss and death and an entry into life, a participation in the kingdom of God. The term as used in the Synoptic gospels is then a very comprehensive one and it includes faith, as part of the process, the last step of it.

Faith is, therefore, an accompaniment of repentance. And throughout, the emphasis falls upon this aspect thereby making clear that there is nothing in man which procures his salvation. If repentance is thought of as merely sorrow, then a man may have something wherein to boast. But a sense of shame and guilt which drive a man to God for pardon and peace is much more than the feeling that one has played the fool. Here evidently one comes to God to receive from Him a boon and a blessing to which he has in and of himself no right. It is for this reason that faith figures more largely in the Synoptics, and the New Testament generally, than repentance. In the Synoptics 'to repent' comes fourteen times, and 'repentance' ten times. But the term 'to believe' or 'to have faith' (*pisteuō*) occurs twenty-nine times, and 'faith' (*pistis*) twenty-four. Faith in one instance in the Synoptics has a passive sense carrying the Old Testament idea of 'faithfulness'.[15] And once also it has the technical sense,[16] which reappears quite frequently in the Pastoral letters. Its use in all other instances is in a religious sense conveying the thought of humble and trustful acceptance of the divine mercy. Throughout the Synoptic gospels the object of faith is either God or Christ, or faith in the promise of God or of Christ. In the last reckoning, however, there is no difference; for all through, God is seen as acting in and through Christ unto salvation. In parable and in miracle, in teaching and in touch, He is revealing to men the measureless love and forgiving grace of the Father. Christ shows the true nature of God as pardoning love. Christ manifested the Fatherlike heart of God; and by Him was sent to be Saviour. The message of the Synoptics is then the essential Christian message for all men at all times, 'Repent and believe the gospel'.[17] And the continual attitude of the trusting soul is this: 'Lord, I believe; help thou my unbelief'.[18]

This fundamental fact of faith as the appropriating condition of salvation is also enforced in other terms. To take on Christ's yoke; to come to Him; to confess Him before men; to follow Him: these are all equivalent expressions. They may, of course, bring out more clearly the continuous attitude, but they also imply an initial act, the decision of faith. But the important thing throughout, whatever the term used, is that of a right relation to Christ as the personal mediator of salvation. Thus in the end, for example, to believe His words[19] is to believe in Him. For the gospel is not something distinct and different from Him. He is the gospel; He is the salvation of God. While, then, faith is the ultimate requisite for the experience of salvation, and the condition of forgiveness, it is such a faith as issues in love of God who through Christ has wrought for man such a good work.

This brings us to the 'what' of salvation. The question is 'what, according to the Synoptics, is involved in the experience of salvation?' It certainly means 'to be saved'. We have seen how, read against its Old Testament background, the idea of salvation tended to be equated with that of rescue from trouble or recovery from sickness. And in a spiritual sense this is what salvation means. For the trouble from which one is delivered is an affliction of the soul. Christ did not promise that life for the believing man would be free from trial—in the world we would have trouble and persecution for His sake. And the sickness which is healed is that of the heart. It is not said that the believing one shall be free from all life's ills. It was also noted how, in the story of the Rich Young Ruler, to inherit eternal life, and to enter the kingdom of God, were synonymous with being saved.

The experience of salvation is also the experience of being forgiven. The Synoptics have much to say on this topic. There are three words meaning to 'forgive'. There is the word 'to set free' (*apoluein*) which is found once.[20] Luke uses the term 'to be gracious to' (*charizesthai*) twice.[21] But the general expression is 'to remit', or 'let off' (*aphiēmi*), which comes some thirty-seven times.

The teaching of Jesus was an elaboration of the declaration of Psalm 86:5, that God is good and ready to forgive. In petition and parable, in prayer and proclamation He made clear that God is always willing to hear the cry of the truly penitent and to pardon their sins. The petitions of the Lord's prayer, or more correctly the disciples' prayer, tell us that it is no vain thing to ask our heavenly Father for forgiveness. For God's willingness to forgive is here assured under certain conditions. Some of our Lord's parables make the same point. Of special note here is that of the prodigal son and the story of the Pharisee and the publican. The first of these makes the point that forgiveness is free and full. The story does not profess to state the grounds upon which the penitent is forgiven; its purpose is to declare the fact that there is forgiveness for all who return to the father's home. There is no cross in the story except in the aching heart of the father. Nor indeed is Jesus Himself in the tale. This does not make the gospel of the Synoptics the gospel of the Father. Jesus here was emphasizing one aspect of the truth; He taught what the religion of His time had woefully obscured, that God is good and ready to forgive. And that was a lesson which was needed. For had not the Scribes and Pharisees virtually held out little hope for 'the people of the land', and virtually no hope at all for the outcast and the gentile?

But if the story of Luke 15 illustrates the fullness and the freeness of forgiveness, that of the Pharisee and the publican unfolds the condition of it.[22] The Pharisee pleaded his own merit and the publican his own misery. And it was the publican who went away with a lightened heart and a livened spirit. Trustful humility is the condition of forgiveness; and without that the moral Pharisee remained wrapt in his own goodness, unaccepted and unhealed. In His own prayer from the cross, 'Father, forgive them, for they know not what they do', Jesus gave public acknowledgement to His own faith in the Father who was willing to forgive. His proclamation, in that hard saying, that all manner of sin and blasphemy shall be forgiven the sons of men except that against the Holy Spirit, was not intended to limit the forgiveness of God. It must rather have had the effect on those who heard of showing how broad and bountiful was the love of God that could extend so far and forgive so much.

There was, however, something even more significant in the Synoptic doctrine of forgiveness. Not only did Jesus teach that God was willing to forgive, but He declared His own right to forgive. In the gospels, it has been said, the really new thing is the forgiveness of sins. Yet Jesus did not teach forgiveness as a general truth. He granted it as a fact. No prophet ever took it on himself to forgive men. The story of the paralytic man shows that Jesus not only declared forgiveness, He embodied it.[23] The account is found in all three synoptic gospels and shows that it made a deep impression, for we are told that the people wondered, praised God, and acknowledged that some unprecedented and superhuman power had been entrusted to a son of man. It was indeed the claim that Christ made of having the power on earth to forgive sin which disturbed the Pharisees. They reasoned, 'who can forgive sins but God alone?' But they did not draw the right conclusion from the evidence before them as the man took up his bed and went his way.

Akin in significance to that of the paralytic man is the

93

story of the sinful woman.[24] Jesus assured her that her sins were forgiven, that her faith had saved her. When Simon, in whose house Jesus was guest, protested at the presence of a woman who was 'a sinner' and at the acceptance by Jesus of the lavish outpouring of her love, Jesus replies that 'her sins, which are many, are forgiven, for she loved much'. Yet He was not declaring that her love was the condition of her forgiveness. This rather is the force of the 'because' (*hoti*)—because you see this lavish outpouring of her love, you may know she has been forgiven much. Her repentance and her acceptance had taken place before her grateful love was manifested. The one who fancies he has little to be forgiven will love but little. But if in the end we are all unprofitable servants who of us has not much that needs remission.

It is in the context of the teaching of Jesus about God's forgiveness that the command given to men to forgive is to be understood. His teaching of an almost unlimited forgiveness of man by man is something of which pagan ethics knew nothing. And even Jewish ethics was not over generous in this regard. It was taught that man could only ask for forgiveness thrice. But Jesus set no limit to forgiveness either in the number of times, until seventy times seven, or in the extent of persons, all men and even enemies.[25] Yet Jesus does enjoin the necessity for repentance if forgiveness is to be real; for it is an ethical act and involves personal relationships. Therefore it is declared, 'If thy brother sin reprove him, if he repent forgive him'.[26] Such reproof and such forgiveness are marks of genuine love.

In one passage (apart from the petition in the Lord's prayer, 'forgive us our trespasses, as we forgive them that trespass against us') a close connection between God's forgiveness of man and man's forgiveness of others is admitted.[27] It is only the one who can forgive who can be forgiven. This is no *lex talionis*—no law of retaliation. It is not being said that God will show mercy only when it is shown to others. The point is rather that God cannot forgive the one who will

94

not forgive, for an unforgiving spirit reveals an unrepentant heart. And where there is no full repentance there can be no real forgiveness.

There is another idea involved in the experience of salvation which has special exposition in the Pauline epistles, but is very much implied in the Synoptics. To be saved is to be justified. The word for justify (*dikaioō*) means to be pronounced 'not guilty' on trial; that is, to be cleared of blame. In this sense in the Old Testament God can be said to be justified. His character is seen to be free from the evil which unbelief, hasty thought, or inadequate insight might bring against Him.[28] So, too, God's servants can be 'justified', cleared of wrongful accusations. In the kingdom of heaven the 'righteous' shall shine as the sun.[29] In the Old Testament God is said to justify the righteous,[30] but not the wicked.[31] There are, however, two passages in Isaiah in which there is a hint of the New Testament doctrine of God's justification of the ungodly.[32]

In the gospels the basis of justification is the attitude which discounts any personal merit. Here, once again, the parable of the Pharisee and publican (Luke 18) is instructive. The Pharisee sought to justify himself, whereas the taxgatherer laid no store on what he was, but threw himself on the mercy of God. He went down to his house justified rather than the other. It was the one folly of the Pharisees generally to seek to 'justify themselves'.[33] But God knows the heart. The evidence of one's acceptance by God is the words of the lips.[34] In the gospels then salvation is to be saved from the wrath of God, to be fully forgiven, to be justified freely by God's grace.

There is the final question of the 'where' of salvation. From what has been said it will be clear that salvation is to be found in Christ. The question poses itself, what do the gospels teach about the grounds on which salvation comes to the trusting soul? Now it is evident that there is no theory about this in the Synoptics. Those healed, those forgiven, knew it as an experimental fact. They did not ask where exactly did the healing power or the forgiving word reside, in the word spoken or in the one who spoke it, or in God in whose name the word was spoken? The truth is that the means whereby Jesus accomplished salvation is variously expressed. He certainly did represent His message as possessing in some sense a saving value. Those who learned of Him would find rest unto their souls. He was known as 'the teacher';[35] and His message rang with 'authority'.[36] It is, however, essential to note that the word He spoke had saving value only because it was His word. In a very real sense what He spoke was what He was. It is impossible to keep Christ's words separate from His person. Thus was His teaching a means for the seeking and saving of the lost. For thereby those who heard were directed to God and their need of Him; thereby, men were led to a truer understanding of the requirements of righteousness and the shame of sin, and thus to an awareness of the forgiving mercy of God and the demands and privileges of His kingdom. But not only is it impossible to separate Christ's words from His person, but also, it is not possible to separate His work from His person. What He says is what He is, and what He is is what He does. As Messiah He came to save men, to forgive them, and to justify them, and as Messiah He suffered and died. His suffering and dying must then have some vital connection with His saving purpose.

What then is the significance of His death in relation to the saving of men? One fact is clear; the idea of the cross was latent in Christ's mind from the first. At the baptism His Sonship was attested and assailed. He knew He was there as God's Messiah identifying Himself with humanity. He underwent John's baptism 'unto repentance', thus becoming numbered with the transgressors. He read the roll in the synagogue of Capernaum and took to Himself what Isaiah attributed to the one on whom the Spirit of the Lord rested.

Quite evidently the cross was no surprise to Jesus. He

knew that a time was sure to come when He, the bridegroom, would be taken away. Throughout His career He was truly His own as well as truly human and the shadow of the world's sin lay upon it from the first.

But the idea of the cross was proclaimed by Christ with clarity after the great confession at Caesarea Philippi. All three Synoptics introduce our Lord's express teaching concerning His death at this point.[37] A new epoch was begun in His ministry; His audience was not now so much the multitude as the twelve; and His subject was not so much the kingdom as Himself, and in particular His death. It was when they had discovered His Messiahship that He began to teach them the implications of it; what the title really involved for Him. From now on they must understand that the cross is the way appointed for the Lord's anointed. He must die; but not by any outward constraint; not because the wheel of history which He took into His hands was too powerful for Him and flung Him back to death. He must die; but rather by an inward necessity. His death is something He must accept if He is to fulfil His saving work. In referring to the coming cross Christ is, then, speaking out of a sense of vocation and not merely out of a view of His historical circumstances. It is beyond question, therefore, that there was in the mind and teaching of Jesus a connection between His suffering and death and His work of seeking and saving the lost. But it is still to be asked, What is the connection? Two passages are important in this regard. The first shows Christ's death to be a ransom for sin;[38] and the second declares Christ's death to be a covenant concerning sin.[39]

Much discussion has gone on about Christ's reference to His death as a 'ransom'. We may take it that the ideas which the passage preserves were integral to the thought of Jesus; here indeed the concepts of Son of Man and the Suffering Servant blend. The passage more than any other reveals Jesus's own conviction about His death. In classical usage

97

the term for ransom (*lutron*) was uniformly applied to expiatory sacrifices and this is the idea here. A ransom is not wanting at all except where a life has been forfeited. What Christ is saying then is that the forfeited lives of men are liberated by His own life of self-surrender. By giving His life man is freed from bondage and death. The thought which Christ Himself verbalizes here is restated by the apostle Paul;[40] and because it is found in a Pauline letter this does not mean that the writer of the gospel 'Paulinized', but rather that the apostle sat at the feet of His Saviour.

In the passage dealing with the institution of the Last Supper the idea of covenant has an Old Testament background. Mark states, 'This is my blood of the covenant shed for many'; Matthew adds, 'for the remission of sin'; Luke has the words 'new' and 'poured out for you'. There is an Old Testament background for a covenant made with blood in Exodus 24. By linking the Supper with the Passover some scholars note that the Passover had no reference to sin. Thus any connection of the Supper with the idea of atonement is denied and Matthew's words 'for the remission of sin' are considered an addition made by the Church. But the probable background is the new covenant of Jeremiah 31. This is connected with forgiveness of sin (v.34). Thus Jesus was proclaiming here the cost at which this new covenant which had forgiveness of sin as its blessing was established, that is, His poured out life. The covenant blood is then sacrificial blood, and with this is associated propitiatory power. And it is shed 'for many'. Here Isaiah 53 is linked with Jeremiah 31. The one who initiates the new covenant at the cost of His life is the Servant who in this way justifies many. Salvation is then based upon the death of the cross and whatever we owe as sinners to the love of God we owe, fundamentally and finally, to the death of Jesus. Like the ransom He paid, so the covenant He made is 'for many'. This clause does not set a limit to the extent of Christ's work. Quite the contrary, it suggests rather that the benefits of His self-sacrifice go beyond that of the lost sheep of the house of Israel.

The new element however is the command 'to drink' and 'to eat', 'each one of you'. There was nothing corresponding to this in the sacrificial system. The wine represents the blood: but the drinking of blood was forbidden by the Law. Israel did not share in the life of their sacrifices. But we are to share in His. His life was made available to us through His death. There is thus the personal appropriation; what is 'for many' is 'for you': for each to take and eat and drink.

THE FOURTH GOSPEL

When we turn to the Fourth Gospel what we owe to Christ is usually presented as eternal life. The word suggests more than everlastingness. It is life of a new quality; the God-type life. It is best understood in contrast with death, to that which is perishing.[41] Life apart from God is the ethical destruction of the soul, the forfeiture of man's true destiny as a child of God. But the life which Christ brings is one of fellowship with God, a life which by its nature is raised above the limits of time and space.

In John's gospel the dominant thought is redemption through revelation. It is life eternal to know the only true God and Jesus Christ whom He has sent. In Christ God makes Himself known to men and in making Himself known redeems them.

Yet it is not true to say that John grounds the significance of Jesus upon the incarnation. Christ came in the flesh as the Word, as the Life, the Way and the Truth. But the death of Christ is brought to the fore in a great variety of ways so as to demonstrate the fact of its utmost significance for the redemptive act.

1 Chapter 1 : 29

'Behold the Lamb of God, which taketh away the sin of

LIVING DOCTRINES OF THE NEW TESTAMENT

the world.' Here the important point is that it is the 'lamb' who deals with man's sin. John, son of Zacharias, was the first to identify the One who came to him to be baptized as gathering up in Himself all the strands of ancient prophecy and ritual relating to the lamb in the religion of Israel. In contrast with the successive statements and sacrifices of the Old Testament, in which a lamb of the flock has a central place, His is the lamb *of God*. As such He takes away the sin of the world. He is the act of God. There is a whole theology in the title 'Lamb of God'. Discussion continues whether the background of the Baptist's declaration is the Paschal Lamb of Exodus 12:3f., or the sacrificial Lamb of Isaiah 53:7. In favour of the former is the fact that Jewish festivals appear to have a special interest for the writer of the Gospel. Against the identity, however, point is made of the fact that the Paschal Lamb had no specific reference to sin. It should be noted, on the other hand, that the blood of the lamb in Exodus was the sign and the seal of salvation.[42] The latter suggestion has special appeal by reason of the fact that in the passage in Isaiah the word *amnos* is used in the Septuagint and is the same as occurs in John the Baptist's declaration. John seems to have been meditating particularly on the prophecy of Isaiah, as did the eunuch on a later occasion, since he quotes from chapter 40 the day before.

Others, noting the tenderness of the lamb to whom reference is made in Jeremiah 11:19, 'I am like a gentle lamb which is led to the slaughter', consider this to have been the source of the Baptist's affirmation concerning Jesus. The passage concerning the Jewish ritual of the lamb slain at the morning and evening sacrifice[43] is thought by some commentators to be the more likely background of the words of John.

Too much effort, it seems to us, has been expounded in seeking to link what John declares with a limited or specific Old Testament passage. The fact is rather that a lamb having relation to the sin, the need, and the worship of the people has a place of particular significance throughout the progressive revelation of God's plan of salvation in the Old Testament. It runs right through the whole unfolding record of the history of salvation. If Exodus tells us of the necessity of the lamb, then Leviticus may be said to specify the purity of the lamb—it must be a lamb without blemish. Isaiah suggests the personality of the lamb—*He* is brought as a lamb to the slaughter. But it was left to John the Baptist, the last of the prophets, to affirm the identity of the Lamb. Fundamental then to the use of the term in the context of God's purpose of grace for mankind is the idea of sacrifice. For the Baptist, the One who had come to him to be baptized with the baptism unto repentance was seen here identifying Himself with man's sin. The Lamb of God, it was disclosed to John, He must be—the Lamb upon whom the Lord was laying the sins of the world.

2   Chapter 2 : 19

'Destroy this temple and in three days I will raise it up.' The evangelist comments that Jesus spoke this concerning the temple of His body. The section has been severely handled by critics. The main bone of their contention is that it does not fall naturally into the context. But could it not be that the idea of His death was very real to the beloved disciple? He, therefore, finds himself dragging it in, where it may not well fit, just because the fact of Christ's cross was central in his thoughts about Jesus. Instinctively, he would find here the key to what is mysterious in the words of his Lord. At any rate the words stand as a testimony to what was understood of the importance for man of the death of Christ.

3   Chapter 3 : 14

'As Moses lifted up the serpent in the wilderness, so must the Son of Man be lifted up.'[44] The evangelist's comment on the use of the same expression 'lifted up' in a later reference is that 'this he said to indicate by what kind of death He was to die'.[45] The phrase was virtually a technical one for crucifixion. The lifting up was, then, His death on the cross in which He was to reveal Himself and by which He was to draw men and through which He was to save them. It is by beholding the Lamb, by believing on the crucified Son, that life eternal comes.

4 Chapter 6 : 51-53

Here the reference is to eating the flesh and drinking the blood of the Son of Man. The starkness of this declaration horrified His Jewish listeners and some of His followers. Christ has already, in the context, identified Himself with the true manna, the bread of heaven, by declaring that whosoever eats shall live forever. He sums up with the statement, 'and the bread which I shall give for the life of the world is my flesh'.[46] He then goes on to distinguish between 'flesh' and 'blood'. By using 'flesh' in a general sense our Lord was stating the virtue of His humanity as the Word made flesh living for us: by the 'blood' He was indicating the virtue of His life as subject to death. The believer must become partaker of both. The Son of Man lived for us and died for us, and He communicates to us the saving effects of both as we participate in Him. There is, of course, no suggestion here of a literal eating and drinking. The whole passage is figurative and Jesus Himself ruled out any such crude interpretation with the remark that 'flesh is of no avail'.[47] It is the Spirit that gives life: and His words are both. To believe in Him as the One who has given Himself in death for men is to eat of His flesh and to drink of His blood. Thus he says, 'he who comes to me shall not hunger, and he who believes in me shall never thirst'.[48] At the end of the discussion, Jesus declares in so many words that those who do not believe do not eat.[49]

5   Chapter 10 : 11

'I am the good shepherd: the good shepherd giveth his life for the sheep.' It is further asserted[50] that His dying is something which He controls. The whole section teaches that His death is vicarious; it is 'for the sheep'. This was the meaning and the motive of it. It was voluntary; for He laid it down of Himself. His death was not for Him an incident in His life, as it is for us. It was the aim of His life; it was His vocation. And His death was victory; for He took it up again and thereby showed His conquest of sin and the grave.

6   Chapter 12

This chapter contains several allusions to Christ's death. The corn of wheat must fall into the ground and die before it can bring forth fruit. Verse 27 refers to the troubling of His soul in view of the 'hour'. He is to drink 'the cup'. The way in which He is moved by it, shrinks from it, and accepts it, all reveal the place it holds in His mind and in the mind of the evangelist as well.

There are other passages, such as John 15:13 'Greater love hath no man than this, that a man lay down his life for his friends', and John 17:19 'For their sakes I consecrate myself' which have also the cross in view. The implication of the first is that to lay down one's life for others is a great thing. And of the second, that men cannot sanctify themselves; this Christ does on their behalf in His consecration through death. His work for men is His supreme act of self-sacrifice. The sacrifice of His life is consummated in His death. Here the last offering of self was made. And the fruits of that voluntary, vicarious and victorious deed are communicated to those who become true branches in the true vine. The story of the Passion itself, so vividly told by John, is the crowning proof of the significance of the death of Jesus both for Christ Himself and the evangelist and for all who believe. Throughout the gospel of John the person of Christ is related to His work. He did what He did because He is who He is. Equally, throughout, while there is emphasis on the benefits of His death, we are made aware that He is such an One whom death cannot finally hold. The Victim is always the Victor; and He will give eternal life to whom soever He will because He is life. In John the life, death, and resurrection of Jesus are all of a piece; and all unite together to make the fourth gospel the Book of Salvation.

SCRIPTURE REFERENCES

1. Lk. 2:11; cf. 1:47
2. Mt. 1:21
3. Cf. Ex. 14:13
4. Cf. Neh. 9:27; see Ex. 14:14; I Sam. 14:45; etc.
5. Cf. 2 Sam. 22; Ps. 18
6. Cf. Ps. 34:6
7. Cf. e.g. Mk. 3:4; Lk. 7:50; 18:42; etc.
8. Mt. 8:25; 14:30
9. Cf. e.g. Mk. 8:35; see Mt. 10:22; 24:13; Lk. 13:23
10. Mk. 10:17 (Mt. 19:23; Lk. 18:26)
11. Mt. 18:11-13
12. Lk. 5:17
13. Cf. Is. 45:23-24; 49:31-34; 60:1-12; Jer. 31:31-34; Ezek. 36:26-28
14. Cf. Mt. 6:20; Lk. 12:21
15. Mt. 23:23
16. Lk. 18:8
17. Mk. 1:15; cf. 6:12; Lk. 13:3, 5; 15:7; etc.
18. Mk. 9:24
19. Cf. Lk. 1:20
20. Lk. 6:37
21. Lk. 7:42, 43
22. Lk. 18:9-14
23. Mt. 9:1-8; Mk. 2:1-12; Lk. 5:17-26
24. Lk. 7:36-50
25. Cf. Mt. 5:43; 18:22
26. Lk. 17:3
27. Lk. 6:37; cf. 11:25-26
28. Cf. Job 8:3; see Lk. 7:29
29. Mt. 13:43
30. Cf. Deut. 25:1; 1 Kings 8:23; 2 Chron. 6:23

31. Cf. Ex. 23:7; Prov. 17:15; Is. 5:23
32. Is. 50:8; 53:11
33. Lk. 16:15
34. Mt. 12:37
35. Mk. 10:17
36. Mt. 7:29; etc.
37. Cf. Mt. 16:21; Mk. 8:31; Lk. 9:22
38. Mk. 10:45; cf. 20:28
39. Cf. Mk. 14:24; and parallels.
40. 1 Tim. 2:6
41. Jn. 3:16; 10:28
42. Cf. Exod. 12:1; see 1 Cor. 5:7; 1 Pet. 1:18, 19
43. Cf. Exod. 29:38-46
44. Cf. Jn. 8:28; 12:32
45. Jn. 12:33
46. Jn. 6:51
47. Jn. 6:63
48. Jn. 6:35
49. Jn. 6:64
50. Jn. 10:17f.

8

The Kingdom

The idea of the kingdom was a constant theme in the teaching of Jesus; so central indeed is it that it is difficult to speak about it without reference to all the main issues of the gospel. It is a term which holds within it a number of antitheses. Jesus used it in several different contexts which show that He regarded it as present and yet as future; as a process of development, and also as a state to be revealed cataclastically in power; as now among men, and at the same time as something transcendent.

The conception was with Jesus all through His ministry. He began His preaching with the announcement that it was 'at hand';[1] and on the very eve of His crucifixion. He spoke of it and anticipated a union with His disciples therein.[2] In between this first and last instance Jesus gave stress to the significance which the kingdom-concept held for Him both by proclamation and by parable. Thus Mark has some thirteen references; Matthew forty-eight and Luke thirty-four. His parables were in the main about the kingdom and the gospel is spoken of in Matthew 9:35 as the gospel of the kingdom.

Matthew prefers the phrase 'the kingdom of heaven' while Mark and Luke have 'the kingdom of God'. There are two passages in Matthew[3] in which he has simply 'the kingdom'; and there are three Synoptic references to 'His kingdom' or 'my kingdom'.[4] On the whole the phrase 'the kingdom of heaven' is to be preferred as the more original for the reason that it occurs in the so-called *Logia* of Matthew, those parts of his Gospel which are though by some to be sayings of Jesus compiled by the ex-taxgatherer himself (although others deny that the *Logia* referred to by Papias is something different and prefer to equate it with the Gospel of Matthew as a whole). Be this as it may, Matthew's phrase would appear to be the one used by Jesus because of its Jewish flavour. And it was more directly to the people of Israel that His teaching was directed. As the second and third evangelists wrote for Gentile believers they would naturally modify a Jewish expression out of consideration for them rather than that the author of the first gospel would modify an expression used by Jesus. It is hardly likely, as some have argued, that Jesus used the phrase 'the kingdom of heaven' so as to avoid the divine name. He had no such inhibitions; it was for calling God His Father that He was crucified. It is virtually beyond dispute that no difference of meaning is to be sought in the two expressions, especially since the two terms are used interchangeably in the first Gospel.[5] Maybe the genitive addition would in each case convey the idea better to the two types of audiences. Thus to the Jew the kingdom *of heaven* might mark the transcendent character of the kingdom which Jesus had come to inaugurate in contrast to the notion of a present realm of pomp and paraphernalia. For the Gentiles the kingdom *of God* would give stress to the monotheistic and theocratic nature of it. But in either case emphasis would fall upon the idea of a divine kingship. God is here presented as possessing royal majesty; and the kingdom is centralized upon God as King.

The concept of the kingdom was familiar to the Jews. It has parallels in the Old Testament Scriptures.[6] The cognate expressions, 'throne', 'herald of good tidings', and the like, were in the minds of the people at large. Thus were the prophetic declarations of the coming kingdom rooted in the Old Testament conception of God's relation to His people. The very phrase itself was current in Israel.[7] By using it

Jesus connected Himself with the messianic hope of the nation. Yet even in making the association Jesus was at the same time marking a difference. For with Him the term received new meaning. From the beginning He sought to stress that the kingdom was something larger, and more spiritual, than the Jewish state had ever been or could ever become. Thus, however the concept was rooted in the Old Testament, its meaning cannot be confined thereto; for the more Jesus raised it above the popular notions the more sharply did it contrast with them.

Jesus proclaimed the kingdom as something new; the time of preparation was gone and the time of waiting was over. It was this 'newness' which caused the people's astonishment. It was a strange view even for His disciples when He asserted that humility was the test of greatness within the kingdom, and that membership within it was grounded upon certain moral factors. There were spiritual and ethical qualities proper to life therein. When viewed in connection with Himself the new element in His conception is revealed. His work as Messiah was to bring men into the kingdom in which is eternal life and salvation. Such an emphasis undercut from the beginning all nationalistic, humanistic and legalistic conceptions of the kingdom. Thus is the theocentric nature of it emphasized. This means that the term for kingdom, *basileia*, would be better translated as 'kingship' or 'rule'. Kingdom suggests too much the idea of organization and location. God's 'kingdom' is His 'sovereignty'. It is this very concept of kinship which lies at the basis of all God's dealing with His people in salvation and with the world in judgement. His sovereignty is exercised in redemption and rule; thus is He the Saviour-King. Yet God's dominion is not an impersonal and abstract concept. The kingship of God has become personal in Christ who is proclaimed in the Gospels as both Saviour and King.[8] It is for this reason that many of the kingdom-parables centre upon the personal.[9] At the same time, the kingdom is presented as an order of existence;

as the realm of God's saving activity and the domain of God's kingly rule.[10]

Throughout the teaching of Jesus concerning the kingdom is the antithesis between the idea that the kingdom is come, and is yet to come. It is at the same time 'now' and 'not yet'. As present it is to be entered; for within it is life. It is God's rule accepted and acknowledged. In this sense 'the kingdom' is begun with Christ's messianic mission as 'the salvation of God'.[11] On the other hand, the kingdom is to be entered when Christ returns.[12] To this future manifestation of the kingdom the apocalyptic glory of the Gospels belong. If 'now' the kingdom is the sovereignty of the King as Saviour, 'then' the kingdom will be the sovereignty of the Saviour as King. As the inaugurator of the saving rule of God, Christ underwent suffering and humility; as the inaugurator of the kingly rule of God, Christ shall come in triumph.

These two aspects of Christ's messianic purpose, as the One who comes to His rule by way of suffering, come together in the title of 'Son of Man' which Christ used of Himself. In this way Christ related Himself to the kingdom as the One whose suffering initiates it and whose triumph consummates it. It is for this reason that 'the coming of the kingdom of God' and 'the coming of the Son of Man' are two ways of referring to the same reality.[13] The Son of Man is He who is the Saviour-King. He has suffered and He will triumph. The figure of the Son of Man is, therefore, determinative of the rule of God. It is He who is central to it both in its present and future reality. Christ the Lord exercises divine sovereignty both in grace and glory. His is the kingship both in its 'redemptive-historical' aspect as well as in its 'eschatological-cosmic' aspect.

Jesus began His ministry with the proclamation that the time is fulfilled and the kingdom of God is at hand.[14] The phrase 'at hand' means that it has arrived; it is present. The 'day' of the fulfilment of Isaiah's prophecy is now here.[15] It is the day of salvation—the acceptable year of the Lord. John

the Baptist was the herald of the kingdom; since that time
the kingdom of God is preached and men press into it.[16] So
from the days of the Baptist the kingdom forces its way
onward.[17] In this sense the kingdom is a realized actuality:
it is a fulfilment. As God's saving initiative in history, the
kingdom has brought the past into the present and the
future within the actuality of history. For the kingdom has
come with power. The realm of evil has been shaken by His
coming. Satan's rule has been broken. The devil offered
Jesus the kingdoms of the world if He would worship him.[18]
By His rejection of the temptation and His proclamation
of the rule of God Jesus shook Satan's hold. His casting out
of demons was a signal proof that the kingdom of God had
appeared among men.[19] The grace of God has appeared
bringing salvation: that is the theme of God's present rule.

But there is an end to history, an *eschaton*, when the Son
of Man shall appear 'in His kingdom',[20] 'with power'.[21] It
will be a coming for judgement.[22] And then shall the
righteous shine forth as the sun in the kingdom of their
Father.[23] In this sense the kingdom is an awaited event; it
is an expectation.

The preaching of John the Baptist of repentance (*metanoia*,
a change of mind), prepared the way for the announcement
of the idea of the kingdom as a spiritual entity in contrast
with the Jewish notion of a revived Davidic monarchy under
a Messiah of great pomp. John associated the Kingdom of
God with the person of Jesus; and all through the Gospels
the account of His life and ministry find their fundamental
significance within this context. Jesus and the kingdom are
integral to each other. He embodies the kingdom as its
living representative on earth. In bringing the salvation of
God to man Jesus establishes the kingdom as the reign of
God in human hearts.

From the standpoint of the Gospels, not only did Jesus
embody the kingdom in Himself, but His miracles are to be
regarded as revelations of it and His parables as illustrations

of it. There is a close connection between the moral claim of Jesus and His exercise of supernatural power. They are part and parcel of His unfolding of the essential nature of the kingdom of God as theocentric. The miracles are a vindication of the kingship of God; they are demonstrations of His dominion. They show the superiority of the spiritual over the material even though some of the miracles were themselves of a material nature. But in this way they declare that the salvation of God is concerned with the whole man; and that the reign of God relates to the total life. The miracles, one and all, have a definite eschatological character as messianic deeds of salvation. Even the so-called nature-miracles demonstrate the reality of God's present rule, but they also point on to the end when all nature shall be renewed at the coming of the Son of Man in His kingdom.

The parables, too, for the most part are related to the kingdom. A very broad division of them would be a twofold classification into parables of grace and parables of judgement. And these two ideas unite, as we have seen in the concept of the kingdom in its present and its future aspects. Perhaps they would be more precisely classified as ethical and eschatological parables. In both groups, specifically kingdom-parables preceded by the formula, 'The kingdom of heaven is like . . .', will be found. It is these parables which draw out the most significant characteristics of our Lord's teaching about the kingdom. These can best be studied according to their distribution in the synoptic gospels. Thus Mark sets forth in the Seed Growing Secretly the necessity on the part of those who sow the seed to depend upon the power of God to give an increase. The Sower illustrates how differently the Word is received. The Mustard Seed speaks of its mighty growth from small beginnings: the Leaven shows how gradually and quietly its teaching permeates society. The Lost Sheep refers to the willingness of the Lord to gather the strayed into the safety of the kingdom.

Luke, in the parables peculiar to him, sets forth the more

ethical values of the kingdom. The Friend at Midnight and the Unjust Judge teach the care of God for His children in spite of delays, and also the necessity to persevere in prayer. The Watchful Servant bids the members of the kingdom to watch for the *Parousia*. The need for humility is emphasized in the parables of the Chief Seats and the Pharisee and the Publican; and specially in the latter is it made clear that salvation is by grace alone. The Great Supper shows how the blessings of the kingdom are withdrawn from apostate Jews and given to others.

Matthew in his special kingdom-parables teaches in the Tares that good and evil remain side by side until the final harvest. In the Hid Treasure and the Pearl of Great Price the superlative value of the kingdom is set forth. The Drag Net, like the Tares, tells us that good men and bad will remain as belonging to the kingdom until the end. That reward is due to God's grace and not to human merit is stressed in the Labourers in the Vineyard: while the Talents contain a warning that membership within the kingdom requires honest activity. Taken in broad sweep then the teaching of the parables concerning the kingdom is that it is at the same time a gift and a task. To be in it one must know the rule and realm of God in one's heart; and in that realization live within the kingdom in full prospect of its future consummation. Yet some will be apparently in the kingdom whose works and ways will at the end-time show them not to have been of it. Our Lord's teaching about the kingdom both generally and in His parables, taken together with His own Messianic consciousness and the Sermon on the Mount, unite to make clear that He regarded Himself as the new King, His Church as the new Israel and His word as the new Law.

One issue remains for comment—there is the question of the relation between the kingdom and the Church. The fact is that when we pass from the gospels to the epistles of the New Testament we are aware of a new mode of expression, if not of thought. There are still references to the kingdom[24] but the idea does not dominate as in the gospels, although when it does occur it has the same general significance as in the teaching of Jesus. It is a present reality; and as such is open to those who own the kingship of Christ in spiritual salvation.[25] Thus is the kingdom not one of food and drink but of righteousness, peace and joy in the Holy Spirit.[26] In Colossians 4:11 Paul has a good word to say about his fellow workers unto (*eis*) the kingdom. As in the gospels, 'the kingdom' has in the Pauline letters a future goal; it is to be manifested at the *parousia* of Christ.[27] But some will not 'inherit' it.[28] It is the rich in faith who, according to James, are the 'heirs of the kingdom'.[29] Hebrews refers to the kingdom which cannot be shaken as something possessed by faith.[30] 2 Peter speaks of the richly provided entrance into the eternal kingdom of our Lord and Saviour Jesus Christ for those who have made good their calling and election.[31]

In comparison with the Gospels, however, these references are few. With the decreasing usage of the term in the New Testament there goes an increasing usage of that of Church. The question, therefore, arises as to whether there is not a connection between the two. Does it mean that the kingdom-concept has given way to the Church-concept; or that the Church-concept is but another term for the kingdom-concept? Both these views have their advocates; there are those who argue for an absolute difference and those who assert an absolute identity. Into the discussion we do not intend to enter here except by way of barest reference.

Those who contend for an absolute distinction between the kingdom and the Church—the *basileia* and the *ekklēsia* —point out that the term Church occurs but three times in the gospels, and then only in Matthew's record.[32] They deduce from this, even if they allow the passages to be authentic, that Christ never intended to institute a Church as an organized community. For such exegetes, then, the whole teaching of Christ is thrown into an eschatological context which in their view excludes the idea of the Church. Others desirous of identifying kingdom and Church have sought to find the Church-concept in the references to the 'flock', and to His 'sheep'.[33] Special point is made of the gathered disciples then considered to be the nucleus of the Church. The conclusion is then drawn that Jesus spoke of the kingdom because it would be more understandable to Jews. But the kingdom community He formed, came to be called, especially under the impact of Gentile ideas, the Church, the *ekklēsia*. In Matthew 16:18,19 some sort of relationship is made between Church and kingdom 'upon this rock I will build my Church . . . I will give you the keys of the kingdom of heaven'. But even this juxtaposition of the two terms seems to rule out the idea of absolute difference and of absolute identity. The kingdom seems to be a wider and more general concept. The Church is the company of those who have received the kingdom; the community which prays, 'Hallowed be thy name, thy kingdom come, thy will be done on earth as it is in heaven'. Those who are truly in the Church are really in the kingdom; and being in the Church, the body of Christ, they are called upon to extend the kingdom by making effective the rule of God in the lives of men.

SCRIPTURE REFERENCES

1. Mt. 4:17; Mk. 1:15
2. Mk. 14:25
3. Mt. 8:12; 13:38
4. Mt. 13:41; 16:28; Lk. 22:30
5. Mt. 6:10, 33; 12:28; 21:21, 43
6. Cf. 1 Chron. 28:5; Dan. 2:44; 4:3
7. Cf. Mk. 15:43; Lk. 14:15
8. Cf. Mt. 1:12; 2:2; 18:11; 21:5; 25:34; 27:29; Lk. 1:47; 2:11
9. Cf. Mt. 13:24ff.; 18:23ff.; 20:1ff.; etc.
10. Cf. Mt. 8:11; 26:29; Lk. 14:15; etc.
11. Cf. Mt. 3:2; 4:17; 5:3; 6:33; 12:25; etc.
12. Cf. Mt. 7:21; 13:43; Mk. 9:1; 10:37; etc.
13. Cf. Mt. 10:23; 13:41; 16:23; Mk. 9:1
14. Mk. 1:15

15. Lk. 4:18, 19
16. Lk. 16:16
17. Mt. 11:12
18. Mt. 4:8f.
19. Cf. Mt. 12:28; Lk. 11:20; cf. Mt. 8:29; Mk. 1:24; 5:7; Lk. 8:28f.; etc.
20. Mt. 20:21; cf. Mk. 10:37
21. Mk. 9:1
22. Mt. 25:34
23. Mt. 13:43
24. Cf. Rom. 14:17; 1 Cor. 4:20; 6:9; 15:24, 50; Gal. 5:21; Eph. 5:5; Col. 1:13; 4:11; 1 Thess. 2:12; 2 Thess. 1:5; 2 Tim. 4:1, 18
25. 1 Cor. 4:20; 15:50; Col. 1:13
26. Rom. 14:17
27. 2 Tim. 4:1
28. 1 Cor. 6:9, 10; Gal. 5:21; Eph. 5:5
29. Jas. 2:5
30. Heb. 12:28
31. 2 Pet. 1:11
32. Mt. 16:18; 18:17
33. Cf. Mt. 10:16; 25:33; 26:31; Mk. 14:27; Lk. 12:32; Jn. 10:2f.

9

Final Things

It is much more than a mere paradox to say that the first things in the Gospels is their presentation of the last things. Their theology, like any sound theology which is true to its biblical perspective, involves an eschatology, a doctrine of end events. Everything that Jesus had to say is significant; but none more so than His teaching concerning final things. Yet it is not easy to state simply what exactly is to be understood by the data provided by the records; and the most diverse theories have been built up respecting, for example, the *Parousia* and the judgement. It is certain that Jesus lived at a time when Jewish apocalyptic thought was much to the fore. How far He took over these ideas is hard to say. But of one thing we may be certain—that only whatever was truth therein He could have retained. The two outstanding features of apocalyptic thinking, viz., that the Kingdom lies in the future and that it will come by the immediate act of God, are evidently present in His teaching; and also the view that the rule of God had a contemporary realization in the obedient hearts of God's faithful people. The teaching of the Gospels presents, then, God's sovereignty both as an experience and a hope. It can thus come either quietly and unexcitedly into men's lives in the here and now or suddenly and dramatically in the future. The fact remains, however, that while Jesus may have laid hold upon current ideas He gave to them His own significance and orientation. When the fullest allowance is made for whatever views congenial to

116

Him were close at hand, no less emphasis must be given to what has been called 'the holy originality of Jesus'. Some aspects of the synoptic eschatology have already been considered under such subjects as the kingdom, the Son of Man and other titles for Jesus. It remains to consider the teaching of the gospels regarding the *Parousia*, the Resurrection, Judgement, Life Beyond and the Final State.

1 The Parousia

The Greek word *parousia* has now become popular to express the Manifestation, the Appearing, or the Second Coming of Christ. There is clear evidence in the teaching of Jesus that He did preach a finalizing of human history in which He was the decisive actor. The consummation of temporal events was essentially related to His manifestation and appearing. It is thought by some scholars that it was a Jewish view that the end would come in the form of a catastrophic transformation culminating in the advent of the Messiah Himself from heaven. Be this as it may, it is evident that Jesus both by assumption and direct speech regarded the end as taking place in connection with His own coming again 'in power and great glory'. When we consider how deep was Christ's personal concern for the bringing about of the kingdom we are immediately aware of how His view of things must have differed from all those floating ideas which were by comparison tentative and theoretical. There was an ethical quality in His teaching which is given particular stress in the parables of the kingdom and which is often brought out under the analogy of natural growth. At the same time, He adhered, in a way which cannot but impress the reader of the New Testament, to the catastrophic view of the final event.

But there is no obscurity in the teaching of Jesus about His final advent.[1] Jewish theology had really no concept of a second advent of the Messiah. The gospels are, however, specific in this regard: someday, sometime, Christ will return and openly proclaim God's sovereignty over man and nature. Then will Christ irresistibly establish the kingdom in final triumph. Part at least of the meaning of the petition, 'Thy kingdom come', is to be found here; in the constant prayer of the Church on earth for the consummation of history, and the climax of God's purpose of redemption for the world. There are some *Parousia* passages which focus for us the manifestation of Christ in apocalyptic glory. Mark 14:62 (cf. Lk. 22:69; Mt. 26:64) refers to the Son of Man sitting at the right hand of power and coming in the clouds of glory. The words are Christ's own in answer to the high priest's question, 'Who art thou?'. Luke 17:20-18:8 comes in answer to the question of the Pharisees concerning the time of His coming. In it Jesus drew attention to certain events in the history of Israel in which God acted in judgement and stated that so would it be when the Son of Man is revealed.

Mark 13 is often referred to as 'the little Apocalypse'. It is impossible in our view to explain its presence in Mark and its parallels in Matthew (chapter 24) and Luke (chapter 21) as a Christian adaptation of an original Jewish work; nor is it to be taken as the Evangelist's own composition or the putting into the mouth of Jesus beliefs about the future which the early Church wanted accepted. It seems clear from a reading of the section that two questions were put to Jesus although in the minds of the questioners they may have been one. Jesus asserted that the great temple, whose stones His disciples had admired, would be laid in ruins. They ask, according to Mark's account, 'When shall these things be?' that is, 'When shall be the downfall of Jerusalem and what shall be the sign of His coming and the end of the world?' The disciples may have run the two events together, for in their minds there could be nothing more catastrophic and final than the ruin of the holy city. Actually

118

Jesus answered the questions separately. He spoke first about
the signs of His coming and the end of the age. He declines
emphatically to give a specific date but specifies antecedents
of the end. These are the appearances of false Christs; wars
and rumours of wars; times of persecution; the evidence of
spiritual decline; the progress of the gospel. Having thus
spoken, Jesus then turns to answer the other question. He
made it clear that the destruction of Jerusalem is not a sign
of His immediate return in glory. The phrase 'when then'
of Matthew 24:14 is an introductory formula signifying,
'now to answer your first question'. And in answering it He
alludes to Daniel's prophecy of armies desolating the land
and desecrating the temple. Having answered the two questions, that with regard to the end of the world and that with
regard to the destruction of Jerusalem, both events are then
brought into immediate proximity; and this for the reason
that the latter is a first edition of the former. By thus running
the two events together into one Jesus can say, 'This generation shall not pass till all these things be fulfilled'. By this
He meant, not that the generation then living was to witness
the end, but that in that generation all the things which form
the incipient stage in the development would appear. It is,
indeed, significant that in the first age of Christianity the
buds of most things in the Church's history appeared; the
success of gospel preaching, anti-Christian tendencies,
persecutions, heresies, schisms, and the rest. When they
reach their legitimate issue then shall the end be. The destruction of Jerusalem was an end, the end of the old age, the
end of an epoch. And all the signs which heralded it would
have their parallel and fullness in the final end, the end of
the present age. The end of the old age was cataclastic and
sudden; and so, too, will the end of this one be. Luke (cf.
21:24) makes it clear that a considerable period was to elapse
between the first ending and the second. There would be a
long dispersion of Israel. 'The times of the Gentiles' must
first run its course. The expression indicates a period when

the Gentiles have their opportunity of enjoying the promises of God, corresponding to the times of God's gracious visitation enjoyed by the Jews to which Christ referred in His lament over Jerusalem. By many of His parables these two facts of the kingdom are enforced; there is a period of waiting and there is a cataclastic ending.

The one great truth taught in all the *parousia* passages is that Jesus will come again for judgement and to rule. The Day is connected with judgement. It is nowhere stated or implied that His coming will mean a universal salvation of mankind.

2 The Resurrection

The doctrine of the resurrection of the body is a leading topic in the New Testament doctrine of last things. In the gospels it was explicitly stated by Jesus in His reply to the Sadducees who denied the resurrection of the body.[2] Other passages, too, clearly state the same truth.[3] But while Christ's words are both luminous and emphatic, the supremely significant thing, which flashes a flood of light on the subject, is Christ's own resurrection. Here He is the first-fruits, for His resurrection is both the actual commencement of the Christian resurrection and the indication of its nature. The resurrected life is not bound by the limitations of space as is our present physical life. In His answer to the Sadducees Jesus took occasion to correct their crude conception of the nature of the risen life.[4] In all His teaching Jesus restricted resurrection to the redeemed. Some are accounted worthy to attain that age and the resurrection of the dead.[5] Quite evidently some are not worthy. Resurrection is the inheritance of the saved; there is no resurrection for the wicked.

3 Judgement

The fact of a coming judgement is definite in the Gospels.

The great prophetic discourse concludes with the most solemn declaration of the final judgement of the world when all men are gathered before God. There they are judged either by the historical gospel preached to them for a witness, or by its great ethical principles, the law of charity written on their hearts. Those who have refused the gospel and rejected its moral dictates are sent away to keep company with the devil and his angels.

4 Life Beyond

One of the most striking things about the teaching of Jesus is the comparative scarcity of His references to death. Whatever He feasted His eyes upon He never feasted them upon the grave. Yet He spoke often about His own death. It is this absence of reference to death which separates Jesus from the Stoical teachers of the era. On one or two occasions He refers to death as a sleep. Jairus' daughter, He said, is not dead but sleepeth; and in John's gospel He refers to Lazarus in a similar way. When Jesus said that death was a sleep He was not using the language of poetry. It was because He meant it that they laughed Him to scorn. Death in His view was supremely a sleep—a sleep to wake.

For Jesus the real death is that which is spiritual. The son in the far country, separated from his father's home and heart, was dead. Yet while Jesus had little to say about death He had much to say about the life beyond into which one wakes after the sleep of death. It is clear that for all—the righteous and the wicked—there is beyond death a conscious existence. Death in the teaching of Jesus was not an annihilation but the loss of certain powers. It is not the extinction of that in which these powers reside. The 'sleep' of which Jesus spoke is not that of the soul. In Matthew 22 Jesus declared that by designating Himself the God of Abraham, Isaac and Jacob, God was not the God of the dead but of the living. The declaration was used by Him as an argument for the life beyond. The patriarchs were not extinct, not non-existent.

The life beyond the grave for the redeemed was viewed by Jesus as a state of blessedness. Lazarus was carried by the angels into Abraham's bosom, and the dying robber was assured of Paradise in company with Jesus. On the other hand, as the story of Dives and Lazarus makes plain, the state of the unrighteous is one of conscious suffering. Although we have only fleeting glimpses in the Gospels of the condition of the wicked between death and the judgement, these glimpses indicate that already they have begun to endure the penalty of their wickedness.

5 The Final State

Christ's words about heaven and hell are notable for several reasons. One is their spirit of restraint and reserve. He refused to answer curious questions. They ask, 'Are there few that be saved?' His answer was to remind those who asked to 'strive to enter'. Another feature of our Lord's teaching is the symbolic character of its representations.

Jesus made clear that man's destiny was either heaven or hell. Indeed, He said more about the latter than about the former. There is a sense in which heaven is a reward. Mark 12:25 refers to those who are accounted worthy to attain that world and the resurrection from the dead. From Luke 19:12-27 we learn that the reward corresponds to fidelity and industry. From Matthew 25:14-30 it appears that the reward corresponds to natural gifts and abilities; and Matthew 20:1-6 that the rewards are according to opportunity. At the same time heaven is the realization of an end appropriate to those who enter. In no place, however, is one's entry into heaven conditioned on one's own goodness. This is only, as we saw in our chapter on Salvation, assured to those who have faith in the redeeming act of Christ. Yet one's place is somehow conditioned by one's performance.

In this way the teaching of Jesus unites the doctrine of faith and works. We enter heaven by the faith that works and yet our position is dependent upon the works of faith. We are saved by faith; and we are judged by works.

The concept of hell cannot be expunged from or explained away from the teaching of Jesus. Figures of speech there are, but these do not annul the dreadfulness of the doom; indeed the figure must fall short of the reality. The words of Matthew 25:41 (cf. Mk. 9:48) which speaks of 'eternal fire', and Matthew 8:12 which speaks of 'outer darkness' convey the terribleness of hell. And there can be no doubt that the punishment of hell is conceived by Jesus as eternal. He thought of the state of the wicked in the realm beyond as one of activity not of unconsciousness. In Mark 3:29 Jesus declares that sin against the Holy Spirit has no forgiveness because it is an 'eternal sin'; it is sin, that is, of a quality which has within it the principle of timelessness. Such expressions as 'the undying worm' and 'the quenchless fire' convey the same impression. Eternal punishment cannot be less than eternal, any more than eternal life can be. In the last reckoning heaven is being with God in the enjoyment of His presence; and hell is being excluded from His presence and hating all that is of God.

But the teaching of Jesus makes clear that the present world is the place wherein one's future and final destiny is secured. It is the man without the wedding garment who is expelled from the king's feast; the unprepared virgins who have forgotten their oil supply who are shut out; the idle servant who failed to take reasonable risk who is cast into outer darkness. For such there is 'weeping and gnashing of teeth'.[6] The question of the 'justice' of eternal hell is not raised in the Gospels for the reason that there sin is regarded as more than an unfortunate slip. Hell is for those who refuse to forsake sin as an offence against God. It is the failure to lay hold on the offer of eternal life. And this very offer of love is itself proof that hell is not incompatible with

God's love. It is love which has made a way for man to rise to the sublime abode. It is man's own sinful folly which refuses such a love and prefers the sin which carries within it its own wages of eternal death. Thus in the end, seen in its true perspective, there is no doctrine so right and true as that of heaven and hell. It is in harmony with the very nature of things, and with God's spiritual government of the universe. What could be more just and fair than that there should be a heaven for the righteous and a hell for the wicked? The message is a needed one, too, in an age which has become sentimental and soft. The awful reality of sin rules out any nice concept of sin. The sin that doomed Jesus to the cross, which is not itself met and mastered in experience at the cross, will work out its tragic and eternal effect on all who prefer to have it so.

There is in the Fourth Gospel no real eschatological problem. There is, to be sure, occasional reference to the end, but the main interest is centred upon eternal life through faith in Jesus Christ in the present. John has an amazing way of blending the physical and the spiritual. His gospel presents us with what has been called a realized eschatology. Eternal life, for example, is conceived as a present reality rather than as a coming boon. So, too, is it with the judgement; now is the judgement of this world. This realized eschatological approach has, however, been overdone; and especially so when used to discredit the eschatology of the Synoptics. But it is a conclusion which can only be maintained by shutting the eyes to all that John says.

Jesus does identify His coming with the Spirit's descent,[7] and with His rising again from the dead.[8] But when this is admitted the contention does not follow that the eschatological ideas of the Synoptic gospels are entirely absent from the Gospel of John. There are many references to the resurrection at the last day.[9] Thus while we may grant that John's interest lay in the present, he is not uncertain about the future.

Two statements which appear contradictory can then be

set side by side. In 8 : 15 Jesus declares that 'I judge no man',[10] and over against this in 9 : 39 He says, 'For judgement came I into the world'. How are two such statements to be reconciled? Christ came not to judge but to save; in this sense He does not judge the world in any personal way. He does not pronounce judgement; He offers salvation. Yet none the less while He came not to judge, He came for judgement. It is by relation to Him that men will be tested. It is by reference to Him that the ultimate decision will be taken; by reference to Him the final destiny will be fixed. Thus while in this day of grace He does not judge, His presence is the touchstone of judgement. In this way John conceives of judgement as a present attitude and a final act in relation to Jesus. Now is the judgement of this world; now men are relating themselves to Christ or failing to do so. Now is Christ set forth for the judgement, but there is to be a resurrection to judgement.[11] The fact of the final judgement is clear from 5 : 28-29, 'Do not wonder at this, because the time is coming when all who are in the grave shall hear His voice and move forth: those who have done right will rise to life; those who have done wrong will rise to hear their doom' (NEB).

SCRIPTURE REFERENCES

1. Cf. Mt. 24 : 27f.; Mk. 8 : 38; 13 : 26f.; 14 : 26f.; Lk. 21 : 27
2. Cf. Mt. 22 : 23-33; Mk. 12 : 18-27; Lk. 20 : 27-40
3. Cf. e.g. Mt. 8 : 11; Lk. 13 : 28, 29
4. Cf. Lk. 20 : 35, 36
5. Lk. 20 : 35
6. Mt. 25 : 30
7. Jn. 14 : 18
8. Jn. 16 : 16
9. Cf. Jn. 6 : 39, 40, 44; 11 : 24; 12 : 48 etc.
10. Cf. Jn. 12 : 47
11. Jn. 12 : 48

THE
BOOK
OF
ACTS

10

The Book of Acts

The Book of Acts serves as a bridge between the Gospels and the Epistles. It gives us the background history of the churches of the Epistles. It describes that basis of Christian life out of which sprung both the Gospels and Epistles. The story begins at Jerusalem and ends at Rome: and between these two points questions are settled, principles carried through and divinely implanted tendencies indicated. Although it is not the intention of Luke to give summaries of apostolic doctrine yet the book does make clear the gospel of Christ as understood in the teaching and preaching of the primitive Church. Some have contended that the Book of Acts can be shown to reveal the main clauses of the Apostles' Creed; and more particularly the section of it which states belief in God and the Father, Almighty, in Jesus Christ His only Son our Lord, and in the Holy Ghost. There is certainly justification for the contention.[1] Leaving aside for the present the doctrine of Christ and of the Holy Spirit, quotation can be made to support the presence of other statements of the Creed.

In relation to both Jew and Gentile the doctrine of God is suited to each context. He is thus 'the God of Abraham, Isaac and Jacob'; the 'God of our fathers', who 'spake by His holy prophets'.[2] There are only three references to Him as 'Father'.[3] Two of these have to do with the Father's promise of the Spirit. No idea of a universal Fatherhood of God can be sustained from the Book of Acts, except in the one possible statement by Paul to the people of Athens.

To the Gentiles God is declared to be the Maker of heaven and earth,[4] although in the adoring faith of the Church He is also acclaimed as the divine Creator of all.[5] Acts has much to say about the Church which in the experience of grace is 'holy' and in the purpose of grace is 'catholic'. Texts showing belief in the significance of baptism, in the forgiveness of sins, in the resurrection of the body and the life everlasting could also be marshalled.

From the point of view of theology the main interest of Acts for us is its doctrine of Christ, salvation, and the Holy Spirit.

1 The Person of Christ

As regards the Christology of Acts both the recorded preaching of Peter and Paul reflect the same broad features, although the approach is different. The significant thing, however, is that from the first there was a doctrine of Christ.[6] This means that for the preachers of the Church there was no gospel apart from Christ. Indeed what strikes us as we read these fragments of primitive preaching is that it all centred around the person of Christ. What was proclaimed were facts about Jesus. What was of prime emphasis in the message of the early heralds of the good news was the living reality of Christ; and for them being who He is, was what gave value and meaning to what He did.

Inevitably Peter started from the historical Jesus; with the One he knew and with whom he had kept company. While on earth Jesus was among men as a Man approved of God by the signs and miracles which He did.[7] He was anointed by God with special power.[8] This approval and this anointing declare Him to be both Lord and Christ.[9] His unique position is attested by His resurrection from the dead and exaltation at the right hand of the Father. The designation 'Father'[10] slips naturally from the lips of Peter who must have had in the background of his mind the disclosures in the Upper Room when Jesus spoke so intimately of 'my Father' and 'I and the Father are one'. It is the Jesus whom Peter had known, and who is now vindicated as Lord and Christ, who communicates the power of the Holy Ghost,[11] heals,[12] forgives,[13] and is ordained to be the Judge of all.[14] The ringing assurance is, then, Jesus Christ, He is Lord of all.[15]

The one place where the title Son of God occurs[16] is shown by manuscript evidence not to be part of the text. But if Jesus is not actually called Son of God in our present sources, He is presented in such terms as to put Him beyond explanation in human categories. He is seated at the right hand of God, participating in the divine glory and sharing with God in the government of the world.[17] His lordship is specially mentioned.[18] In the Septuagint use of the designation *Kurios* (Lord) as a name for Jehovah, it is not easy to escape the conclusion that the application of it to Jesus could have suggested anything other in Jewish minds than that He possessed a superhuman character.[19] There is a strong assertion of His sinlessness.[20] He is the true Object of faith[21] and the giver of salvation.[22]

As Christ He is the focus of prophecy—to Him bear all the prophets witness.[23] As Christ He must suffer.[24] It is no matter of surprise, therefore, to find Him referred to in the most natural way as the Suffering Servant of Jehovah,[25] and as the Lamb for the slaughter of Isaiah 53.[26] The whole content of the primitive proclamation can be given its summary form in Peter's own words: 'Neither is there salvation in any other, for there is none other name under heaven given among men whereby we must be saved'.[27] The conviction is steady throughout the Book of Acts that all spiritual blessings which man can possess and God can bestow either here or hereafter are because of this Christ who lived, died, rose again from the dead and reigns as Lord. He stands on

God's side confronting men with the offer of God's salvation.[28]

Jesus is not presented as the first Christian or as the founder of the Christian Religion. As the Lamb brought to the slaughter and the Lord at the right hand of God, as the Suffering Servant of Jehovah and the Prince of Life, He is the sum total of all that Christianity means. The preaching of the primitive Church was, therefore, anchored in Jesus, but the anchor of the Church's faith and gospel is within the veil, where the Jesus of history is the Christ of faith.

Brought into the context of the Apostles' Creed all that is there detailed concerning Him is stated in Acts. He suffered under Pontius Pilate;[29] was crucified, dead and buried;[30] He descended into hades;[31] rose again the third day.[32] He ascended into heaven and sits on the right hand of God.[33] From thence He shall come to judge the living and the dead.[34]

2 Salvation

The supreme significance of Jesus for men is as the forgiver of sins. As such He was set forth to grant 'remission of sins'.[35] Christ, the risen and exalted One, forgives. And nothing greater; no gift more divine, can be offered to men than this. To know one's self forgiven, to be at peace within, and with God above, is the good news of the gospel. But for such there must be repentance.[36] Without such a change of mind regarding sin and one's own native standing before God no salvation is possible. That is the contrast between Saul of the Old Testament and David the king. Saul was the self-sufficient man who had never a sense of sin. The most he could confess was that he had played the fool and erred exceedingly; he felt his folly but never sensed his sin. David was made of different stuff; he sinned more grievously than Saul. But he was a saint withall; for he bothered about his sin, realized the fact of it, and confessed it. So David can write Psalms, for David has something to sing about. Saul has no song—there was no awareness in him of the need to repent.

The place of faith is made crucial in apostolic preaching. It was through faith that the lame man at the gate Beautiful was made to walk.[37] The preaching of the gospel opened 'the door of faith to the Gentiles'.[38] The short statement of 'the gospel of the grace of God'[39] is, 'Believe on the Lord Jesus Christ and thou shalt be saved'.[40] In repentance and faith 'the way of salvation is entered':[41] it is therefore of interest that the early believers came to be called the people of 'the Way'.[42] To be 'in the Way' is, therefore, to be of 'the Faith'.[43]

In full apostolic language the blessings of faith in Christ are stated. By faith the hearts of all who believe are cleansed by the Spirit[44] and sanctified.[45] Virtually a full declaration of 'the message of salvation'[46] is given by Paul in the synagogue in Antioch in Pisidia.[47] The sermon is parallel to that of Peter's on the day of Pentecost.[48] Peter's word ends with the focus upon the name of Jesus Christ in whom is found remission of sins.[49] Paul's message ends with what amounts to a summary of all he has to unfold in his Roman and Galatian letters: 'it is through him that forgiveness of sins is now being proclaimed to you. It is through him that everyone who has faith is acquitted of everything for which there was no acquittal under the Law of Moses.'[50]

Because it is not said in so many words that forgiveness is related to the death of Jesus it must not be concluded, as some have been all too ready to conclude, that there was no cross in the primitive gospel. This is very far from the truth. It is quite evident that throughout the preaching, as we have it recorded in Acts, that the death of Christ was regarded as having atoning value.

The death of Christ is treated from two sides, the manward and the Godward. It was a crime on the part of the Jews.[51] On the other hand, it is clear that the death of Jesus was part of the divine purpose. It was no surprise to God:[52] all the prophets have borne witness to the truth that 'Christ must suffer'.[53] The fact then that the sufferings of Christ had a part in God's plan, and that God's plan is revealed in His purposes of grace to pardon the sins of those who believe, indicates the connection between Christ's sufferings and the forgiveness of sins. And had not Peter and the others heard Him say that He must suffer and that repentance and remission of sins should be preached in His name among all nations? Had they not heard Him say more definitely that He gave His life a ransom for many and shed His blood to seal the new covenant for the remission of sins? If they did not understand these things then, now in the light of Pentecost they surely did. Once when Christ mentioned His dying this same Peter said, 'Far be it from thee, Lord; this shall not be unto thee!' Then he had said, 'Perish the thought'; now he was declaring that men would perish without the thought, without the fact. With the passing of the idea of the kingdom as spatio-temporal there passed the idea of a Messiah of mere Israelitish splendour. Peter has learned that the kingdom is spiritual and eternal and in this context the sufferings of Christ had significance for those who would enter therein. The gospel from the first was, then, that 'Christ died for our sins according to the Scriptures'. And the primitive Church was well established in the faith that the death of Jesus exerted a saving influence in the forgiveness of sins.

By the use of two significant terms the Church of Acts has laid bare its full conviction that the cross of Christ is crucial in salvation. The use of the word 'servant'[54] brings Jesus into relation with the Suffering Servant of Jehovah of Isaiah. Upon Him the Lord laid the iniquity of us all; He was wounded for our transgressions; by His stripes we are healed. For an explanation of the death of Jesus the first Christians naturally turned to the Servant passages in the prophecy of Isaiah.

In Acts chapter 8 there is the account of the conversation between Philip and the Ethiopian minister of state. The

134

chancellor was reading of the death of one led like a lamb to the slaughter. Philip is able to enlighten him with regard to His identity—the Lamb of God, Jesus of Nazareth. It is He who was led to Golgotha, and in His death assures forgiveness of sins to those of all nations who repent and believe the gospel. So He came like Moses as the Redeemer of Israel;[55] and through faith in Him to purify a people for the Church which God has purchased with His own blood.[56]

3   The Holy Spirit

A great deal has been written about the Holy Spirit in the Book of Acts. And from every point of view it is a vital issue since it has relevance to the Church's doctrine, life and witness. But the task of putting the main ideas into brief compass is no easy one. Inevitably something vital may be omitted or some particular view falsely stated. But these are risks which have to be taken. We propose to deal first of all with the subject in what we may call a homiletical manner, then give a doctrinal statement and finally a practical direction.

The Book of Acts emphasizes the continued activity of the Risen Christ. The third Gospel records what Jesus did in the days of His flesh, and Acts takes up the account of 'all that Jesus began both to do and to teach since He was taken up'. It is for this reason that the Book of Acts has been called the Book of the Holy Ghost. It is His presence which pervades it and His power which makes it.

The subject of the Spirit in Acts in a homiletical manner can be taken up in two ways. First by way of broad sweep. We notice:

(a) The Foundation of the Church in the outpouring of the Spirit. Jesus gave commandment to His apostles whom He had chosen through the Spirit.[57] The warrant of their commission was to baptize in the Holy Spirit.[58] They waited until the Holy Spirit came upon them and so the Church as the habitation of God through the Spirit was born (Ch.2).

(b) Service in the Church is dependent on the gift of the Spirit. For every work this was the one necessity. The first officers 'were full of the Holy Ghost'.[59]

(c) The Fellowship of the Church is conditioned upon the presence of the Holy Spirit.[60]

(d) The Advance of the Church is the work of the Spirit. It was the Spirit who inspired Stephen, prompted Philip, and directed Paul.[61]

(e) The Sins of the Church are sins against the Spirit.[62]

The subject may also be set forth in more specific ways by reference to the activities of the Spirit. We note:

(a) His Coming. Acts chapter 2 records the historic fulfilment of the promise of Jesus to send to His people 'another Advocate'.

(b) His Speaking. The Holy Spirit spoke through the prophets of old.[63] The Old Testament was regarded by the Church as the voice of the Holy Ghost. And the Holy Spirit spoke through Jesus.[64] All that Jesus said here on earth He said through the Spirit. But the Holy Spirit speaks still[65] and in the hearing of His voice there is blessing, and in speaking by Him there is power.

(c) His Separating. It was the Holy Spirit who set Paul and Barnabas apart for their special ministry.[66]

(d) His Sending. The two apostles set aside by the Church which heard the voice of the Holy Spirit are 'sent forth by the Holy Ghost'.[67] They were men sent by God, and God-sent men are a godsend for the Church.

(e) His Vindicating. The story of Ananias and Sapphira records their attempt to deceive the Holy Ghost and trifle with God. They lie against the Spirit, and the presence of the Spirit who is holy was vindicated by their swift and terrible removal.

(f) His Indicating. There are references to the decisive action of the Spirit both in indicating the dangers of a path,[68] and the rightness of a decision.[69]

(g) His Comforting. In 9:31 we have the statement that the Churches walking in the fear of the Lord and in the comfort of the Holy Ghost are multiplied. Specially fulfilled in such an experience was Christ's words about the coming Spirit.

(h) His Empowering. Everywhere throughout Acts we see demonstrated the assurance of Christ that power will come with the coming of the Holy Ghost. The whole of Luke's record is indeed an evidence of this very fact.

(i) His Guiding. In 11:12 Peter recounts how he was told by the Spirit to go without doubting to Caesarea. Paul was aware of both the restraints and constraints of the Spirit in his missionary work.[70]

(j) His Witnessing. The Holy Spirit whom Peter declares is given to those who obey God, is among men as the Divine Witness to the realities of the gospel.[71]

(k) His Filling. This is one of the recurring statements about the Spirit in Acts. The idea is that of abundance, adequacy and authority. The filled Church and the filled life were abundant in grace, adequate in power, and authoritative in witness.[72] It was because of the abundance of the Spirit's presence, the adequacy of the Spirit's power, and the authority of the Spirit's voice that the Book of Acts can record the strength of the Church's life, the swiftness of the Church's expansion, and the success of the Church's witness.

Turning to the subject of the Spirit from a doctrinal perspective, what has been already said provides a useful context. Acts is the gospel of the Spirit, and contains a manifestation of the Spirit almost as distinct as the Gospels do of the Son.

The fact of the Spirit as a divine personality is clear throughout. The Spirit is no mere 'sweet influence'. The Spirit speaks of Himself and is spoken of in personal terms. Very specifically the Spirit comes before us in Acts as a Divine 'I'.[73] Paul and Barnabas are said to be separated by the Spirit 'for me'.[74] The various activities of the Spirit stated above,

137

are one and all personal activities. He speaks, He separates, He sends, and so forth; all of which show the rightness of the prefixed personal pronoun, 'He—the Holy Spirit'.

Equally, too, the Spirit is from God. On Jesus the Son of Man the Father bestowed the Spirit for His life and service in the world. Now exalted in His glorified human nature to the throne of the Father, the Son pours forth the Spirit upon the Church for its life and service.[75] At the same time the Spirit is the promised gift of the Father,[76] which He has poured forth upon all flesh at the last times.[77] The presence of the Spirit is the life-giving power of God among men. He is the giver of spiritual gifts and the source of inspiration. By His authority the Church is directed and its leadership appointed. But He who is of God is no less God. Only by God can God be glorified and His work done. And Acts demonstrates the Godness of the Spirit in all that He does. In the Gospels Jesus declared that blasphemy against the Spirit is the final sin, so in Acts is it demonstrated.[78] The significant fact is that here there is an explicit assertion of the deity of the Spirit; for to lie against the Spirit is to lie against God.[79]

In a special sense, then, this is the age of the Spirit. Thus Acts chapter two is to be read as the coming of the Spirit to the Church. The 'day of Pentecost' was, of course, one of important significance in the calendar of the Jewish Church. It was the feast of harvest, the day of first fruits.[80] It took place a 'week of weeks' after the Passover, and was the occasion for special readings in the synagogue. These selected passages (Exod. 19; Ps.29; Ps.68; Ezek. 1; Hab. 3) are all marked for their display of God's power in might and majesty. Thus was it on the day of Pentecost when the Spirit came. The feast was 'being fulfilled' at the time when its meaning was filled full. The colours of the old economy, radiantly beautiful and full of suggestiveness as it was, were being eclipsed, fading into the dawn of the day of the Spirit's coming in all His fulness. The prophetic was merging into the historic. There in the temple court by Solomon's gate, as I believe, were gathered the disciples who had come fearfully to keep the feast. And in the midst of it the Spirit came upon them and those who had gathered came to witness what was taking place. They were with one accord in one place; but the place is nothing, the accord is everything. It is for certain that it was for the sake of those others that there were the accompanying phenomena of the rushing mighty wind and the cloven tongues like fire. The material phenomena which accompanied His coming were temporary, but the facts which they symbolized were eternal. The manifestations were passing the meaning was permanent. The outward drapery of the Spirit's advent went, but He remained. And the whole Book of Acts is evidence of the abiding presence of the Spirit in His Church. The wind, the tongues, the fire will go—and yet they will remain. They will remain in the Spirit: for the Spirit is the breath of God, life-giving; the Spirit is the voice of God, truth-speaking; the Spirit is the fire of God, soul-cleansing.

It remains to say a word concerning the Spirit by way of practical direction although it could equally well be referred to as closing spiritual counsels. It does not belong to our purpose to be precise at this point, but these observations should however, be made. First is the need to remember that the Book of Acts is not a theological treatise. It does not purport to be a blueprint for Christian experience. What is clear throughout it is that the wind of the Spirit blows where He wills. God has no mould for His saving action. He comes to every man down His own secret stairs. This means that the terminology of Acts is not meant to mark the exact stages or grades of experience in the Spirit.

At Pentecost the Spirit came by a sovereign act of God. The disciples waited for His coming. Yet it was not as a consequence of their praying or their merit that He came. The Spirit came as a gift from above. He came to be in the world as the creator of spiritual life and to reveal the things of Christ which accompany salvation. In Acts the work of the Spirit in effecting man's salvation is variously stated in relation to its beginning and its continuation. Many terms are used. Some of these would seem to see the Spirit's presence from differing perspectives. On the one hand there is the divine activity in relation to either the Father or the Son as when the Spirit is said to be poured out, or forth, or given.[81] Then there are terms which denote the Spirit's own action as when He comes upon,[82] falls upon,[83] rests on.[84] On the other side there is the reference to being 'baptized with',[85] and 'being filled with' the Spirit.[86] From the subjective point of view the Spirit is received[87] as a gift.[88]

The baptism of the Spirit seems to refer to the oneness of the Church in Christ. That is why we have in Acts two pentecosts. In chapter 2 there is the coming of the Spirit to the Jewish Church, and in chapter 10 His coming to the Gentile Church.[89] It was in the Spirit then that the Jewish and the Gentile Church were 'baptized' and made one in Christ. The word had been said, 'Ye shall be baptized with the Holy Ghost not many days hence',[90] and the fulfilment of that word is found for the Jewish Church in chapter 2 and for the Gentile Church in chapter 10. The presence of the Spirit is an assurance that there is the possibility of new life for those who receive Him. It is indeed in the very reception of Him that the new life in Christ begins. But He would possess in fullest measure those who have received Him so that the fruits of His indwelling may be seen in experience and the fact of His infilling may be known in witness.

None who read the Book of Acts with serious intent will make too much of the Holy Spirit; and yet there can be a pre-occupation with the Spirit which is not of the Spirit. For always and at all times the Spirit would glorify the Son who died that we may live. Still, it is only a church and an individual believer who recognizes the Senior Partnership of the Spirit[91] that will be a match for the demands of the day.

SCRIPTURE REFERENCES

1. Cf. Ac. 2:22-24, 32, 33; 3:13-15, 18; 4:10; 5:30-32; 10:36-43; 13:27-31
2. Cf. Ac. 3:13, 21; 7:1f.; etc.
3. Cf. Ac. 1:4, 7; 2:33
4. Ac. 14:15; 17:24
5. Ac. 4:24; 7:50
6. Ac. 5:28
7. Ac. 2:22
8. Ac. 4:27
9. Ac. 2:36; cf. 10:36
10. Ac. 2:33
11. Ac. 2:33
12. Ac. 3:16
13. Ac. 5:31
14. Ac. 10:42
15. Ac. 10:36
16. Ac. 8:37
17. Ac. 5:31; 10:36, 42
18. Ac. 2:20, 25, 35; 4:26; 10:36; etc.
19. Cf. Ac. 2:25, 36; etc.
20. Ac. 3:14; 4:27
21. 3:16; 10:43
22. Ac. 3:25; 4:12; 5:31
23. Ac. 3:18; 10:43; cf. 2:25; 8:28f.
24. Ac. 3:18
25. Ac. 3:18, 26; 4:27, 30 RV.
26. Ac. 8:32f.
27. Ac. 4:12
28. Ac. 2:38; 3:18-20
29. Cf. Ac. 1:3; 3:13, 18; 13:28; etc.
30. Cf. Ac. 2:23; 3:15; 4:10; 5:30; etc.
31. Ac. 2:31
32. Ac. 10:40
33. Ac. 1:11, 22; 2:33; 5:31
34. Ac. 1:11; 3:20-21; 10:42
35. Ac. 5:31; cf. 10:43
36. Ac. 2:38; 5:31; 17:30
37. Ac. 3:16; cf. 14:9
38. Ac. 14:27
39. Ac. 20:24; cf. 14:3
40. Ac. 16:31
41. Cf. Ac. 16:17
42. Ac. 9:2; cf. 18:26; 19:9, 23; 22:4; 24:14, 22
43. Cf. Ac. 6:7; 14:22; 16:5; 24:24
44. Ac. 15:8, 9
45. Ac. 26:18
46. Ac. 13:26

47. Ac. 13:14ff.
48. Cf. esp. Ac. 2:22-36 with 13:26-37
49. Ac. 2:28
50. Ac. 13:38, 39, NEB.
51. Cf. Ac. 2:23; 3:15; etc.
52. Ac. 2:23; etc.
53. Ac. 3:18
54. Ac. 3:13; 4:27, 30, NEB.
55. Ac. 7:37
56. Ac. 20:28
57. Ac. 1:2
58. Ac. 1:5
59. Ac. 6:3; cf. 6:5; 7:55; 9:17; 11:24; 13:2-4; etc.
60. Cf. Ac. 4:31; 8:14; 9:31; etc.
61. Ac. 2:14; 6:10; 8:29; etc.
62. Cf. Ac. 5:3, 9; 8:18-20; etc.
63. Cf. Ac. 1:16; 28:25
64. Ac. 1:1, 2
65. Ac. 8:29; 13:2
66. Cf. Ac. 13:3
67. Cf. Ac. 13:4; etc.
68. Cf. Ac. 11:28; 21:4
69. Ac. 15:28
70. Cf. Ac. 16:1, 2, 10; etc.
71. Ac. 5:32
72. Cf. Ac. 2:4; 4:8, 31; 6:3; 13:9; etc.
73. Cf. Ac. 10:19, 20; 13:2
74. Ac. 13:2
75. Cf. Ac. 2:38; 10:45
76. Ac. 2:33
77. Ac. 2:15f.
78. Ac. 5:1-11
79. Ac. 5:4, 9
80. Cf. Lev. 23:15-21
81. Cf. Ac. 2:17, 18; 8:18; 10:45; 15:8; etc.
82. Cf. Ac. 1:8; 19:6
83. Ac. 8:16, 10:44; 11:15
84. Ac. 2:3
85. Ac. 1:5; 11:16
86. Ac. 2:4; 4:8, 31; 13:9
87. Ac. 2:38; 8:15; 10:47
88. Ac. 5:32; 8:18; 11:17
89. Ac. 10:44; cf. 11:15-18; 15:6-11
90. Ac. 1:5
91. Ac. 15:28

THE

PAULINE

LETTERS

11

Christology

It has been said that the theology of Paul is 'the theology of a converted man'. Certainly Paul was no mere academic theologian; he had been found by Christ and knew himself to be His herald. For Paul Christ was vividly and dramatically alive; and he went out into the world with heart aflame to proclaim a Saviour and not to expound a system. In the days when Paul set out as God's servant to preach that Christ is the Son of God, what carried him through with such glorious success was not skill of statement and precision of doctrine, but a clear vision, a firm conviction, and a full love for the Lord who had redeemed him. History has too many evidences of those who have taken it upon themselves to systematize Paul's doctrine the more accurately, only to miss Paul's Christ the most completely. It must then be kept well in the forefront of our minds that all that the apostle has to say about Christ comes warm from a heart throbbing and thrilling with devotion and emotion. The gospel as Paul proclaimed it was Christo-centric through and through; to him Jesus was absolute in the message and experience of salvation.

Two considerations, however, are important for a right approach to a summary of Paul's Christology. It must be premised, first of all, that what the apostle has to say respecting Christ is in essential harmony with the primitive gospel. Paul did not introduce a strange Christ into the theological world. He was not the originator of another gospel.[1] He did not 'Paulinize' the gospel by adding other accretions, for example, the Son-of-God Christology. The truth is rather that all Paul's great central conceptions, on grace, on justification, on salvation through the blood of Christ, on final things, as well as every item in his so-called 'higher Christology', came straight to him out of the heart of Jesus's message. The other point to be made is that Paul's Christology was coloured by the fact that his first encounter with Jesus was with Him as the glorified Lord. It is just here we have the living and dynamic centre of his understanding of Christ. He first found Christ on bended knee; and it was this glowing experience which is reflected in all he has to say about Him. For the original disciples the astonishing thing was that the Jesus, whom they knew and whose companions they were, and who had been put to death as a common criminal, should now be exalted to the throne of God. To Paul the very reverse was the astonishing thing. He had been confronted by the living Christ on the Damascus road and his immediate reaction was to acknowledge Him as Lord. The One who had so overwhelmed him by the sheer grace of God was declared to be the exalted Jesus.[2] He was seen by Paul's new inner sight to have a place in the realm of divine lordship. For Paul the glory of Christ lay in the humiliation which brought Him within the human sphere to accomplish His divine work of salvation. For the other disciples the wonder lay in His exaltation from the human sphere having died a death which was revealed to be on account of man's sin.[3] Peter saw the glory of Christ against the background of His lowly ministry. His thought travelled from the Christ of the Galilean road to the Lord of the excellent glory: Paul's took the reverse direction; for him the amazing thing was that the Lord of the eternal throne should meet him on the Damascus road.

Paul's gospel, then—'my gospel' as he speaks of it[4]—was not something learned at second-hand. It came to him directly by the revelation of Jesus Christ.[5] It was given to him from above. He can consequently declare what was so personally and dynamically real in his own experience, that 'No man can say that Jesus is Lord except by the Holy Ghost'.[6] Thus Paul's gospel was no invented message, no borrowed faith, but Christ's gospel—the veritable gospel of God.[7]

The transforming experience on the Damascus road brings into focus what was to be the heart of Paul's proclamation throughout the following years. Stabbed awake in his conscience by the appearance of Christ, Paul found himself made aware of the identity of Jesus as the Lord. And it was this fact which was to become central in Paul's gospel: Jesus, He is Son of God,[8] and very Christ.[9] This was the essence of his message, the focus of his preaching. Christ is exalted Lord —it was with this affirmation of faith and with this expression of devotion that Paul's Christian life began. He saw that Lordship as basic for man's salvation and ultimate for the world's destiny. From Christ, the glorified Lord, stems all the redeeming influences and flows all the moral power requisite for the transformation of man into the image of Christ, for the perfecting of the Church, and for the renewal of the universe in righteousness.

The phrase 'in Christ' occurring constantly in Pauline writings is pregnant with the sense of Christ as the divine reality in which the whole of Christian experience gets its reference and its explanation. It is 'in Christ' that man is made nigh to God. It is 'in Christ' that life forever more is assured:[10] it is 'in Christ' that God causes us to triumph:[11] it is 'in Christ' that we are 'under the eyes of God':[12] it is 'in Christ' that the veil which lay on the minds of the Jewish people as they read their ancient Scripture is done away:[13] it is 'in Christ' that man is made anew:[14] it is 'in Christ' that God reconciled the world unto Himself:[15] it is 'in Christ' that we are blessed of God with every kind of spiritual blessing:[16] it is 'in Christ' that God will gather together all things:[17] it is 'in Christ' that the promises of God are authenticated.[18] The use of the phrase could be continued almost indefinitely to make His name all the more glorious. In Him we have our completeness, for in Him there is nothing lacking.[19] Clearly all that is of God is to be found 'in Christ'; and little of God can be found apart from Him. He who thus gathers men into relationship with God by taking them up into His own life, is Himself no less than divine Lord.

The lordship of Christ is the decisive factor in the Church. The Church is His,[20] as it is God's.[21] Here is a relationship which does not detract from God but which rather exalts Christ to the status of deity. It is from this conviction of the absolute right of Christ as Lord within His Church that all the ethical demands of the New Testament derive. The believer is related to Christ as the slave to Master, and his highest ideal is to be made 'captive to the obedience of Christ'.[22] The inner power controlling all his motives is the overwhelming love of Christ who loved him even when he was yet a sinner.[23] As one bought with a price he must glorify the Lord who bought him. Christ is therefore 'the head of His body, the Church, and the fulness of Him who filleth all in all'.[24]

His lordship extends to the universe and beyond.[25] The whole created cosmos was ushered into existence by Him as the creative principle of the work of God; and although Paul does not refer to Christ as the Word—the *Logos*—it 'trembles on his lips'. The universe as a created reality is His doing; and He is the 'chain band' of all existing things. In Him all that is 'holds together'.

Thus the lordship of Christ is all-embracing; over Jew and Gentile, rich and poor. He is the same Lord to all who call upon Him.[26] To His lordship all will be subject.[27] To this Christ, prayer is made in the fullest confidence that He is able royally and richly to fulfil. Paul besought the Lord thrice, and it is clear that the Lord he sought was the Christ he knew.[28] To call upon the name of the Lord Jesus Christ was virtually a synonym for Christians. To do anything for His sake is the true norm of service to God.[29] By the application of the term Lord (*kurios*), the uniqueness of Christ as standing in the place of the Jehovah of the Old Testament is made manifest.[30] For Paul indeed the title 'Lord' had a lofty significance. It had ceased in fact to be a title and had become the sacred expression of a personal devotion to God encountered in Christ into which went the gratitude, the love and the loyalty of his redeemed being. In Romans chapter 8 Paul's hymn of praise gathers in intensity as it proceeds, moving from the death of Christ to His rising again from the dead, and thence to His session at the right hand of the majesty on high, and reaches its climax at the point where the imagination fails, His intercessory presence above. If in Philippians 2 he travels down from the throne to the tomb, in Romans 8 he ascends from the grave to the glory. Thus for Paul is Christ set forth as the whole of Christianity on its objective side, as God's very presence among men for our salvation. Yet what Paul has to say about Christ is entirely at one with those who were 'in Christ' before him. Paul was in no sense a 'second founder of Christianity'. He was not the second after Christ but one among those 'in Christ'. Paul's emphasis upon the lordship of Christ is in harmony with all that his predecessors in the faith of the gospel knew of Him. From the beginning Christ was seen as occupying the throne of the universe. In Paul, as in the earlier sources of the New Testament, Christ's resurrection and exaltation are united with the reality of His lordship. It is those who confess that Jesus is Lord and believe in their hearts that God raised Him from the dead who are the saved.[31]

As the exalted Lord He is not far off and unheeding. He is ever-present within His Church, indwelling the hearts of His redeemed. He is the never-failing Guide, Comforter and Leader.

Paul never uses the title Son of God except with a profound sense of reverence and gratitude; and it scarcely ever comes except in passages in which the apostle is contemplating the high themes of Christ's place and purpose.[32] Taken in conjunction with his emphasis upon the lordship of Jesus, his references to Jesus as Son of God gain an enriched connotation in which His essential divineness comes luminously to the fore. Thus in certain places the specific relationship of Christ with God is stated even more absolutely as 'his Son',[33] and even more intimately as 'his own Son'.[34] The declaration of Colossians 1:13, 'the Son of His love' must not be taken to read that He is a Son because loved, but quite the reverse. He is loved because He is Son. It is as Son He came into the world. And since His Sonship runs back beyond time's beginning, any idea that the title came into use to express Messiahship is ruled out. There was no such use made of it in Jewish literature; and in any case Paul himself did not attempt to establish an identity between the messianic title 'Christ' and that of Son of God. The substance of his creed was not 'Jesus is the Christ', but 'Jesus is the Lord'. This, the earliest of the creeds, was Paul's faith and Paul's gospel. When, therefore, the apostle speaks of Him as Son of God he is not referring to Christ's revelatory action. He is stating something about His being, not about His function. Functional Christology, as now in vogue in some quarters, gets little support from Paul, although few expressed more fully and profoundly than he what Christ has done for men.

The suggestion that Paul initiated the 'Son of God Christology' can have no substance from the one passage adduced to support it, namely Romans 1:4. Certainly Paul does here bring the Sonship of Christ into conjunction with the resurrection. Christ is described as coming of David's line according to the flesh and declared to be the Son of God in power according to the Spirit of holiness by the resurrection from the dead. Does this mean that the Pauline Christ is designated Son of God only after the resurrection? It cannot mean this. No such adoptionist Christology can be deduced from this one verse: and in any case such an understanding of Christ would be contrary to the whole tenor of the apostle's teaching. The word in the original (*horizō*), signifies that although Christ was Son of God before the resurrection, yet He was openly appointed ('declared', AV) such among men by this transcendent and crowning event. 'The divine state,' comments Godet, 'which followed the resurrection is a recognized not an acquired state.'

The title Son of God, then, is not to be taken as expressing messianic function or as referring to messianic dignity. It indicates rather the pre-mundane and essential unity of life between Christ and God. Nothing less than this assertion will do justice to Paul's intention by his use of the title Son of God, His Son, and His own Son.

In 1 Corinthians 15:44-49,[35] Paul refers to Christ as 'the last Adam' and 'the second man'. The title suggests the idea of Him as the Founder of a new humanity. In Him, as Representative, a new, that is, a redeemed humanity, takes its rise. The first Adam began a natural history; by him came death; he is a creature and perishable. The last Adam stands at the head of a new humanity; by Him is resurrection. He is of heaven. The contrast between the first Adam, as a living soul, and the last Adam, as a quickening Spirit, brings out the fact that as such Christ is not merely within the natural order. He is a Being above nature by reason of the fact that in Him is life. He has life of Himself and is capable of communicating it to those who are united to Him by faith. The new principle of life which is His to give is the over-flowing of that Spirit of holiness which is the innermost reality of His being.

This reference to the last Adam as a quickening Spirit raises the question of the relation between the exalted Christ and the Spirit.[36] With the specific doctrine of the Holy Spirit we shall be concerned in the next chapter; but meanwhile we may note that the apostle does link the Spirit closely with the person of Christ as the redeeming reality within the human heart. Yet the relation is not one of absolute identity. The trinitarian passages[37] make clear that the relation is that of vital union.[38]

This exalted Lord, this divine Son, this 'second Man' is necessarily, for the apostle, the 'prius' of all. He antedates creation as He initiates salvation. Both have their beginning and ending in Him. It is through Him that all things are, and that we exist.[39] In Colossians 1:15f. Paul brings Christ into relation to creation as 'first-born'; to God as 'image'; to the Church as 'head'. As 'first-born' (*prototokos*) Paul is not including Christ in creation, but quite the reverse. Christ stands outside the created order, for all things are the result of His creative activity. In relation to creation He takes the place of 'first-born', as being 'before it' in time and 'over it' in sovereignty. In relation to God He is the image. He embodies God. In Him God is shown forth. With the term 'image' may be associated the designations 'wisdom and power'. These two are brought together in 1 Corinthians.[40] The concept of Christ as God's Wisdom has also an echo elsewhere in the Pauline literature.[41] Some have sought to interpret the reference by Paul to the 'spiritual rock' that accompanied Israel on her journeys by the same concept, considering that the apostle might have had in his mind a comment by Philo on Deuteronomy 8:15: 'The rock of flint is the Wisdom of God from which he feeds the souls that love him'. But this is most unlikely. By referring to Christ as the 'wisdom of God' the apostle had, of course, an Old Testament background for the use of the phrase. In, for example, Proverbs 8:30 the act of creation is attributed to Wisdom which throughout the chapter is personified. In creation then, Christ is the active Wisdom of God: and so, too, in redemption. In Proverbs 8:38 it is said that whoever finds Wisdom finds life. In Christ is the wisdom in which true life is found.[42] The thrust then of Paul's reference to Christ as Wisdom is to say that all the Jews sought in the Wisdom which is of God is found in Christ.

Christ is also 'the power of God'. For the man in Christ 'the power of God' is not some influence directed upon him by remote control. For faith, God's power is centralized in Christ. Thus the kingdom of God is not 'in word' but 'in power'.[43] To be gathered in Christ's name is to be gathered in His power.[44] The gospel is, therefore, God's power for man's salvation.[45]

In fine, then, Christ is the 'image of God'; in Him God is clearly seen. Christ is 'the wisdom of God'; in Him God is surely known. Christ is 'the power of God'; in Him God is truly felt. Something of the unbegun Sonship and the universal Lordship of Christ is compressed by Paul in the moving declaration of Colossians 1:15f. which comes out finely in Lightfoot's paraphrase. He is 'the perfect image, the visible representation of the unseen God. He is the Firstborn, the absolute Heir of the Father, begotten before the ages; the Lord of the universe by virtue of primogeniture and by virtue also of creative agency. For in Him and through Him the whole world was created, things in heaven and things in earth, things visible to the outward eye, and things cognizable to the outward perception. His supremacy is absolute and universal. All powers in heaven and earth are subject to Him. This subjection extends even to the most exalted and most potent of angelic beings, whether they be called Thrones or Dominions or Princedoms or Powers or whatever title of dignity man may confer upon them. Yes, He is first and He is last. Through Him, as the mediatorial Word, the universe has been created; and unto Him, as the final goal, it is tending. In Him is no before or after. He is pre-existent and self-existent before the worlds. And in Him as the binding and sustaining power, universal nature coheres and consists.'

For all his emphasis, however, upon Christ as exalted Lord, as Divine Son, as Cosmic Agent, Paul was not altogether indifferent to the historic reality of the human Jesus. True, he does not make mention of His miracles, His prayerfulness, His faith, His habits among men. At the same time the view that Paul was so pre-occupied with the exalted Christ that he virtually turned Christianity from being a historic faith into a mere Christ-mysticism has little foundation in fact. It is not true that the Epistle to the Hebrews was written as a corrective to Paul; as an attempt to make secure again the Jesus of history.

2 Corinthians 5:16 has been urged as a warrant for the assumption that Paul did not bother himself with the Synoptic figure of Jesus. But the meaning here is not that Paul had no concern for the historic facts of Christ's life, but with the important truth that spiritual things must be spiritually interpreted. To know Christ in a fleshly way is not to have a real spiritual understanding of Him. Whether Paul did actually know Christ during the period of His days in the flesh is uncertain, although it seems likely. In this passage he suggests that he did formerly know Him in a human manner, but that now, in contrast, he knows Him in a living fellowship.

From the record of his sermons in Acts there are evidences of Paul's knowledge of the historical facts of the life of Jesus. He was probably well aware from his pre-Christian days of the kind of apologetic for Christ of which Stephen's speech was an example. After his conversion Paul was baptized and certainly not without some knowledge of the Christ whose name he had taken upon him. He must have been acquainted with some of the facts about Jesus during the three years in Arabia. He went up to Jerusalem on a special fifteen days mission according to Galatians 1:18, and there he talked with Peter. He went up to interview Peter—'to history' (*historēsai*) him; only, of course, that is not good English. Paul worked for long periods in company with Barnabas, John Mark, Silas, and Luke, all of whom were certainly in possession of the facts of the life and teaching of his Lord. It is incredible to suggest that he would not have learned from them something of these matters, or that he was not interested in what the Lord, in whom he gloried, said and did. For Paul the fact is rather that he regarded a saying of Jesus as the highest authority he could quote. Only when he has no commandment as such from the Lord does he admit his own commandment, though he believes himself to be inspired of the Spirit.[46]

A study of the Epistles of Paul reveals his knowledge of the historic Jesus. There is much obviously presupposed for he was writing from faith to faith and for faith's understanding. His epistles were not missionary propaganda; they were for the churches who were in possession of the historic facts. There are, however, impressive passages in which he refers to Christ's entry into human history. He was 'made of a woman, made under the law'.[47] He set an example of courage under persecution.[48] He instituted the Last Supper, was killed upon the Cross. Of His character outlined in the factual story of His life, Paul has much to say. The glory of the believer is to be conformed into the image of Christ; to express, for example, 'the meekness and gentleness of Christ'.[49] 1 Corinthians 13 is nothing if not a portrait of the Saviour. Paul not only quotes the authority of Christ but records the unwritten saying of His: 'Remember the words of the Lord Jesus how He said it was more blessed to give than to receive'.[50] Such injunctions as 'Judge not that ye be not judged'; 'Be careful for nothing' and the like are more than an echo of our Lord's teaching.

For Paul, then, it is a real Jesus who is Lord. Yet His Sonship is not the deification of a human Jesus. It is Paul's clear teaching that Christ's Sonship has no temporal beginning; it goes back into the eternity of the Divine Being. It is the very incidental way Paul states the fact of Christ's pre-existence which shows how deeply rooted it was in the faith and message of the gospel. He refers to the Son's being 'sent'.[51] And he makes it clear at the same time that He is 'sent' because He is the Son and not that He becomes a Son by fulfilling a special divine calling.[52] A passage such as 2 Corinthians 8:9 shows that the apostle sees the incarnate life against the background of a pre-temporal glory. The epic passage Philippians 2:5-7 is the apostle's most deliberate declaration on the subject. On the face of it the meaning here is plain; Bethlehem did not begin His story. He who ever was became, in undertaking the humiliation of servanthood, what He wasn't. As the 'spiritual rock' it was He who kept company with ancient Israel on their way.[53] The Son of God in whom love divine became actual in human history is one for whom time itself is irrelevant. This pre-existence of Christ is not a notion borrowed from an alleged Jewish-Hellenic idea of a pre-existent 'heavenly man'. The evidence for such is too slender: and Philo's 'heavenly man' is not anything like what the apostle says of Christ. Philo called his 'heavenly man' the 'first'. Paul's is emphatically 'the last'. For those who will persist in interpreting the gospel in humanistic terms any floating idea will readily be called in to their aid. But Paul did not so learn Christ. For Him the pre-existence of Christ was the result of a spiritual reading of the fact of redemption into which he had been brought by Christ's saving deed on the cross. Paul knew by the simple contemplation of faith that the glory he encountered in Christ was too Godlike to be acquired by any human life however devout. It was a glory to be shared and yet never diminished; it is the very glory of God which is seen in the face of Christ Jesus.[54]

Paul will, therefore, not hesitate to associate God and Christ in the closest possible way. We have seen how he applies to Him without hesitation the term Lord (*Kurios*) which the Septuagint uses to translate the Hebrew 'Jehovah'.[55] Furthermore, the Old Testament 'day of the Lord' or 'day of Jehovah' becomes for Paul, without any awareness that he is doing violence to truth, 'the day of Christ'.[56] There can, therefore, be no doubt in Paul's mind as to the true status of Christ. He is essentially Divine—fully within the area of Deity. Equally with God, He is the source of all spiritual blessings for the people of God.[57] He does for us what God does and is for us what God is.[58] He bears the character of God.[59] He performs the activities of God.[60] He exhibits the finality of God.[61] He is consequently the One in whom God is seen absolutely.[62] In Him the very fulness of God took up its permanent abode in bodily form.[63] While originally in the fullest possession of Godhead, yet He did not maintain this exclusive state as a prize to be held to, but took to Himself the form of man and in that state lived a life of obedience even unto the death of the cross.[64] He emptied Himself of all the honour that His divine status demanded and renounced His pre-existent glory, humbling Himself to our position, and in that condition of humanness submitted Himself to a slave's place and a criminal's death for mankind. And for such an excess of obedience and love He was reinstated at the throne of God; and received again the glory which He had with the Father before the foundation of the world.

Can it then be fairly contended that Paul hesitated to apply to Him the appellation 'God' in the very fullest sense? He has made Him so Godlike that He cannot be less than God. In a number of passages Christ is brought into the most intimate conjunction with God in a way which suggests that there is no incongruity in moving from the one to the other.[65] In 2 Thessalonians 1:12, the statement 'the grace of our God and Lord Jesus Christ' seems to make the identity definite and thus to assert Christ's absolute Deity. Titus 2:13 (cf. v.10), assuming its Paulinity, most certainly makes Jesus Christ our great God and Saviour. True to Paul's Christology is, therefore, his doxology of Romans 9:5. It is a much debated question whether the words 'God over all blessed for ever' are to be taken as a further description of Christ or as a separate doxology referring to the Almighty. The structure of the sentence favours the first. It is on dogmatic grounds only that some have refused to allow that Paul is here making an unequivocal assertion of Christ's essential Deity. The suggestion that such a declaration must be regarded as 'too

advanced' for him begs the question. Such a thesis can only
be entertained by misreading the faith of the primitive
Church and is due to a failure to grasp the reality of Paul's
own intense experience and the actuality of Christ's own
divine self-disclosure. It cannot be reckoned as outside the
faith and the proclamation of Paul, therefore, to make this
full and final confession. The words of Romans 9:5 may,
then, be taken to read 'Christ . . . over all God blessed for
ever', and thus, as H. R. Mackintosh says, they are 'an
explicit assertion of Christ's deity'. Such an assertion is the
only natural and legitimate climax of Paul's Christology, as
we have seen the outlines of it in what has gone before.
Confession is made throughout of God the Father and of the
Lord Jesus Christ.[66] The two are not confused; yet they are
intimately related. We are thus led on naturally to the great
trinitarian passages of the Pauline letters, in which the work
of the Father, Son and Spirit is unfolded in relation to man's
redemption. God is known as Father, through the Son by
the Spirit.[67] The 'Trinitarian form of experience' with the
trinitarian benediction[68] make no less secure, however, the
unity of the Christian experience of God. It is God who is
known as Divine Father, through Him who is Divine Son
and in Him who is Divine Spirit. This is both the authentic
voice of revelation as it is the living reality of experience.
Therefore, to confess Christ's Deity is simply to give Him
His right name. In truth the whole New Testament Christology is but the unfolding of the proclamation made at His
birth; 'of Mary was born Jesus, who is called Christ'.[69] He is
the anointed One. His name is to be called Jesus, for He
shall save His people from their sins. He is the atoning One.
And they shall call His name Emmanuel, which being
interpreted is, *God* with us.[70] And He is the abiding One.

It is within the context of Paul's high view of Christ's
Person that the so-called 'subordinationist' language he uses
in other passages must be understood.[71] None of these statements can be taken as detracting from the absoluteness of

Christ in relation to the Father. Such a notion would be altogether foreign to the apostle's thought. It is in such passages that Paul does have in mind Christ's 'function' as Mediator. For Paul Christ is the one and only Mediator;[72] and as such He who fully shares in the Godness of God, acts for the Father and with Him in the divine purposes of grace in creation, revelation and redemption. It was in the reality of the flesh and the fullness of obedience that the Son accomplished God's saving work for man. In the obedience of faith the Son is 'subject' to the Father; and the relationship is one of perfect love, not of variance, hostility or difference. And when His work of redemption is completed, and all things have been gathered up in Christ, then shall the Son deliver up the kingdom to the Father, that God, the Triune One, may be all in all.

Without, then, a hold on Christ there is no hold on God at all. For in the knowledge of Christ no mistake can be made about God.

SCRIPTURE REFERENCES

1. Cf. Gal. 1:16f.
2. Ac. 9:5
3. Cf. Ac. 2:22, 23
4. Cf. Rom. 2:16; 2 Cor. 4:3; Gal. 2:2; 1 Thess. 1:15; 2 Thess. 2:14
5. Gal. 1:16
6. 1 Cor. 12:3
7. Cf. Rom. 1:1, 16; 15:16, 19; etc.
8. Ac. 9:20
9. Ac. 9:22
10. 1 Cor. 15:18, 19
11. 2 Cor. 2:14
12. 2 Cor. 2:17
13. 2 Cor. 3:14
14. 2 Cor. 5:17
15. 2 Cor. 5:19
16. Eph. 1:3
17. Eph. 1:10
18. Eph. 3:6
19. Col. 2:9, 10
20. Rom. 16:16; etc.
21. 1 Cor. 1:2; 11:22; 15:9; etc.

22. 2 Cor. 10:5
23. Cf. Rom. 5:8; 2 Cor. 5:14
24. Eph. 1:22
25. Eph. 1:21
26. Rom. 10:12, 13
27. Eph. 3:11; Phil. 2:11; etc.
28. Cf. 2 Cor. 12:2-10; cf. v. 9
29. Cf. Ac. 9:16; Rom. 15:30; 2 Cor. 12:10
30. Rom. 10:13; cf. Joel 2:32
31. Rom. 10:9; cf. Rom. 8:34; Eph. 1:19, 20; Col. 3:1
32. Cf. Rom. 8:32; 1 Cor. 1:9; Gal. 2:20
33. Rom. 1:9; 5:10; 8:29; Gal. 1:16; 4:4; 1 Thess. 1:10
34. Rom. 8:3, 32
35. Cf. Rom. 5:12-21
36. Cf. above p. 47ff.
37. Cf. 2 Cor. 13:14; Eph. 1:3-11; 2:18; etc.
38. Cf. Rom. 8:11; 1 Cor. 6:11; 12:3; 2 Cor. 3:17; 4:14; Gal. 2:17; etc.
39. 1 Cor. 8:6.
40. 1 Cor. 1:24
41. Cf. 1 Cor. 1:30; 2:6, 7; Col. 2:3
42. Cf. 1 Cor. 1:17ff.
43. 1 Cor. 4:20
44. 1 Cor. 5:4
45. Rom. 1:16; cf. 1 Cor. 1:18; etc.
46. Cf. 1 Cor. 7:10, 12, 25, 40; 9:14
47. Gal. 4:4
48. Rom. 15:2f.
49. 2 Cor. 10:1
50. Ac. 20:35
51. Gal. 4:4; cf. Rom. 8:3
52. Cf. Mt. 21:37
53. 1 Cor. 10:4
54. 2 Cor. 4:6
55. Cf. 1 Cor. 1:31; 2 Cor. 3:16; 10:17; Eph. 4:8; 2 Thess. 1:9
56. Cf. Joel 2:1; Amos 5:18; 1 Thess. 5:2; cf. 1 Cor. 5:5; Phil. 1:6; 2 Thess. 1:9
57. Rom. 1:5, 7; 1 Cor. 1:3; 2 Cor. 1:2; Gal. 1:3
58. Cf. Rom. 4:4; 1 Cor. 15:10; 2 Cor. 5:18; 10:8; 12:8; 13:10; 17:9; Gal. 1:16; Phil. 3:12; 2 Thess. 3:5; etc.
59. Phil. 2:5
60. Col. 1:16; etc.
61. 1 Tim. 4:1; etc.
62. Col. 1:15
63. Col. 2:9
64. Phil. 2:7, 8
65. Cf. Rom. 1:7, 9; 1 Cor. 1:3; etc.
66. 2 Thess. 1:12
67. Cf. Rom. 8:15; 2 Cor. 1:21, 22; Eph. 1:4-21; 2:18; etc.

68. Cf. 2 Cor. 13:14; Eph. 1:4-21
69. Mt. 1:16
70. Mt. 1:21, 23
71. Cf. 1 Cor. 3:21; 11:3; 15: 28
72. 1 Tim. 2:5; Cf. Gal. 3:20

12

The Holy Spirit

1 Preliminary Statement

It is almost impossible to gather into a brief chapter all
that the apostle Paul has to say about the Holy Spirit. For
the Holy Spirit is related by him to every aspect of salvation,
to our justification, our sanctification, our service and our
glorification. In every one of his letters with the exception
of his postcard note to Philemon, he refers to the Spirit.
There are about one hundred and twenty allusions to the
Holy Spirit in his writings. Thus to become a Christian is
for the apostle to receive the Spirit,[1] and to live as a Christian
is to walk by the Spirit.[2] Viewed objectively, Christianity is,
for Paul, the grace of God in Christ; viewed subjectively it
is faith through the Spirit. Thus the gospel of our salvation
may be summarized as, by grace in Christ; or as, through
faith by the Spirit.

We have seen in an earlier chapter that the Spirit's presence
was foreshadowed in God's special relation to Israel. But a
new age began at Pentecost. A new Israel was constituted
by the coming of the Spirit, so that the Spirit's indwelling
presence is the new factor in history and the new experience
for the people of God. Everywhere in his epistles Paul
emphasizes this unique and supernatural character of the
Christian gospel. It is through the Spirit that man comes to
newness of life,[3] and is made a new man,[4] and a new
creation.[5] Those in Christ are no longer 'in the flesh' but 'in

162

the Spirit', because of the indwelling of the Spirit of God.[6] To be made a man in Christ is to be made new through the Spirit. The Gospels themselves, as we have noted, represent Jesus as emphasizing that His work was done by the Spirit. The apostle, too, refers to the Spirit's activity in the humanity of Jesus,[7] but he does not, anymore than do the Gospels themselves, leave us with a Jesus who is no more than a Spirit-filled Man.

According to Paul it is the Spirit's activity in men which creates the new relationship with God which is best expressed as union with Christ. It is in the fellowship (*koinōnia*) of the Holy Spirit that men are sure, through the grace of our Lord Jesus Christ, of the love of God. The epistles are none other than an exposition of the Spirit's action in the life of the believer and the believing community. The Spirit's operations gave rise to new spiritual gifts within the Church. The apostle's teaching regarding spiritual gifts springs out of his conception of the Church as the body of Christ constituted by the Spirit. The Holy Spirit is the life-giving principle distributed throughout the body. And it is by the Spirit that the believer makes his response to the Lordship of Christ.[8] The underlying motive of all service for Christ and relationship within the fellowship of faith is love shed abroad in our hearts by the Holy Spirit.[9] Far-reaching and comprehensive then, is the place Paul gives to the Spirit. Thus, whereas in the Pauline theology the Son of God is the root of all human relationships with God, it is the Holy Spirit who is the creative source and living energy of man's redemptive relation with God in Christ. From one point of view the sphere of Christ's activity is wider than that of the Spirit's, for Paul sees Christ as the agent of creation as well as the mediator of salvation. It is within the sphere of salvation that Christ's work overlaps with that of the Spirit, so that the regenerative activities of divine grace are attributed both to the Son and the Spirit. New life from God is in Christ and in the Spirit;[10] and the believer is indwelt by both,[11] as is the Church.[12] The bond that unites believers is Christ and the Spirit.[13] In Romans 8 intercession for believers is made by the Son and the Spirit,[14] and through both the filial spirit of adoption is given.[15] In the experience of grace is begun a spiritual warfare of flesh and sin against the indwelling Son and Spirit.[16] Not only are all the graces of the new life, including both our justification and sanctification, attributed to the work of each,[17] but all the charismatic gifts are derived equally from both.[18]

2   Epistolary Summary

There seems to be in the Pauline letters evidence for fuller treatment of the presence of the Holy Spirit as the apostle's fellowship with Christ deepened. For Paul, to know Christ was indeed to know more of the Spirit, and to be fully taken up with Him is to be filled with the Spirit. This does not mean that Paul's doctrine of the Spirit was the result of an analysis of experience. Both the Old Testament and Paul's own specific revelation of Jesus Christ helped to shape the apostle's doctrine of the Spirit. Too much cannot then be made of a suggested development in Paul's teaching on the Spirit; yet a suggestive way of following his understanding is to take the general order of the composition of his letters.

A beginning can then be made by looking at the Thessalonian epistles. There are only four allusions to the Spirit here.[19] It is thought that all he has to say in these passages goes little beyond what could be found in the Synoptic Gospels. But this is important in itself as it shows how akin and harmonious with the teaching of the primitive Church is the Pauline doctrine, and rules out of court the oft repeated accusation that he was an innovator of other ideas unknown to the first disciples. The little that he has to say, however, shows that the idea of the Spirit was a factor well known in the experience of these early believers and in the life of the Church. Paul had no need to explain his teaching; it is taken for granted that the Thessalonians were no strangers to the Spirit's presence. His word among them from the first was 'in power, and in the Holy Ghost';[20] and it was received by them 'in much affliction, with joy in the Holy Spirit'.[21] It was the Spirit that wrought the change which turned them from idols to serve the living and true God. God calls to holiness; but the one who despises man, despises God who has given us His Holy Spirit.[22] We have been chosen by God in Christ through sanctification of the Spirit and belief in the truth.[23] The words of 1 Thessalonians 5:19 may suggest that the apostle was urging the uncritical use of spiritual gifts which he had occasion later to curb at Corinth. Thus the NEB has for the injunction, 'Quench not the Spirit' (AV, RSV), the translation, 'Do not stifle inspiration'. But Phillips seems to have preserved best Paul's intention: 'Never damp down the Spirit, and never despise what is spoken in the name of the Lord'.

In the second series of letters, those to the Romans, the Corinthians and the Galatians, the apostle gives a large place to the Spirit. Here Paul makes clear that it is by the Spirit's incoming and indwelling that the Christian life is begun and maintained.[24] At the same time he relates closely the Spirit's presence in man with man's own redeemed and renewed spirit. It is by the power of the Spirit that mighty signs and wonders were wrought by the apostle during his missionary work.[25] It is through the power of the Spirit that hope is made sure,[26] and by love of the Spirit that prayer is strengthened[27] and in sanctification of the Spirit that gospel ministry is sweetened.[28] It is the Spirit who distributes to the believing community those gifts which make for the general good.[29]

Of the letters of the first imprisonment only Ephesians has significant statements on the subject of the Spirit. In it the Church is seen as the building of God in which God dwells through the Spirit.[30] Through Christ access is found into the new redeemed community unto the Father by the

Spirit.[31] Therefore, believers must endeavour to keep the unity of the Spirit,[32] a unity created by the Spirit and only maintained in Him.[33] The Spirit strengthens the inner life of the believer[34] and seals Him as God's property until the day of redemption.[35] The Christian must, therefore, take the Spirit's sword and fight the good fight of faith.[36] The Spirit is not to be put to pain,[37] as He can by unChristlike talk and walk. Rather, no place must be given to the devil,[38] but every place to the Spirit.[39] For, as the Epistle to the Philippians says, there is available 'the supply of the Spirit of Jesus Christ'.[40]

The two certain references to the Holy Spirit in the Pastorals are in line with the Pauline teaching. It is by the Holy Spirit who dwells within that, 'That good thing committed' unto Christ is kept 'against that day'.[41] And by the renewing work of the Spirit the grace of God which is salvation is brought to man.[42]

3 Specific Relationships

Throughout his epistles the apostle brings together the Spirit and other concepts sometimes by way of association and sometimes by way of contrast. In drawing out some of these relationships we are led to see more clearly his teaching on the Holy Spirit.

(a) The Spirit and Faith

Although Paul's great central doctrine is justification by faith, an act absolutely of God to which man makes his response by faith, there are passages in which faith and the Spirit are brought into the closest association. In 2 Corinthians 4:13 the apostle speaks of 'the spirit of faith'; but this could as surely be read with a capital S, for faith is of the Spirit. It is God who gives to every man the measure of faith.[43] The Corinthian believers are reminded that the apostle's preaching was in demonstration of the Spirit, and thus their faith does not stand in the wisdom of men, but the power of God.[44] The unspiritual man cannot grasp what belongs to the Spirit of God.[45] Only the Spirit received from God knows what God is.[46] Faith is, therefore, bestowed by the Spirit, and is itself a condition of receiving the Spirit.[47] To have the Spirit is then for Paul to have faith; and to have faith in God's act in Christ is to be justified. Consequently by virtue of the Spirit in our hearts we experience the divine sonship and are adopted into the family of God.[48] And all the blessings of that new relationship, its peace, its joy, its liberty, are assured in the Spirit.[49]

(b) The Spirit and the Christian life

Everything which belongs to our salvation is made available for the believer in and by the Spirit. The Spirit is not only the source of the believer's faith, as we have seen, but He is also the secret of the believer's fruit.[50] Love, the supreme grace, is the gift of the Spirit.[51] Saving knowledge is of the Spirit;[52] and it is by His power the Christian lives, and under His seal the Christian is secure.[53]

(c) The Spirit and the Church

We have seen from the Book of Acts how the early Church, in which Paul was Christ's supreme servant, was led on and out by the Spirit. All through his letters the same awareness of the Spirit and His place within the Church as its Senior Partner is stated or implied. The Church, as the *koinōnia*, the fellowship, is the creation of the Spirit;[54] and Paul's own ministry, as God's ambassador, was under the Spirit's control.[55] Paul planted the local congregations by the power of the Spirit,[56] having preached the message of Christ in the Spirit's eloquence.[57] In one Spirit all believers are baptized into one body.[58] The Spirit is the principle of unity by whom the entire community of believers are bound together in a common life in God.[59]

(d) The Spirit and the spirits

There can be no doubt that Paul regarded the present world as in some way the theatre of activity for evil spirits. He talks, therefore, about the 'spiritual hosts of wickedness in the heavenly places',[60] and warns against 'seducing spirits and doctrines of demons'.[61] He knew something of the 'wiles' of the 'commander of the spiritual powers of the air, the spirit that now works in the children of disobedience'.[62] Satan is the god of this world[63] who hindered the apostle's work and afflicted his person.[64] There is then, in contrast with the Spirit of God—the Holy Spirit—'a different spirit'.[65] This is 'the spirit of the world',[66] otherwise characterized as 'the spirit of bondage',[67] 'the spirit of stupor',[68] 'the spirit of fear'.[69] It is clear from what Paul has to say, especially in his letters to the Corinthians and his experiences as recorded in the Book of Acts, that evil spirits as well as the Holy Spirit could take hold of men and make their presence felt by means of uninhibited ecstasy and extraordinary workings.

By what criteria, then, is the true presence of the Spirit of God to be demonstrated? These can be singled out somewhat as follows. *First,* by a full acknowledgement of the Lordship of Jesus. No man speaking in the Spirit can ever say Jesus is cursed.[70] That would be to contradict the central confession of the Gospel and would be to blaspheme the Holy Spirit. Anyone who gave voice to such a verdict upon Jesus would have lost whatever understanding of divine things he might have had. That would be to do despite to the spirit of grace and to slip down into perdition. Thus no man can say that Jesus is Lord, in the full measure of faith, except by the Holy Spirit.[71] It is from a 'different spirit' to assess Jesus as less than that; as it is the essence of saving faith to confess with the mouth Jesus Christ as Lord and to believe in the heart that God has raised Him from the dead.

A *second* criterion of the presence of the Holy Spirit is loving unity in the fellowship of Christ. The first letter to the Corinthians is designed to show that pride of place, jealousy of another's gifts, strife among brethren, are not of the Spirit of God. Those who act in this manner are not really 'spiritual'; for these things are not of the Spirit. Paul is sensitive to the fact that in the Corinthian Church gifts which should have been used to bind together the community of believers into a fellowship of brotherhood, were the occasion of disruption and division. To bring disunity into the Church of God is to be carnal,[72] and is to bring destruction into the temple of God which is holy because of the Spirit of God who dwells in its members.[73] The Corinthians were zealous for spiritual gifts, but are reminded that they are to seek them for the good of others.[74] There is an evident danger in being more concerned with the gifts of the Spirit than with the Spirit who gives them, and thus to remain in the stage of childhood.[75] There is always the peril of the spiritual nursery; to be coaxed and coddled instead of meeting life's stern demands. But Paul would stress that God never saves us the trouble of growing up, of seeking to attain to the fullness of the stature of Christ. To remain as children is to give way to childish chatter, to baby-talk more fitting to the nursery. The child, too, often has its mind on the gift rather than the giver; on what it can have for itself rather than what it can use for others. It is in this way that Paul regarded the gifts of the Spirit in the Corinthian Church. They sought them for their own sake, for the status they would give and for the thrill they might bring. As a result they became 'puffed up' like a bellows; all 'fizz', like inflated wineskins. Thus Paul seeks to show that not all who boast of the gifts of the Spirit are spiritual. He would have them know that the Spirit is not here to excite uninhibited emotional experiences, but to be the source of spiritual power and the spring of Christian character. This is the deeper

169

reading of the Corinthian letters. Far more important than these special moments and movements of the Spirit, is the reality of the Spirit's presence judged in the light of the higher valuation of love. All that transgresses the principle of holy love makes for disorder and division, and is not of the Spirit at all, but of our own making.

It is for this reason that there appears in the Pauline letters a gradual discouragement of the gifts of the Spirit with their appeal to the Church in its first immaturity, and a corresponding encouragement of the fruits of the Spirit in conformity to the likeness of Christ. The proof of the Spirit is not revealed in fluctuating loyalties, and passing moods, but in a steady spiritual outlook, a unique type of Christian character, a strenuous service for Christ and a devoted commitment to the divine purposes for the world. This means that for a *third* criterion of the Spirit's presence there must be a growing approximation to the ideal of Christ. It is by the Spirit that we are initiated into divine sonship in Christ.[76] Where this sonship is known, the Spirit is present.[77] It is of the Spirit to act within the sphere of this sonship to make fruitful its implications in the life.[78] The believer must then 'walk in the Spirit' and bear 'the fruit of the Spirit'. All that the Pauline letters mean by being a Christian is comprehended under what he has to say about the Spirit. It is by the Spirit we are set free from the law, from sin and from death. All the moral forces and factors which constitute Christian experience and secure Christian character are by the Spirit's power.[79]

Thus is the Spirit regarded as the spirit of faith,[80] of life,[81] of meekness,[82] of wisdom,[83] of sanctification,[84] of holiness.[85] It is the Spirit who makes for spirituality in the Church; thus for Paul the Spirit is specifically Christian.

4 Resultant Doctrine

In the light of what we have gathered about the Spirit in

the Pauline writings it is possible to state more precisely his doctrine of the Holy Spirit. To begin with we note the Spirit's relation with God. He is called the Spirit of God,[86] and the Spirit of Him that raised Jesus from the dead.[87] He is of God and knows His mind.[88] He is given to man by God.[89] Yet there is a distinction between God and the Spirit; although the same results are attributed to the Spirit as to God.[90] The Holy Spirit is, then, a divine transcendent Being possessing of Himself a Divine objective reality.

There is also a relationship insisted upon between the Spirit and the Son. The Spirit of God is the Spirit of Christ[91] and God sent forth the Spirit of His Son.[92] Passages such as 1 Corinthians 15:45 and 2 Corinthians 3:17 associate the Spirit and the Son in the closest intimacy, yet they are not absolutely identified. They are distinguished, yet united: united, yet distinguished. Throughout, Paul does not permit us to regard the Holy Spirit as an 'It'. The Spirit carries personal attributes and performs personal acts. He can be lied to, grieved, and so forth. And the Spirit leads, speaks, helps, and the like. What, therefore, Paul has to say on the subject is, in spite of its practical nature, sufficient to provide the basis for the later formulated doctrine of the Church of the threefold existence in the one Divine Being. Again and again there is the association of Father, Son and Holy Spirit,[93] which shows, that in the gospel as Paul had received it and experienced it, it was not improper to refer to the Holy Spirit as a Divine Other in whom he had come to know the Father through the Son, in a personal way.

SCRIPTURE REFERENCES

1. Cf. Gal. 3:3-5; Rom. 8:9, NEB.
2. Gal. 5:16
3. Gal. 4:6
4. Col. 3:10
5. 2 Cor. 4:16; Gal. 6:15
6. Rom. 8:9
7. Cf. Rom. 8:11; Gal. 4:29; etc.

8. 1 Cor. 12:3
9. Rom. 5:5
10. Cf. Rom. 14:17; 2 Cor. 5:17; 6:6; etc.
11. Cf. Rom. 8:9, 10; Gal. 2:20; Col. 1:27
12. 1 Cor. 3:16; 12:27
13. Cf. Eph. 4:3, 4; Phil. 1:27; 2:1; 4:2
14. Rom. 8:26, 34
15. Cf. Gal. 4:4-6; Eph. 1:5
16. Cf. Rom. 13:14; Gal. 5:16-25
17. Cf. Rom. 15:18, 19, 1 Cor. 1:2, 30; 2:4; 5:4; 6:11; 1 Thess. 4:8;
    etc.
18. Cf. 1 Cor. 12:4-6
19. Cf. 1 Thess. 1:5, 6; 4:7; 5:19; 2 Thess. 2:13
20. 1 Thess. 1:5
21. 1 Thess. 1:6
22. 1 Thess. 4:7
23. 2 Thess. 2:3
24. Cf. Rom. 8:9, 26; 1 Cor. 3:16; 6:11; Gal. 3:14; 4:6; etc.
25. Rom. 15:19
26. Rom. 15:13
27. Rom. 15:30
28. Rom. 15:16
29. Cf. 1 Cor. 12:4f.
30. Eph. 2:22
31. Eph. 2:18
32. Eph. 4:3
33. Cf. Eph. chs. 2, 3, 4
34. Eph. 3:16
35. Eph. 1:13; 4:30
36. Eph. 6:17
37. Eph. 4:30
38. Eph. 4:27
39. Eph. 5:18
40. Phil. 1:19
41. 2 Tim. 1:14
42. Tit. 3:5
43. Rom. 12:3
44. 1 Cor. 2:5
45. 1 Cor. 2:14
46. 1 Cor. 2:12
47. Gal. 3:2, 14
48. Cf. Rom. 8:15, 16; Gal. 4:6
49. Cf. Rom. 7:2, 6; 14:17; Gal. 5:22; 1 Thess. 1:6
50. Gal. 5:22, 23
51. Cf. Rom. 15:30; 1 Cor. 13; Col. 1:8
52. Cf. 1 Cor. 2:7-10; Eph. 1:17, 23; etc.
53. 2 Cor. 1:22
54. 1 Cor. 3:16, 17; etc.

55. Rom. 15:18, 19
56. Cf. 1 Cor. 2:4; Gal. 3:2; 1 Thess. 1:5, 6;
57. Cf. 1 Cor. 2; 2 Cor. 3
58. 1 Cor. 12:13
59. Cf. 1 Cor. 3:16; Eph. 2:18, 22
60. Eph. 6:12
61. 1 Tim. 4:1
62. Eph. 2:2, NEB.
63. 2 Cor. 4:4
64. Cf. 2 Cor. 12:7; 1 Thess. 2:18
65. Cf. 2 Cor. 11:4; 2 Thess. 2:2
66. 1 Cor. 2:12
67. Rom. 8:15
68. Rom. 11:8
69. 2 Tim. 1:7
70. 1 Cor. 12:3
71. 1 Cor. 12:3
72. 1 Cor. 3:1
73. 1 Cor. 3:16, 17
74. 1 Cor. 14:12
75. 1 Cor. 14:20; Eph. 4:14, 15
76. Gal. 4:6
77. Rom. 8:14
78. Gal. 5:22, 23
79. Rom. 8:23; cf. Gal. 5:22, 23
80. 2 Cor. 4:13
81. Rom. 8:2, 10
82. 1 Cor. 4:21; Gal. 6:1
83. Eph. 1:17
84. 2 Thess. 2:13
85. Rom. 1:4
86. Rom. 8:9; 1 Cor. 3:16
87. Rom. 8:11
88. Cf. Rom. 5:8; 1 Cor. 6:19; 1 Thess. 4:8
89. 1 Cor. 2:11, 12; Gal. 3:5
90. Cf. Rom. 15:16; 1 Thess. 5:23
91. Rom. 8:9
92. Gal. 4:6
93. Rom. 15:13-19, 30; 2 Cor. 13:14; Eph. 2.18, 21, 22; etc.

13

Man

Like most of the Pauline theology, Paul's doctrine of man is not given in any formulated manner. Some of his statements, of course, presuppose accepted Jewish views, but then the roots of the Christian message are in the Old Testament, and in the Old Testament Paul was well versed. Much of Paul's psychological vocabulary, in spite of his use of such Greek terms as 'mind', 'conscience' and 'inner man', is Hebrew in form and content.

It was certainly not Paul's business to set forth a detailed anthropology or psychology. He was more concerned to bring man a gospel of salvation which touched him in the whole area of his human nature and need. His data about man are consequently experimental in form and practical in aim. His references, therefore, to man's structure are occasional; and are found usually in the context of Christ's soteriological work and the apostle's proclamation of that saving deed. It is on this account that Paul, for example, makes mention of the 'weakness' of human flesh and to the action of the Spirit of God within him quickening him to 'spiritual' life.

The Pauline doctrine of man presupposes the truth of the Genesis account of man's creation. In Romans 9 he insists on the right of God as sovereign Creator. The whole passage stresses that in making man as He has done, God was but revealing Himself to be the God that He is. In his sermon on Mars' Hill the apostle quotes approvingly the words of the heathen poet Aretus to the effect that all men are God's offspring. Paul's use of the words was intended to convey the truth that man is more than a piece of clay. He has a spiritual element in him, a 'God-shaped blank' at his very heart which can only be filled at the last by the God whom he had come to declare.[1] Paul believed without doubt that man was made in the image and likeness of God; he is a combination of dust and deity.

Allied to his full acceptance of the Old Testament understanding of man's origin, Paul sees human solidarity as a fundamental postulate of his doctrine of sin and salvation. By 'one man' sin entered into the world, bringing with it sinnership and death to all.[2] The organic unity of mankind lies at the foundation of Paul's doctrine of universal sinfulness due to the first transgression and of the provision of salvation for the race in Christ. Evidently the doctrine of human solidarity was for the apostle more than a requisite for a theology; it was part of his preaching.[3]

Due to his characteristic emphasis on personal experience, Paul finds it necessary to make reference to the elements of man's psychological nature. 'Flesh' (*sarx*) and 'spirit' (*pneuma*) are Paul's most characteristic terms to contrast the lower and higher elements in man. The former term occurs ninety-one times in the Pauline writings of which the larger number (fifty-six to be exact) have a physical connotation. This number can be broken down further. Twelve cases refer to the actual physical body. It was in this sense, for example, that Paul speaks of his thorn in the flesh.[4] In eleven instances the idea of kinship is to be understood as when the apostle writes concerning his kinsmen according to the 'flesh'. Eight of the eleven uses of the word with this meaning occur in the epistle to the Romans.[5] In fourteen places the term covers the sphere of present existence as when the apostle speaks of the life that he lives in the 'flesh'.[6] There are nineteen references in which *sarx* conveys the idea of fleshly weakness. In some way a deficiency is suggested, as, for example, when it is declared that 'not many wise men not many noble after the flesh are called'.[7] By far then the greater number of occurrences of the term 'flesh' (almost two-thirds) have a primary physical connotation. Common to all these uses of the term is the idea of the 'flesh' as human nature conditioned by the body.

There is another use of the term *sarx* in the Pauline theology which has a moral or ethical sense. In this context the concept 'flesh' and 'spirit' have moved from one of contrast to one of conflict. Man's moral and ethical struggles are then to be seen as a battle between his higher and lower natures. The lower nature is the *sarx*, and with it sin finds an ally. There are thirty-five instances of the use of the term in this sense, and it occurs more frequently in Romans (cf. chs. 7 and 8) and Galatians (cf. ch. 5). But it is also to be found in other contexts.[8] Sometimes the 'flesh' is personified, and is said to possess will and desires, and so becomes the antagonist of the Holy Spirit and of the new spirit which grace creates in us.

The very close connection between sin and the flesh[9] raises the question whether Paul regarded the flesh as itself evil. There are those who do not hesitate to credit to him such a Gnostic conception. But a careful reading of what the apostle has to say about the connection between sin and the flesh prohibits such a rash conclusion. For one thing Paul clearly distinguished sin from the flesh and when he does treat of sin's origin he describes it as a voluntary act of transgression and in no sense the necessary outworking of human nature. The fact that the body can be cleansed and sanctified[10] is decisive against any identification of sin with the flesh. In Romans 8 (cf. v.11) Paul refers to the quickening of the mortal body, and in the context he is dealing with the flesh. In all his epistles Paul declares for the resurrection of the body, and this would be inconsistent with the view that it is essentially evil. He insists, too, on the reality and integrity of Christ's human nature and argues at the same time for

His sinlessness, a fact which suggests that in the apostle's thinking he did not consider the flesh to be sinful.

Yet *sarx* is not a mere name for man's weakness as a creature in contrast with God. True the flesh is 'corruptible',[11] and subject to death.[12] None the less Paul gives a more positive ethical content to his idea of *sarx*. Thus while flesh is not itself sinful it is that part of man's nature which gives sin its opportunity. It provides sin with its ready basis of operation. *Sarx* is that element in man upon which sin impinges and to which it attaches itself. In broad sweep, then, while Paul does not teach any Gnostic notion of the essential evil of matter, he does regard the flesh as somehow permeated by the presence of evil, which issue in 'the works of the flesh'.[13] Consequently the flesh can be said to resist God[14] and find satisfaction in mere outward religious ordinances.[15] By *sarx* then is to be understood human nature as conditioned by the fall.

The contrasting term 'spirit' (*pneuma*) is found 146 times in the Pauline epistles and covers broadly the Old Testament meaning of the word *ruach*, except that the sense of 'wind' is not in Paul and the idea of 'life' or 'breath' is almost absent. Two main thoughts are then associated with Paul's use of the word. First is the psychical sense. In about half the passages with this meaning the word refers to the higher nature of the Christian man and can hardly be distinguished from the activity of the Divine Spirit. There are, therefore, statements, for example in Romans 8, where it is not easy to say whether the word should have a small 's' or a capital; whether, that is, the reference is to the renewed spirit of the redeemed man or the Divine Spirit within the believing man.[16] But for the rest the term certainly connotes an element in man's natural life.[17] Paul does not teach that man by nature is without *pneuma*. The human spirit is not a gift super-added to man when he believes. It is a reality of man's personality, a constituent of his nature, a distinguishing mark of his being. It is that element in man in which he is

177

most akin to God. It is the non-material part of man which relates him to the eternal world. Man's spirit is the higher aspect of man, the Godward aspect which provides that point of contact in man's nature for the regenerative action of God's Spirit. The term *pneuma* then broadly covers these two ideas; the capacity of man for God, and the action of God in man. A discussion of the supernatural use of the term belongs to the doctrine of salvation on its Godward side, and is there more particularly connected with the doctrine of the Holy Spirit.

There is a contrast between the spirit as the higher aspect of man's nature and the flesh as the lower; and this comes out in several ways. There is a contrast in a natural sense as, for example, when Paul speaks of being absent in the flesh and present in the spirit.[18] There is also a contrast in what we may call a 'popular' use of the terms. In this regard 'flesh' and 'spirit' are interchangeable. In 2 Corinthians 7:5 Paul tells the Corinthians that in the trials and disappointments which befell him his flesh found no relief, while in 2:13 he says his spirit found no relief.

There is, as suggested above, a contrast between spirit and flesh in a moral sense. It is indeed a contrast which issues in a conflict between the higher and lower nature of man. The higher nature approves the law of God; it is the element of spirit. The lower nature with its sensuous impulses stirs to wrong choices and actions. From this moral sense Paul easily passes over to the ethical conception. A passage such as Romans 6:19 indicates this transition. Moral weakness belonged to the Roman Christians but they are called to yield their members as instruments of righteousness. Passages such as Romans 8:3 and 6:6 speak of 'sinful flesh' and 'sinful body' and present us with the strictly ethical use of the term 'flesh'. In certain places, for example in 1 Corinthians 2:14,15, 'fleshly' and 'soulish' are used as synonyms in contrast with 'spiritual'. In Romans 8:3-9 the apostle contrasts sharply between the two terms. Paul speaks

178

of a 'flesh of sin' but it is the ethical principle which he has in mind. The spiritual man is the one who cultivates his higher nature in the Spirit.

The term body (*sōma*) and soul (*psuchē*) would seem to represent the outward and inner aspect of the human individual. But this would not be a full characterization of Paul's usage. Of course, the apostle does have for 'body' the sense of the human organism, either living or dead; and this sixty-six of the eighty-nine occurrences of the word.[19] On fifteen occasions it designates figuratively the 'mystical body of Christ'. On one occasion, in Colossians 2:11 it means 'reality' in contrast with the shadow. In a number of instances the term is less expected. In 1 Corinthians 6:15 it is applied to the whole human being, and in this connection needs to be read in the light of 1 Corinthians 12:27. In Romans 6:6 there is a reference to the 'body of sin', and in 7:24 to 'the body of this death'. In both places Paul seems to have in mind the body as under the influence of sin and belonging to death. Neither is proper to the body as such; they are aliens which have invaded. The body is occupied territory. By the expression 'the body of the flesh' which appears in Colossians 2:11 Paul evidently means the body given over to the carnal instincts of 'the flesh'.

Not as frequent as might be thought is the use of the term 'soul' in the Pauline letters. It is found on thirteen occasions and means generally the life principle. Twice in Romans it is used of the 'person'.[20] At other times Paul makes the term an equivalent for individual life.[21] Yet the idea of the soul as itself distinct from the body is to be found, which justifies the contrast between the body as the outer and the soul as the inner aspect of man's being.[22]

Having broadly designated the 'flesh' as the lower and the 'spirit' as the higher, and now the 'body' as the outer and the 'soul' the inner element of man, the question arises whether Paul was a dichotomist or a trichotomist. Did he conceive of man as composed of two elements—a body and a soul, or of three—a body, soul and spirit?

In certain passages Paul contrasts flesh and spirit in such a way as to suggest dichotomy. For example in 1 Corinthians 5:3 he speaks of being 'absent in body' but 'present in spirit'. In Romans 7 there is the contrast between 'flesh' and 'spirit'; while in Romans 8:6 Paul refers to the mind of the flesh as death and the mind of the spirit as life and peace. These and like passages seem to suggest a division of man into two elements, the one material, the flesh or body, and the other immaterial, the spirit or soul. On the other side point is made of the suggested contrast between 'spirit' and 'soul' in, for example, 1 Corinthians 15:44. It is argued that these are arbitrary and baseless antitheses if there is no specific difference between the two terms. But the point is easier made than justified. For if it is asked wherein lies the difference no clear answer is forthcoming. There is still however, the important verse of 1 Thessalonians 5:23 which seems to demand a trichotomist interpretation. But this one passage is hardly sufficient to build up a theory of Pauline psychology. It was not Paul's purpose to set out a statement of the structure of man's being, he was more concerned with the spiritual dedication of the whole man. He is not, therefore, giving any systematic dissection of human life but rather praying for the Thessalonian believers that they be fully sanctified. The truth of the matter is then, that from different points of view soul and spirit are two aspects of man's one inner nature. Spirit denotes life as having its origin in God, and soul denotes life as constituted in man. Spirit is the innermost of the inner life of man, the higher aspect of his personality: soul expresses man's special individuality. Soul is spirit modified by its union with the body. The *pneuma* is man's nature looking Godward, whereas the *psuchē* is man's nature looking earthward and touching the things of sense.

To complete the picture of man in the Pauline theology reference must be made to the terms 'heart', 'mind' and 'conscience'. The first of these words is not infrequent in Paul. On fifty-two occasions he speaks of the 'heart'. And by the expression he does not mean the physical organ as such. The term is used in a sense more akin to man's psychical nature either as a whole or with reference to one or other of its activities. Yet Paul never takes the heart for the total individual as a living embodied person. By heart Paul means generally the inner life of man; on fifteen occasions he refers it to the whole psychical nature:[23] and on thirty-seven occasions to a specific element of man's psychical nature. Sometimes it refers to the emotional state of consciousness;[24] sometimes to its intellectual activities;[25] sometimes to the decision of the will.[26] The term is then broadly the same as in the Old Testament except that the intellectual use has decreased with the employment of the new term *nous*, mind.

The word *nous* was much in use in Greek philosophy, and the Stoics made it common currency. It occurs twenty-one times in Paul's writings and denotes man's natural rational activity.[27] In 1 Corinthians 14:14,15, Paul contrasts mind with the ecstatic state. In Isaiah 40:13 where the Hebrew has the phrase *ruach Yahweh* ('the Spirit of the Lord'), the Greek of the Septuagint has *nous kuriou* ('the mind of the Lord'), and the apostle preserves this phrase in two quotations of the verse.[28] The term has also the significance of practical judgement and is so used by Paul in Romans 14:5. In general the word covers man's reasoning ability and as such can approve the law of God. But the *nous* may become either demoralized, and thus vain, fleshly, corrupt,[29] or it can be transformed by the renewing grace of God until the Christian has 'the mind of Christ'.[30]

The word translated conscience (*suneidēsis*) is found twenty times in the Pauline literature. The term was in frequent use in Stoic writings. It means literally 'joint-knowledge', and appears to denote the reflective judgement which a man has alongside the original consciousness of an act. In the New Testament it has reference to what Kant called the

181

practical reason, or man's moral consciousness.[31] In Romans 9:1 Paul personifies conscience and sets it over against himself as another reliable witness to the truth he declares. Conscience is a possession of every man, a natural faculty by which he can judge his own actions[32] and that of others.[33] The famous passage of Romans 2:14-15 is almost Stoic in tone. The law written in the heart of pagan-man has witness borne to it by his conscience. For the 'conscientious' pagan there is the 'law of conscience', for the Jew the 'law of Moses', for the Christian believer 'the law of Christ'. But the conscience, too, like the mind can become 'defiled',[34] or be 'pure'.[35] In the Old Testament the term 'heart' is often used as an equivalent for the New Testament phenomenon of the conscience; the sense of guilt and the feeling of shame which we attribute to the conscience is in the Old Testament attributed to the 'heart'.

Yet in spite of this excursion into Paul's use of terminology in reference to man it seems right to underscore again that his was no academic interest in a doctrine of man. Paul was much more concerned with man as a being for God who could only fulfil his chief end by glorifying God. He sees man as created by God who despite his rebellion and fall can be restored again after the image in which he was created. He does not regard man as a loose combination of two disparate elements. Man is a unity in himself and it is the whole man that Christ has come to redeem. But for Paul mankind also is a unity, not an army of disconnected units which have no windows through which to look out on others. It is indeed this fact of the unity of the race in Adam which is basic in Paul's doctrine of the involvement of every man in Adam's sin; and the same truth is vital for his gospel that 'all shall be made alive' in Christ. There is the book of nature and the book of grace; 'the book of the generation of Adam',[36] and 'the book of the generation of Jesus Christ'.[37]

1. Ac. 17:22
2. Cf. Rom. 5:12, 19; 1 Cor. 15:21, 22
3. Ac. 17:26
4. 2 Cor. 12:7; cf. 1 Cor. 7:28; Gal. 4:13; etc.
5. Rom. 9:3
6. Gal. 2:20
7. 1 Cor. 1:26
8. Eph. 2:3; Col. 2:18; etc.
9. Cf. Rom. 7:5, 18, 25; 8:3, 5, 8, 13; Gal. 5:16, 17; etc.
10. Cf. 1 Cor. 6:13, 19, 20; 2 Cor. 7:1; see Rom. 6:13; 12:1
11. 1 Cor. 15:50
12. 2 Cor. 10:2
13. Gal. 5:9; etc.
14. Rom. 8:8; etc.
15. Col. 2:23
16. Cf. Rom. 8:4, 5, 13; cf. 1:9; 7:6
17. Cf. 1 Cor. 2:11; etc.
18. 1 Cor. 5:3
19. Cf. Rom. 1:24; 4:16; 1 Cor. 6:13, 15; etc.
20. Rom. 2:9; 13:1; cf. 1 Cor. 15:45
21. Cf. Rom. 11:3; 16:4; Phil. 2:30; 1 Thess. 2:8
22. Cf. 2 Cor. 1:23; 12:15; cf. Eph. 6:6; Phil. 1:27; Col. 3:23
23. Cf. e.g. Rom. 5:5; 1 Cor. 14:25; Eph. 5:10
24. Cf Rom. 9:2; etc.
25. Rom. 1:11; etc.
26. Cf. Rom. 2:5
27. Cf. Rom. 7:35f.; etc.
28. Rom. 11:34; 1 Cor. 2:16
29. Cf. Eph. 4:17; Col. 2:18; 1 Tim. 6:5; 2 Tim. 3:8; Tit. 1:15
30. 1 Cor. 2:16; cf. Rom. 12:2
31. Cf. Ac. 23:1; 24:16; Rom. 2:15; 9:1; 13:5; 1 Cor. 8:7, 10, 12; 2 Cor. 1:12; etc.
32. 2 Cor. 1:2
33. 2 Cor. 4:2; 5:11
34. 1 Cor. 8:7
35. 1 Tim. 3:9
36. Gen. 5:1
37. Mt. 1:1

14

Sin

There is no better place to begin a consideration of Paul's view of sin than with his own triumphant statement that 'where sin abounded, grace did much more abound',[1] or, as it is put in the NEB, 'where sin was thus multiplied, grace immeasurably exceeded it'. For the apostle Paul the great thing was the gospel of salvation which he was given to proclaim. He gloried in the cross of Christ because there he knew sin's sway was overmatched, its awfulness overwhelmed, and its power overcome. Paul has no need, therefore to paint sin's darkness in lighter colours. He has no temptation to make sin less than sinful. Nor, on the other hand, does he wish to go beyond what is true. He can thus take seriously the fact enshrined in the first part of the opening declaration 'where sin abounded', and show how much it does abound, because he is sure of the reality of the gospel that in Christ 'grace did much more abound'. Put the other way round, to fall in line with his own procedure in the Epistle to the Romans, Paul will show what grace superabounds in Christ by showing that sin does abound in the world.

The apostle, then, in order to present the gospel of the grace of Christ has need to deal with that for which his whole message was the answer: he must, that is to say, deal with the issue of sin in its scope, its origin, its cause and its results. But all through he will relate the reality of sin to its cure and conquest in the cross and resurrection of Christ.

Doubtlessly Paul began from his own experience. As a

Pharisee he had sought to live a blameless life according to the demands of the law.[2] He struggled for purity and separation from the evils of the world. But he found that the more he struggled the more he sank: the more separated he became the more stained he discovered himself to be. Before ever he entered into the freedom of the gospel he had learned of the reality of sin's masterful dominion. He had sought to overcome indwelling sin only to become aware of the overwhelming magnitude of the evil which was against him. In those autobiographical passages in which he lifts the curtain upon his own life we are shown how profoundly conscious he became of the fact of sin in his own experience.[3] Bitten deeply then into all he has to say about sin is the forceful argument of his own spiritual history. It is, of course, in the Epistle to the Romans that Paul comes nearest to what may be called a philosophy of sin. He begins with establishing the universal sway of sin. Underlying all he has to say is the view that sin is a religious term. Sin is not just seen as wrong acts, as slips, as vices. In relation to man these are our more generous terms, but sin is fundamentally an offence against God. For Paul sin is a downright contradiction of God's nature, a repudiation of God's holy purposes.[4] In opening his Roman treatise, then, Paul first surveys the Gentile world. Having a capacity for knowing God, men allowed their minds to become darkened and their hearts depraved. They blinded their eyes and can no longer read the signature of Deity on the created universe. The very law written in their hearts they heeded not.[5] They are 'without excuse' and 'worthy of death'.

From the Gentile world Paul turns to the Jewish world. The Jew for all his privileges fares no better. He has an historic position of privilege, but has turned it to no real account. He has a 'law' of which he boasts, but he does not abide by it. So it has become his keenest judge condemning him as a transgressor.[6] Thus in wide sweep the whole world is seen as guilty before God[7] and the verdict is that 'all have sinned and fall short of the glory of God'.[8] The verdict is upheld by Scripture as Paul quotes from the Old Testament to re-inforce it. In this way the apostle, however much he had found sin's reality in his own life, shows that he is not just generalizing his own experience as proof of the universality of sin. He is not seeing the world through darkened glasses. The world is dark. Sin has done that.[9]

From his assertion of sin's universality there is a natural transition to the question of sin's origin. Two ideas can be singled out here. Paul treats of the fact of sin in every man and the cause of sin in each man. There is a sin of principle (*hamartia*),[10] and a sin of practice (*parabaseis, paraptōmata*).[11] The first refers to sin as a world-ruling power, the second to sin as a personally chosen act. With regard to the first it is clear that the apostle traces the sinfulness of mankind in general to Adam's transgression. By the sin of Adam a principle of sin was lodged in the life of humanity. As in Christ all are constituted righteous by the righteousness of one, so in Adam are all constituted sinners in the transgression of one.[12] The crucial passage is, of course, Romans 5:12. Differences among commentators arise from the interpretation of the statement 'for that all sinned'. The question is, how did all sin? Some would answer; simply by following Adam's example; and in so doing they regard themselves as safeguarding the voluntary nature of sin. Others take the words as meaning that all men sinned actually in Adam by reading in place of, 'for that' the phrase 'in him'. In this way they regard themselves as showing that the apostle taught how exactly sin was injected into the whole race. The truth is, however, that the apostle is not so much arguing here for sin's universality as for the universality of death as sin's consequence. Because of sin 'death spread to all men because all men sinned'. Yet the fact remains that Paul is saying that sin, as a result of Adam's fall, got a foothold in the world and has made human life the sphere of its action. Thus there is one sin and the sinning of all. Sin 'entered the world through one man' and 'through one man's disobedience the many are made sinners'. For Paul that was clear and that was true. The fact of death shows the universality of sin. Those who had but little consciousness of sin because of the absence of law, were still subjected to death. Physical death as the consequence of sin belongs to all; all are involved in it.[13] But more profoundly for the apostle, passing from physical death to that of which it is a type, moral and spiritual death, he shows its ultimate effect in man's separation from God resulting from the presence of sin in human nature.

When treating of the cause of sin in each man it becomes clear that he finds it in 'the flesh'. In Romans 7:14 the apostle states that he learned from his own experience that sin taking advantage of the weakness of the flesh made him a slave. In the Pauline teaching then two ideas interweave. Sin was ever there and sin is ever my own. I am involved in the reality of it, and yet acknowledge the guilt of it. Adam introduced it to me and the introduction was welcomed by me. Paul then unites two acts; our connectional relationship with Adam which compels us to say that his fall was not his alone but ours, and our present responsibility through Adam which compels us to say, we are each the Adam of our own soul.

Paul has many ways of saying how much we are affected by sin. Sin dwells within,[14] we are 'sold under sin',[15] we are 'bondservants to sin',[16] the members of the body are 'instruments of unrighteousness to sin',[17] we are 'dead in trespasses and sins'. All such statements reveal something of the all persuasiveness of sin.

He brings sin into relation to other categories which serve all the more to uncover the terribleness of sin's presence and power. We have noted in the previous chapter how he relates sin to the flesh. He does not intend us to conclude that sin is merely sensuous for he also speaks of 'fleshly wisdom' and the 'mind of the flesh'. The flesh is what is 'natural' to man; it is the principle of corrupt nature. He used the term 'man'

in a somewhat similar manner. There is a 'natural man'.[18]
By this he means the principle of human life, with its natural
thoughts, reasonings, desires and the like. By the phrase the
'old man' he has in mind the natural life as yet untouched
by the Spirit; it is the old and unregenerate self.[19] He has
something to say, too, about the 'carnal man'.[20] He seems
to use it in two ways: to designate the 'fleshly', either as the
Esau nature in its sheer godlessness, or as the Jacob nature
not yet made Israel. In a similar manner he uses the word
'body'. Paul had no low view of the body for he knew that
Jesus had a body and he knew, too, that his body of humiliation would be resurrected to become like His body of glory.
He likens the Church to a body and asserted that the body
of the believer is a temple of the Holy Ghost. Yet he refers
to 'the body of sin', and evidently means the body in which
sin operates.[21] Akin to the idea of body there is that of its
members. He finds a law of sin in his members.[22] and as
such 'the members which are upon the earth' must be kept
in subjection.[23]

There are three other relationships which call for comment. Paul connects sin with the devil, with the law and
with the world.

It is certain that the apostle conceived of the devil as the
moral agent of man's ruin. He is the 'god' of this present
world-order and it is his spirit which works in the children
of disobedience.[24] Paul speaks of his wiles[25] and his
snares.[26] It is a grievous thing to fall into his condemnation.[27] The term law is found 118 times in the Pauline
literature and of this number all but fifteen come in the
Epistles to the Romans and the Galatians. For Paul the law
was the whole law; he does not distinguish between the
ethical and the ceremonial. Stressing, especially in Galatians,
that no man is justified by the law, he does not on that
account suggest that the law as such is sinful.[28] Rather, by
the law is the knowledge of sin;[29] the law so to speak brings
sin to light; where there is no law there is no transgression.

The law is established by showing up sin.[30] The requirements of the law shut up all under sin. Paul uses also the
concept of the world, especially in the Corinthian letters,
in something like a Johannine sense. To the Galatians he
describes the pre-Christian life as slavery to the rudiments of
the world; and goes on to assert that through Christ the
world is crucified unto him and he unto the world.[31] In
writing to the Corinthians he condemns the wisdom, the
passing fashion, of the present world-order and declares that
the choice of God rests upon those whom the world least
esteems. The perception of the true worth of things belongs
to those who refuse to be swallowed up in the spirit of the
age and come under the Spirit of God.[32] Under the idea of
the world, then, Paul means that world-spirit which leads
to evil and brings blindness to and ignorance of the true
realities.

Fundamentally for Paul then is the idea of sin as a taking
on of an alien way of life. It is living and acting apart from
God. It is disobedience to God and His law. It brings condemnation[33] and death upon all.[34] Virtually in Paul's doctrine man
is a god in ruins. The sin which he has shown reaches every
man is also shown to affect all the man. In this sense man is
totally depraved; in the sense, that is, that no element of his
make-up has escaped the inroads of evil. He is thus darkened
in his understanding,[35] hardened in heart,[36] an enemy of
God in his mind,[37] weak in will,[38] and defiled in conscience.[39] Being in such a state he will need a radical salvation. It will take a mighty gospel to change all this; to
enlighten his understanding, to transform his heart, to
change his mind, to strengthen his will, and to cleanse his
conscience. And such a gospel Paul has to proclaim. In spite,
then, of all he has to say about the all-pervading character
and the all-perverting nature of human sin he does not shut
us up to a final gloom, because he shuts us up to a faithful
God. All that is required to renew man again after the image
of Him that created him is available, for, 'where sin

abounded, grace has much more abounded'.

SCRIPTURE REFERENCES

1. Rom. 5:20
2. Cf. Phil. 3:5f.; Ac. 26:5
3. Cf. Rom. 7:18f.; 1 Cor. 9:27; 15:9; 1 Tim. 1:15
4. Cf. Rom. 8:7
5. Rom. 1:28-32; 2:14-16
6. Rom. 2:17f.
7. Rom. 3:19
8. Rom. 3:23
9. Cf. Rom. 1:21; 2:19; Eph. 5:8, 11; 6:12; Col. 1:13; 1 Thess. 5:4, 5
10. Cf. Rom. 3:19; 5:12
11. Cf. Rom. 2:23; 4:15
12. Cf. Rom. 5:19
13. Cf. 1 Cor. 5:22
14. Rom. 7:17, 18
15. Rom. 7:14
16. Rom. 6:20
17. Rom. 6:13
18. 1 Cor. 2:14
19. Rom. 6:6; Eph. 4:22; Col. 3:9
20. Cf. Rom. 7:14; 1 Cor. 3:1f.; cf. Rom. 8:7
21. Rom. 6:6; cf. 7:24; 8:10
22. Rom. 7:23
23. Col. 3:5
24. Eph. 2:2; cf. 5:6; Col. 3:6
25. Eph. 2:2; cf. 5:6; Col. 3:6
26. 1 Tim. 3:6, 7; 2 Tim. 2:26
27. 1 Tim. 3:6
28. Cf. Rom. 3:21; 7:7, 12, 14, 16
29. Rom. 3:20
30. Rom. 3:21
31. Gal. 4:2; 6:14
32. Cf. 1 Cor. 1:20-28; 2:12; 7:31; 11:32
33. Rom. 5:16, 18; cf. 8:1
34. Rom. 6:23; 8:2; 1 Cor. 5:16
35. Eph. 4:18; cf. Rom. 1:21
36. Rom. 2:5
37. Rom. 8:7, 8; cf. Eph. 4:14; Col. 1:21; 1 Tim. 6:5
38. Rom. 7:14f.
39. 1 Cor. 8:7; 1 Tim. 4:2; Tit. 1:15

15

Grace

Towards the end of our chapter on 'grace' in the Synoptic Gospels we noted that from beginning to end the life and work of Christ must be read in the category of grace. The story of the cross does not give an account of how the life of Jesus ended; it is a revealing of the basics upon which God's grace is secured and assured. Two broad facts were, therefore, drawn from the record of the gospels. On the one hand, that the saving initiative is with God, and, on the other hand, that any plea to human merit is ruled out. Thus while Jesus is not the source of the term *charis* which summarizes these two facts, His own work as God-man is the source of the 'grace' of which the New Testament speaks. It was the apostle Paul who took up these twin ideas and included them under the one pregnant term *charis*. In this sense grace is specifically a Pauline conception.

While all shades of meaning which we noted earlier are to be found in the New Testament not all of them together convey the richness which the term acquired in the theology of Paul. For him 'grace' was nothing less than the unsought and unbought saving activity of God which made him a debtor forever. The Damascus road encounter with the risen Jesus brought to focus the two basic ideas which unite in the word *charis*; that the saving initiative is with God and that human merit is of no avail. By 'grace' then is meant that salvation has its beginning and its ending in God's eternal purpose as the counterfoil of history. He loves because He would love; saves because He would save. He acts in grace; acts without waiting for a sign or a nod from us. Grace is, then, as it has been put, 'the radiant adequacy of God'. It is not, however, to be conceived of as some mysterious sort of fluid or force imparted through some mechanical channel. Grace is the active love of God; a love which has its cause in God's own being. It is a love spontaneous and unmotivated by not being called forth by any worthiness in those who are the objects of it. It is from the grace of God that all the blessings of salvation flow. In summary form, then, the Christian message is 'the gospel of the grace of God'.[1]

The idea of the absoluteness of grace in man's salvation is specially indicated by the fact that Paul never begins or ends a letter without reference to grace. In neither case is he adhering to a merely conventional usage.[2] By beginning as he does Paul is suggesting the supremacy of grace as the source from which flows all the blessings of the new order into which God's unmerited favour has brought the redeemed soul. Coming at the close the term *charis* was a new thing in epistolary literature. In using it as he does the apostle was virtually authenticating his position as an apostle to whom the grace of God had come. Everything rests on His free grace. At the beginning of his letters Paul always associates 'grace' and 'peace'. While in the salutations the close connection between the two terms is not always immediately seen, the latter word comes nearly always somewhere in the context. The two concepts seem to be associated in the apostle's mind.[3] As the first word of greeting and the last word of salutation, 'grace' sums up for the apostle the totality of the blessings which come from God through Christ. Grace gives stress to the loving activity of God in pardon for sinful men, while peace refers to the inward feeling of calm which comes to the heart of those who have experienced grace.

At the end of 2 Thessalonians, Paul adds to that which he had already dictated to his amanuensis, a 'grace' conclusion with his own hand.[4] Such, he declares, is his sign (*sēmeion*) in every epistle. There is no reason to suppose with Bengel that he was in the habit of appending the 'grace' in a specifically picturesque style of his own, although it may be agreed that if he could he well might, for the word was engraven in multi-colours upon his own heart. Yet Paul had a purpose other than personal in adding his 'grace' benediction. His letters were, as Dryden says 'absent sermons', and the last word for any Church as well as the first is 'grace'. This must remain the dominant note of the celestial symphony as a Pauline epistle dies away.

For Paul, then, 'grace' and 'peace' go together. But the relationship is fundamental. Grace always precedes peace. In this is to be understood the supremacy of grace. It may be that in some of the passages where the two terms are associated the apostle was reminding his readers that if they had the grace of God it would issue in peace among brethren. Some commentators then argue that the word peace (*eirēnē*) was used by Paul in view of friction within the Church. But in most cases this understanding does not suit the context and a much deeper connotation for the word is required. In general then 'peace' signifies more than a request for brotherly concord. The Jews regarded 'peace' as an eschatological hope; the greatest blessing of the messianic reign. For the Christian believers the reign of Christ had begun and there was peace on earth to men of goodwill.[5] Christ had made peace; and become peace in believing hearts. No longer was it an eschatological dream; it was a present reality due to the revelation of God's grace in Christ. Peace, then, springing out of grace is primarily peace with God.[6] It comes as a result of the soul's rest upon God's saving act. But out of this peace with God Paul would have his fellow-believers aware of the peace of God. As justified in Christ we are urged to enjoy the peace of God in the confidence that no one can lay anything to the charge of God's elect.[7]

Looking at the epistles of Paul severally from the perspective of his teaching of grace, notice must be taken of the fact that amid the variety of contexts in which the term occurs the same general idea of God's radiant adequacy pervades. Romans can be broadly divided into almost two equal sections, chapters 1 to 8 emphasizing the theme, all of grace, and chapters 9 to 16 having for its dominating message, grace for all. These headings are not, of course, clear-cut; for throughout, the one idea involves the other. By proving that all is of grace Paul shows incidentally that grace is for all, and vice versa. Both ideas together present us with the wide scope of Paul's gospel. Indeed the word 'all' is the keynote of his message and is found some seventy times in this epistle. It is of particular interest to observe that when the apostle is discussing the theme, all of grace, he deals with the relation of grace and law. For clearly if all is of grace the question must arise, What then of the law? On the other hand, when he has as his main point, grace is for all, then the question is, What of the chosen people, the Jews?

Apart from the salutation and benediction the word grace occurs in Romans seventeen times, and most frequently in chapter 5 (five times). In 1:18 to 3:20 Paul deals with the fact of universal sinfulness and leads up to the conclusion, 'all have sinned'. In this section the word grace does not appear at all; and neither does the name of Christ. In 3:24, having made Jew and Gentile the same under sin, Paul states that there is a full acquittal 'for nothing' by the grace of Christ. Thus grace is something 'given'.[8] It is, therefore, 'not of works'.[9] In grace we have an introduction to God.[10]

In the Corinthian correspondence grace is often brought into relation with Christian life and service: grace is given for gracious living. In 1 Corinthians Paul says that it was according to the 'grace given' he laid down a foundation for the gospel upon which others could rear an edifice.[11] He stresses that his apostolic work is a 'grace given' and is thereby a valid and an effective work. Paul was aware of the absoluteness of grace. He had persecuted the Church, but the grace of God had changed him from a hard-souled persecutor into a warm-hearted preacher. He laboured more abundantly than the rest because of the grace of God which was with him. Paul means more by this than that God and he co-operated as equal partners, although he never speaks of requirements without speaking of resources. But the grace of God was for Paul God's divine adequacy in the strength of which he was able to fulfil his mission.

The Corinthians had apparently suspected the apostle of some equivocation in his attitude towards them. But Paul defends his conduct as the very mark of the grace of God. In the passage which concludes at 2 Corinthians 6:1, Paul appeals to his readers not to receive the grace of God in vain. He does not here call upon them to accept the grace of God which gives a new standing in Christ, but rather to live as befits their life in Christ. Their lives were to be an inviting language, a legible letter. Christ's coming to man's low level is seen by Paul as an act of divine grace.[12] The words 'ye know' with which the verse begins suggests that the grace exhibited in the incarnation was part of his gospel. In this context the apostle is referring to the duty of giving, and his allusion to the grace of Christ giving up His riches is thus singularly appropriate. The call is then for us to show grace, that liberality which benefits others, because we have received of Christ's liberality. In 1 Corinthians the collection is designated a 'service', a 'fellowship', but in 2 Corinthians 8 it is spoken of as 'this grace'. It is here treated in the light of what the apostle had discovered as the final truth of God's nature, His giving, His grace. In 2 Corinthians 12 Paul gives an account of his 'thorn in the flesh'; but he does not seek to induce self-pity, for the apostle never allowed his manuscripts to smack of his medicines. Paul would rather have his readers know of his discovery that the presence of God's grace was a greater thing than the absence of affliction.

In the body of the Galatian letter there are five passages which deal with grace. In chapter 7 there is specified the 'call' of grace.[13] Paul found himself called of God in the grace of Christ; and yet called by the grace of God to be the vehicle of the Son's glory. Galatians 2:9-21 is the epitome of the gospel; and if we had nothing more of Paul's writings than Galatians 2:21 we should be able to grasp his essential message. All else is but a commentary on these few words. The principle of God's salvation is that of grace. To admit that of works would be virtually to say that Christ dies 'for nothing'.[14]

In the Thessalonian letters there are two occurrences of the term grace (apart of course from the opening and closing greetings), and both come in the second epistle.[15] In both passages the eschatological setting is evident. God's final purpose for His redeemed people is that they should be conformed to the image of His Son. The 'end' of 'grace' is the manifestation of the divine glory.

In the so-called Captivity epistles the grace-concept is evident throughout, even in places where the word itself is not found. But specifically the Colossians are reminded that they 'learned to know what the grace of God really is' from Epaphras.[16] Afflicted by insidious heresy, they were in danger of compromising their standing in faith and the gospel of grace. God's saving act comes through no one but Christ and is not received in any other way than by faith.[17] Paul's gospel was no local message: it was for the whole world.[18] Paul gives, therefore, a cosmic context to grace and in the Colossian letter approaches a Logos Christology. The One who is the channel of the world's existence is also central for faith. Thus Jew and Gentile owe their position in the Church to the grace of Christ. Ephesians underscores the freeness and fullness of grace.[19] The Pauline message can then be compressed into one statement which throbs with apostolic devotion: 'For by grace you have been saved through faith; and this is not your own doing, it is the gift of God'.[20]

Those who reject the Pauline authorship of the Pastorals have had to acknowledge that they are much indebted to Paul on the subject of grace. Apart from two references in which the idea of 'thanks' comes[21] the whole tenor of the letters regarding God's dealing with men throughout is Pauline. Grace is linked to justification,[22] and to service.[23] The grace of God has appeared in salvation,[24] teaching us to renounce all ungodliness. Here is the grace of law and the law of grace. It is an authoritative demand of God's free favour that we should live a life of self-mastery. The slave had no right before the law but grace has come to make him a responsible being. The grace of God is then seen in the 'appearing' of our great God and Saviour Jesus Christ; grace has come in His royal epiphany.

In order to fill out the account of Paul's doctrine of grace something needs to be said about the relation between grace and some other aspects of Paul's message.

(a) Grace and the Trinity

In the salutation of his letters the connection between grace and Christ is not so explicit as in the benedictions. The general formula in the latter case is 'The grace of our Lord Jesus Christ be with you'.[25] In 2 Corinthians 13:14 Paul bases his trinitarian benediction on the order of experience. It is the grace of Christ which makes real the love of God; first the experience of grace, and then, through that and only through that, the certainty of the love of God. In 2 Corinthians 8:9 Paul sees the grace of Christ displayed in 'the poverty' which for our sakes He accepted that we might become 'rich'. Thus to preach any other gospel than that of 'the grace of Christ' would be anathema.[26] For Paul the 'grace of Christ' and 'the grace of God' are associated.[27] The absoluteness of Divine grace is the reality of the Divine Christ. To preach absolute grace Paul preached an absolute Christ. It is for this reason he makes an easy transition from the one phrase to the other. Grace is given by God,[28] and in no meagre fashion either.[29] Grace is the generous love of God's gift bestowed in Christ in which all the blessings of the

197

rule of God are begun now in the life of those who have come to faith in Him and will be consummated at the time of the end.

It is by the Holy Spirit that the love of God manifested in Christ is made real to believing hearts. Both the individual and the Church are the dwelling-place of God through the Spirit.[30] In this connection note must be taken of the association between 'grace' and 'power'. God's special 'favour' and God's diverse 'favours' are alike the result of divine grace.[31] It is, therefore, natural to conceive of the relation between them in terms of 'power'.[32] This association between 'grace' and 'power' is given special emphasis in 2 Corinthians 12:9, 'My grace is sufficient for you, for my power is made perfect in weakness'.[33] Between 'grace' as divine 'power', and 'power' as the presence of the Holy Spirit there is, then, a vital kinship. Thus the experience of being 'full of the Holy Spirit' and being 'full of grace and power' is hardly to be distinguished.[34]

(b) Grace and Justification

At Romans 3:24 Paul begins his exposition of God's 'grace as a gift' (RSV). To be declared righteous before God by virtue of our acceptance in Christ is altogether of God's own spontaneous mercy. The grounds of our justification is variously stated, but it is always conceived as an act of grace. Grace points to the ultimate source of God's act of justifying the sinner by His sheer goodwill and compassion.[35]

Paul sees 'the abundance of and the free gift of righteousness'[36] as greater and more powerful than the original taint of nature even when the added stains of actual sinful acts are added, for 'where sin increased, grace abounded all the more'. And grace reigns through righteousness to eternal life through Christ our Lord.[37] This does not allow for any idea of 'cheap grace'. Paul does not admit of the perversion of God's free generosity in an antinomian direction.[38] Instead

198

of sinning that 'grace may abound', the believer is called upon to grow in grace.

Paul's experience had taught him that God gives and God forgives. He was sure that 'all is of grace'; here was the sovereignty of grace. This was the logic of his own sense of being overwhelmed by the mercy of God. But the gospel he received and preached made it clear to him that there was no limit to the grace of God. He saw that 'grace is for all'; here is the sweep of grace.

Yet in no place does Paul state that grace is given to all men. In Romans 3:22-24; 5:17f. and Titus 2:11 the term 'all' is certainly found. But in each case it is clearly restricted by reference to the immediate context. In the first, the 'all' of Romans 5:23 does mean 'all men' in a parenthesis about sinners. But the declaration that 'they are justified by grace as a gift' (RSV) points back to 'all them that believe' in v.22. So in chapter 5:18 the 'acquittal and life for all men' must be read in connection with the assurance that 'those who receive the abundance of grace and the free gift of righteousness reign in life through one man Jesus Christ' (v.17). The RSV translates Titus 2:11, 'For the grace of God has appeared for the salvation of all men', but this could too easily lead to a universalist conclusion if isolated from the whole drift of the New Testament. But even here the preferable translation is 'For the grace of God hath appeared to all men, bringing salvation'. In the three passages, then, the most that can be said is that salvation is offered to all men: in none of them is it declared that all men are saved.[39]

In Romans 3:28 Paul says that man is justified by faith apart from the deeds of the law. Throughout he clearly puts law and grace into antithesis. To follow the law as a way of obtaining salvation is but to increase one's debt,[40] and to fail of the grace of God. But 'Christ is the end of the law unto righteousness to every one that believeth'. The law 'met its end in Christ', yet the law was not just 'ended' by Him. He is Himself its 'end' as a means of attaining to a righteousness acceptable of God. The gospel reveals the righteousness of God by grace through faith. Grace, too, cancels out works as a means of attaining righteousness.[41] A reward is not reckoned of grace;[42] thus to receive grace is to renounce works as the means of justification. Any association of grace and works in salvation is impossible for then would 'grace be no more grace'.

All by the free generosity of God through the self-giving Spirit of Christ is, then, throughout, the Pauline doctrine of grace. Christ's self-giving unto death is the supreme demonstration of grace.[43] For man, He is the incarnate grace of God made available to faith. By grace we are called,[44] and justified,[45] and sanctified.[46] By grace we have an eternal consolation and a good hope,[47] and the strength to endure.[48] Paul would have concurred that he was forever a debtor to mercy alone and but for the grace of God in Christ through the Spirit he would have remained as the chief of sinners to be at the end of the days a castaway.

SCRIPTURE REFERENCES

1. Ac. 20:24
2. Cf. Ac. 15:29; Jas. 1:1
3. Cf. 2 Cor. 13:11-13; Eph. 6:23-24; 1 Thess. 5:23-28; 2 Thess. 3:16-18; etc.
4. 2 Thess. 3:17, 18
5. Cf. Lk. 2:14
6. Cf. Ac. 10:36; Rom. 5:1; Eph. 2:14; etc.
7. Cf. Rom. 15:33; 16:20; Phil. 4:7; etc.
8. Cf. Rom. 5:15; 12:3, 6
9. Rom. 11:6
10. Rom. 5:2
11. Cf. 1 Cor. 3:10; 15:10
12. 1 Cor. 8:9
13. Gal. 1:6, 15
14. Cf. Gal. 5:4
15. 2 Thess. 1:12; 2:16
16. Col. 1:6
17. Cf. Col. 1:6, 13, 14, 27; etc.
18. Col. 1:6
19. Cf. Eph. 1:7; 2:5, 7, 8; 3:7, 8; 4:7

20. Eph. 2:8 RSV.
21. 1 Tim. 1:12; 2 Tim. 1:3, *charin echō.*
22. Tit. 3:7
23. 1 Tim. 1:14; 2 Tim. 1:14
24. Tit. 2:11
25. Cf. Rom. 16:20; 1 Cor. 16:23; 2 Cor. 13:14; Gal. 6:18; etc.
26. Cf. Gal. 1:6
27. Cf. 2 Thess. 1:12
28. Cf. Rom. 15:15; 1 Cor. 1:3; 3:10; 15:10; etc.
29. Rom. 3:24; 5:20; 2 Cor. 4:15; 9:8, 14; 12:9; Eph. 1:7; 1 Tim. 1:14
30. Cf. 1 Cor. 3:16; 12:11, 13; Eph. 1:12; 2:22 etc.
31. Cf. Rom. 1:5; 12:3; 15:15; 2 Cor. 8:9; Eph. 4:7; etc.
32. Cf. 1 Cor. 15:10
33. Cf. 2 Tim. 2:11
34. Cf. 1 Cor. 12:4-11; Eph. 4:7-13; etc.
35. Cf. Rom. 11:6
36. Rom. 5:17
37. Rom. 5:21; cf. Tit. 3:5
38. Rom. 6:1f.; Tit. 2:11-14
39. Rom. 4:16; 1 Cor. 1:18; 2 Cor. 2:15; 2 Thess. 2:10; etc.
40. Gal. 5:3
41. Cf. Rom. 11:6
42. Rom. 4:4
43. Cf. 2 Cor. 8:8; Phil. 2:5f.
44. Gal. 1:15
45. Rom. 3:24
46. Rom. 6:14
47. 2 Thess. 2:16
48. 2 Tim. 2:1

16

Salvation

'For by grace you have been saved through faith; and this is not your own doing, it is the gift of God';[1] in this one declaration we have the very centre of Paul's doctrine of salvation. The amplification of the verse in its context shows that salvation is God's doing in Christ and man's discovery without works. We have seen, in our chapter on Grace, how God's dealings with men as regards man's standing before Him is a 'favour' on His part. Salvation is a gift (*dōrean*); and sinners are justified 'for nothing'. The doctrine of God's free act of mercy in Christ lies at the root of the apostle's teaching on salvation. This is indeed for Paul the superlative wonder of the gospel. For in the gospel of Christ is disclosed to full view the 'secret' which in the Old Testament economy was but fragmentarily shadowed and but dimly grasped.[2] Paul saw with the compelling conviction of the Spirit that what was impossible to attain by the way of law,[3] God had brought to man's own door as His gift in Christ.[4] Thus has He become the Saviour of men by a love for sinners which their rebellion had entirely forfeited, but which His nature could not alter.[5] From first to last, then, the gospel of salvation bears the character of grace. It is a love-gift of God, so rich and royal, that reason, left to itself, is quite unable to comprehend.[6]

By grace, then, is the salvation of God brought to man. But the term salvation is a wide one comprehending all the blessings of the gospel as focused in the purpose of God's grace in Christ, and as found by the experience of man's faith in Christ. We noted earlier how in the Old Testament the idea of deliverance from peril is the basic meaning of the term. Thus in the Exodus story which is the account of Israel's deliverance from her enemies, the word 'salvation' is constant throughout.[7] But there is not lacking altogether a deeper note in which salvation is seen as deliverance from sin.[8] Yet in whatever context the term or its cognates occurs it is always conceived as an act of God. Thus Paul, taking up into his doctrine of salvation all that his own experience of Christ had taught him and what had come to him by divine illumination,[9] drew into the term all the rich treasures that God has made available in Christ.

Essentially and fundamentally, however, Paul's doctrine of salvation is vitally related to the death of Christ; so much so indeed that apart from the Cross there is no salvation at all possible. The central fact in Paul's theology was what was pivotal in his experience, that God saves men through the death of Christ. At Calvary Christ was vicariously related to man's need and victoriously related to man's sin. So Paul gloried in the Cross. It was its message he blazed across Asia Minor. It was with this word he challenged the ritualism of the Jew and the intellectualism of the Greek. It was the same message he proclaimed in the prison in Philippi and the prison in Rome.[10] It was the gospel of the cross which he found as the power of God unto salvation for the man in the mire and the man in the mansion.[11] Everywhere and in all its aspects is salvation related to the cross. For the un-believing Jew and the unhumbled Greek the cross was, to each in his own way, anathema.[12] To those without, the cross was a deed of man; but in the enlightenment of the Spirit, the cross had become for Paul an act of God. To them it was a crucifixion; to him it was the cross. The cross is more than the crucifixion. The crucifixion is what *man* did to Christ; the cross is what *God* did in Christ. Thus for the apostle the cross is significant because of who died there. The prince of glory was the price of salvation. It was the one who being in the form of God and emptying Himself and in utmost obedience went even unto death on the cross who has won for us a complete salvation. Thus the cross is never set in isolation in the theology of Paul. It is never divorced from the person of Christ, nor from the resurrection which followed. It is because the cross is that of the Son of God, because it is vitally linked with the empty tomb, that it becomes God's saving act. The cross and the empty tomb stand together; and it is in this conjunction that the uniqueness of Christ's death shines forth.

Without then the slightest hesitation the apostle relates the cross to the love of God.[13] However dark was the night the Lord went through, the anchor of the cross was secure in the eternal heart of God. It was no view of Paul's that the death of Christ somehow induced God to love us. It was rather the reverse. Paul clearly read the death of Christ as the supreme evidence of a divine love which could not let us go. For Calvary is where God turned to us when we had turned away from Him. Calvary was not something done behind God's back but done in the full light of His presence by His own beloved Son in whom He was always well-pleased.

So Paul grounds the death of Christ in His own love.[14] The cross was His loving act of obedience. He was not there as a passive instrument but as a willing agent. Love divine welled up in the heart of God the Son for us men and our salvation. He bled because He would bless. Golgotha was pregnated with grace; and the dark hilltop felt a divine heart-throb. And from the ground there blossomed red, life that shall endless be.

It is there at the place of a skull that man finds again the shape of his soul. It was there that Paul discovered that the condemning and crippling power of the law was shattered.[15] By becoming 'a curse' for us, the cross redeems us from the curse of the law. It was a shameful thing to be crucified; it was a criminal's death. The cross was no nice affair. We

204

have decked it too much with flowers and hidden beneath them its harsh and horrible reality. To die on a cross was to be reckoned accursed. So the Jews looked at that mud heap outside the city and saw Him who died on the central jibbet as a man accursed. So He was, says Paul—but not for anything He had done. The law proclaimed Him to be outcast, condemned, 'the despised and rejected of men'. He was all that—but 'for us'. He was subjected to the most shameful death, not justly as they supposed, but vicariously—for He bore His shame for us. He exhausted the curse of the law and bought us out from under its sway. The cross relates not only to the rule of law but also to the reality of sin. We have seen that the apostle took sin seriously. To its presence in the lives of all is due our estrangement from God. Christ alone among the sons of men has ever known the meaning of sin, when He took our sins in His own body to the cross. We cannot wade into the deeps of sin's awfulness because we do not know by the merest trifle sin's meaning and measure. Not a fraction do we know. But He knew it in the length and breadth and depth and height. And He knew it so much that He took it to Himself, being made very sin for us.[16] Mark records that with the cross looming dark before Him He 'began to be sore amazed'.[17] Luther found these words the most astonishing in the whole New Testament about our Lord. There was nothing in all the world that could sore amaze the Son of God but the huge totality of human sin. And He had it all 'laid upon Himself', until He was 'made sin'. Sin is so exceedingly sinful, so unspeakably evil, that in sore amazement the strong Son of God was pressed down by it unto death and hell. What do we know of sin? Something of the froth of the cup we know—but of the reality itself we know not the first thing. 'Take away all its terrible wages: take away its sure and full discovery and exposure: take away its dreadful remorse: take away both the first and the second death: take away the day of judgement and the fire that is not quenched—all which is the mere froth of the cup—take away all that, and leave pure sin: leave pure, essential, unadulterated sin—what the apostle so masterfully calls "the sinfulness of sin"'. Take away all that, if we can, and with pure, essential, unadulterated sin we are left: and then remember that 'pure, essential, unadulterated sin' and 'all that' crowded on to the holy soul of Jesus at Gethsemane as He took the cup and allowed its poison to bring about His death on the cross. That is the atonement of the cross; salvation by the death of Jesus. For there at Calvary all sin's sting has been taken by Christ and all sin's cup of woe has been drunk by Him to its very last dregs. Not a drop has been left for us. There on the cross He is doing for us what none of us could ever have done for ourselves much less for another. There He is doing for us what only He could do and would.

So God's deed in Christ for us will be set forth in many ways by Paul, the herald of salvation. It is a substitution. The idea is there in Paul's letters clear as day.[18] Anyone familiar with the Levitical account and who has no preconceived theory to defend must see that the idea was present in its sacrificial system. Yet Paul does not present the substitutionary concept in any mechanical manner. His usual prepositions are 'concerning' (*peri*), 'on behalf of' (*uper*), 'on account of' (*dia*). He was on the cross for us—where we should have been: and yet somehow we were there because He was there. For Paul makes clear the dynamic nature of Him 'taking our place'. He is there for us, but not as it were behind our backs. For as God was in Christ reconciling the world unto Himself so we, so to speak, were gathered up in His act. Thus, as has been said, is salvation by substitution and substitution by incorporation. One died for all and then all died.[19] In the cross everything in sin was made His that sin had made ours, everything in sin except for Him the being a sinner. And all that is in Him becomes ours, for in Him we are made righteous with the righteousness of God.[20]

It is in the context of our union with Christ that the full

force of Paul's salvation theology gets its interpretation. We are identified with Him and He with us. By His union with us He takes our place and bears our sins.

In several passages the apostle introduces the concept of redemption (*apolutrōsis*).[21] The figure is taken from the slave-market; the slave is bought at a price to become the absolute property of his owner. So the death of Christ is the ransom price for our freedom. The question is not raised, and is indeed absurd to ask, to whom is the ransom paid? The fact that is being declared is that Jesus overcame sin's power through the cross, and achieved a spiritual deliverance for mankind. At an infinite cost He paid the price for us. We have been bought out to be His for ever and for ever. We are a purchased people paid for in full by the precious blood of Christ. He died for us—that is substitution: He paid for us —that is redemption.

In Romans 3:24-26 Paul uses the term 'propitiation' (*hilastērion*) in an effort to unfold what Christ accomplished for us on the cross. The word used by the apostle is found in the Septuagint and in Hebrews 9:5 for 'mercy seat', that is, the covering of the ark. But that cannot be the meaning of the term here. The word must be taken in its plain meaning; the death of Christ is the means whereby propitiation has been made for sin. The term implies that there was a just wrath of God against sin.[22] God was not feigning displeasure. To deny the wrath of God is to do violence to Paul's gospel and to nullify the verdict of the human sense of guilt. In the last reckoning Paul is making clear that the death of Christ has to do with the wrath of God. In the cross Christ removed the obstacle in the way of God's love flowing into the heart of man. And in His wrath which was real, is His love which is deep. There is a rainbow around the throne. Thus what His righteousness demanded His love provided. A righteous love cannot be complacent; and the loving righteousness cannot be unheeding. It is then God Himself who has set forth Christ as a propitiation. In the cross God's wrath is seen in judgement; and in the cross God's love is seen in mercy. Thus has Christ done justice to the character of God by providing a propitiation 'in His blood'. The deed is done— the substitute is found; the ransom is paid; the propitiation is made.

There is another of Paul's words which indicates his profound understanding of the cross. It is while we were enemies we were reconciled by the death of the Son of God.[23] And God was in Christ reconciling the world unto Himself.[24] The idea of Christ as reconciler is a fundamental one in the Synoptic Gospels. His every word had healing power. But far beyond the teaching of Jesus in reconciling efficacy divine and inspiring as that is, was Christ's actual identification with sinners. It is here He is seen most decisively as the mediator and minister of reconciliation. It is, however, in the light of the cross that Christ's reconciling work finds its ground and goal. It is consequently to the apostle Paul, whose own experience had validated the fact, that the interpretation of Christ's work in terms of reconciliation (*katallagē*) gets its strongest statement.

It is in the death of Jesus that man's hostility to God finds an answer. And it is in the cross that God's hostility towards man, conditioned by man's sin, is overcome. For there are divine necessities which had to be met, and principles of justice and righteousness which could not be set aside. The cross answered these necessities and satisfied these principles. At the place called Calvary, God and man are reconciled. There God Himself has made reconciliation in Christ. At the cross we have been put back on a friendly footing with God; there is a restored relationship made between God and man in the death of Jesus. By sin man was alienated and made an enemy in his mind towards God.[25] By sin God's heart was wounded and His holiness shrank away from the evil of man. For sin not only stained human life, it also strained divine love. At the cross, then, we see infinite pain in the presence of human sin, uniting with God's boundless

208

and all-comprehensive love. In the atoning work of Christ, God has exhibited His righteousness, expressed His condemnation of sin, and reconciled the sinner to Himself by putting away sin: and in it all and through it all His love shone forth. But the reconciling work of the cross goes beyond the bringing of sinners and God together. It involves the uniting of the races; the bringing of them into one at the cross.[26] Everywhere sin divided. Always the cross unites. Whenever men are not right with God they will be apt to be at odds with each other. It is in right relationship with God that man will find in others a community of nature and interests which lift them above the estrangements of prejudice and the corrosive power of suspicion. It is in Christ that God has been pleased 'to reconcile all things to Himself . . . whether they be things on earth or things in heaven'.[27] Here is the cosmic significance of Christ's cross drawing back a hostile world unto the Father. In the cross all things are reconciled. The universe, cursed with sin's curse, hostile with sin's hostility, is given new status by God's own act in Christ: and thus will there be a new heaven and a new earth in which dwelleth righteousness. Although we cannot say exactly what is meant by things in heaven needing to be reconciled, this is certainly clear that there is no problem of reconciliation which the love that gathered up our sins in the mighty atonement of the cross cannot deal.

Because of the death of Christ God has nothing against us any more: His wrath has been appeased, and His love has found a way. To those who have received the reconciliation[28] has been committed the proclamation of the healing word.[29]

Such is the salvation procured by Christ for us: a salvation which is effective for us because of our union with Him. Indeed salvation and union with Christ are for Paul virtually two ways of saying the same thing. To be saved is to be united to Christ. Union with Christ is Paul's formula for all that he means by salvation. The supremely intimate relation of oneness with Christ in His death and resurrection was what counted in the apostle's understanding of Christ's saving deed.[30] Here was the heart of his own personal religion; the central thing in the gospel. Thus on no less than 164 occasions does the phrase 'in Christ' occur. Salvation for Paul is a living union with God in Christ. And by using it as he does Paul shows how indispensable Christ is for salvation. The formula is not then to be explained away as an 'ecclesiastical formula'. Paul is not meaning by 'in Christ' being 'in the community of Christ', but rather being 'in communion with Christ'. By union with Christ, Paul safeguards his ethics and rescues justification from being a legal fiction. For salvation is not just something for us it is also something done in us.

To be united to Christ is to know our justification; it is to be declared righteous before God.[31] And being united to Christ is to have our sanctification.[32] If justification is God declaring us righteous and sanctification is God making us righteous, as it is often put in the interests of neatness, it needs to be stressed that the two are not finally separate. Both are connected with our union with Christ: and God's judicial act of declaring righteous is closely bound up with our death to sin. To be justified by faith is to enter into a living union with Christ so as to live Christlike justification by faith was for Paul a dynamic and creative experience. It is 'once for all', to be sure; but yet not all at once; for the new life must be unfolded. The righteousness which God confers is 'a righteousness God looks after'. Thus 'in Christ' we know what we are; and 'in Christ' we become what we are.

To know Christ in justification and in sanctification is ours by the Spirit. Justification opens up the way into the new life, and sanctification develops that life in union with Christ by the Spirit. Paul can, therefore, speak of 'salvation in sanctification of the Spirit',[33] that is 'sanctification wrought by the Spirit'. In this union with Christ we are adopted into God's family, becoming children of God.[34] We receive our sonship in His Sonship.[35]

And all is finally of grace through faith. The divine initiative is grace; the human response is faith. For Paul the two go together. The absence of the term faith in the Old Testament[36] has occasioned the statement that there is no doctrine of faith there. But the fact is there clearly enough and is exhibited in the lives of the patriarchs, the prophets and the psalmists. And the occurrence of words such as 'trust', 'rest', 'wait' and the like indicate that faith is regarded not only as 'the queen of the virtues' but also as 'the foundation of salvation'. But Paul brings the word to the fore by using it one hundred and thirty-six times in his writings. For him faith is the whole of the gospel subjectively, as Christ is the whole of it objectively.

For Paul faith was neither a cold approval of doctrinal statements nor yet a blind leap in the dark. There are basic facts about Christ which have to be known and understood before response can be made to the One of whom they speak. Damage has been done when these two aspects of the one saving act of faith have been set apart. Faith is neither assent to facts about Christ to be known, nor trust in a Christ about whom no facts can be known. Faith is a commitment on the basis of a conviction; a trust in One who is known to be worthy of the trust. For faith, then, there must be conviction concerning gospel facts. There is evidence that apostolic preaching involved the recital of certain statements concerning Jesus, the *kerygma* as it is called. These were held to be well authenticated facts, and gospel faith necessitated an acceptance of these facts. Thus Paul after his conversion sought to prove that Jesus is very Christ.[37] Statements in Paul's writings beginning with such a formula as 'If ye believe that . . .'[38] or 'If thou wilt confess that . . .'[39] may be taken as stating the facts which must be acknowledged. And the 'faithful sayings' are another instance of the essential creed of the gospel.[40] Yet it is sure that, for the apostle, faith was more than an implicit faith in even such facts. For in the end no man can be convicted of the gospel facts in a saving way apart from the prior action of God upon his soul. Thus for Paul faith is taking up the facts about Christ and abandoning one's self in confident trust in Him unto salvation. To give over one's life to the sin-bearing love of God in Christ, and to do so without reserve and without condition is what Paul would have us understand as faith. This is that abandoning trustfulness which produces a deep and intimate union with Christ. In those passages in which the apostle speaks of 'the faith of Christ'—for example, 'a man is not justified by the works of the law but by the faith of Jesus Christ'[41]— the apostle is not suggesting a subjective meaning. The reference is not the Christ's faith. Here we have instances of what has been called 'the mystic genitive' which indicates that a man's standing before God is not found in a cold performance of an objective law but it becomes a present reality in close fellowship with Christ. For Christ is not only faith's object, He is also faith's sphere. It is in such a faith that all the blessings of Christ's cross comes to man. Thus the Pauline doctrine of faith unites an acknowledgement of facts with an abandonment to a Person.

SCRIPTURE REFERENCES

1. Eph. 2:18, RSV
2. Eph. 3:4; 6:19; Col. 4:3; cf. 1 Cor. 2:9; 13:2; 14:2
3. Cf. Rom. 3:20; Gal. 2:16; 3:11; Phil. 3:6
4. Cf. Rom. 5:15, 17; 2 Cor. 9:15; Eph. 2:8; etc.
5. Cf. Rom. 8:37; Gal. 2:20; Eph. 2:4; 5:2, 25; 2 Tim. 2:16
6. Eph. 3:3, 4, 19
7. Cf. Ex. 14:13-16:2; cf. Ps. 38
8. Cf. Ps. 139
9. Cf. Gal. 1:11f.
10. Cf. Ac. 16:30; 28:30; Phil. 1:13
11. Cf. 1 Cor. 6:11; Eph. 2:1-4; Phil. 4:22
12. 1 Cor. 2:22-24
13. Cf. Rom. 5:5, 8; 2 Cor. 13:11, 14; etc.

14. Gal. 2:20; cf. 2 Cor. 5:14; Eph. 5:25
15. Cf. Gal. 3:13, 27
16. 2 Cor. 5:21
17. Mk. 14:33
18. Cf. Rom. 4:25; Gal. 1:4; 1 Thess. 5:10; etc.
19. 2 Cor. 5:14
20. 2 Cor. 5:21
21. Cf. Rom. 3:24; 1 Cor. 1:30; Eph. 1:7
22. Cf. Rom. 1:18; 2:5; Eph. 2:5; Col. 3:6
23. Rom. 5:10; cf. Col. 1:21
24. 2 Cor. 5:19
25. Col. 1:21
26. Eph. 2:14f.
27. Col. 1:20
28. Rom. 5:11, RSV, NEB
29. 2 Cor. 5:18, 19
30. Cf. Rom. 6; Col. 3:1f.
31. Cf. Rom. 3:24; 3:25; etc.
32. Cf. 1 Cor. 1:2, 30; 1 Thess. 4:4
33. 2 Thess. 2:13; cf. Rom. 15:16
34. Cf. Rom. 8:16, 17, 21; Gal. 3:16; Eph. 5:1
35. Cf. Rom. 8:15; Gal. 4:5
36. Cf. Deut. 32:20; Hab. 2:4
37. Ac. 9:22
38. Cf. 1 Thess. 4:14
39. Cf. Rom. 10:9
40. 1 Tim. 1:15; 4:9; 2 Tim. 2:11; Tit. 3:8
41. Gal. 2:16; cf. 2:20; 3:22; Phil. 3:9

17

Final Things

We are concerned in this chapter with the doctrine of last things in the Pauline letters; with the final things of the individual, of the Church and of the world. We shall begin with those which touch more directly upon the future of the individual; and in this connection we shall find that the apostle's thought is focused particularly upon the believer.

1 Death

There can be no doubt that for Paul the Christian gospel as it was revealed to him by the Holy Spirit, presented a marked contrast with the faith of his earlier days. In Judaism there was no clear certainty that death did not end man's story. Death came as an unwelcomed guest, for beyond lay the uncertain realm of Hades. Now in Christ all was changed. Christ had brought life and immortality to light through the gospel.[1] He had taken the sting from the sepulchre; and the gloom from the grave.[2] Seen in the glorious light of Christ, death was no longer a terminus but a tunnel. It was not a cul-de-sac, but a channel. In his pre-Christian days, death was for Paul something to be feared. Now he has no desire to cling on to his present life; he yearns to cut loose and put out to sea and find himself immediately at the land whither he goes.

Thus in the doctrine of Paul, death is conceived first as a conquered enemy.[3] Even death cannot separate the believer from the love of God.[4] The last enemy has been met and mastered through Christ, so that he can take leave of life with a Hallelujah shout of victory, 'Rejoice not against me O mine enemy'. All Paul's words about death are couched in notes of triumph. Death is a possession.[5] The believer is not for death; death is for him; it is part of his wealth. It is not the end of life but its beginning. Death is not a deprivation, not a loss, not a defeat, not a calamity. It is, in the experience of grace, a possession, part of the Christian's armoury. It is an opportunity, a resource. For the apostle, death appeared as a ceremony of coronation, the establishing in final triumph of Christ's victory in the human heart.

Yet Paul can view death as a sleep.[6] In this he re-echoes the words of his Lord whose revolutionary conception of death stung the Pharisees to scorn. For neither Jesus nor for Paul was this a mere poetic metaphor. The dead in Christ are not really dead: they sleep; they rest; they will waken again at the trumpet call of God. This is truly the sleep which will knit up the ravelled sleeve of care. This is our great Redeemer's second course. Such a sleep is not a passing into nothingness; not annihilation. Yet Paul's word must not be supposed to give authority to the false doctrine of the sleep of the soul. Such a view would be out of harmony with the whole drift of the New Testament which clearly states that those who have died are not unconscious.[7] It is Paul's sure confidence that to be absent from the body is to be present with his Lord.[8]

For Paul indeed death was a going home.[9] It is a way through to something better. It is not a submerging into nothing but an emerging into something; it is not a ceasing to be, but a coming to be. It is not a re-incarnation, but a renewing. It is the beginning of a new life, that is to say, a heavenly life.

In sum, then, for Paul death holds no terrors. As a man in Christ he knows that death has been vanquished by Christ's death. Yet for those who have not 'died' to sin and been made 'alive again' in Christ, the awful reality of death remains. The wages of sin is death—death both physical and spiritual, and eternal.[10] It is sin that gives death its sting.[11] Death uses sin as a poison to extend its empire and to terrorize its captives. But Jesus Christ has robbed death of its power. And if so be it yet retains a remnant of its grim sovereignty and was the last foe to yield to the triumph of the cross, it is still an inspiration for living to be assured that its dark horror has been mastered and its final banishment made certain. In His death, death itself, physical, spiritual and eternal has been destroyed for all who have plucked the healing leaves from the tree of life on Golgotha's hill.

2 Immediate State

One thing seems irrefutable from a study of Paul's theology: he could not have countenanced the concept of a purgatory. This would be quite at odds with his understanding of Christ's work as meeting all the requirements of the law. We are saved by grace apart from works and this must be kept steadily in mind in considering the few passages where the idea of purgatory is supposed to be implied.[12] Yet if there is not a purgatory in the sense of a purgation by punishment of one's sins there does appear to be a 'waiting' period for the believer between death and the final glory of heaven. It seems clear that there is an interval during which the soul continues consciously without the body. 'Unclothed' is how Paul describes it.[13] It is at the last trump that this mortal shall put on immortality.[14] To the Romans Paul writes that 'not only the creation, but we ourselves, who have the first fruits of the Spirit, groan inwardly as we wait for the adoption of sons, the redemption of our bodies'.[15] And he tells the Philippians that he with them awaits a Saviour, the Lord Jesus Christ, 'who will change our lowly body to be like his glorious body'.[16] At death, then, in Paul's doctrine, the believer is surely 'with Christ', but still awaiting the full benefits of his redemption, that of his body. He has no need of a time of probation or a period of purification: the Saviour's merits are enough. But he must wait until Christ comes in final glory and then with the whole company of the redeemed he shall be 'clothed upon with a habitation which is from heaven'.

3 The Resurrection

It is important to note that in dealing with the resurrection Paul has specifically in mind that of believers. True in 1 Corinthians 15:42, he uses the expression 'the resurrection of the dead',[17] but clearly it was that of the saved which was in his mind throughout. It is 'in Christ' that life for evermore is assured. Those who are united to Christ share in His victory over death. It is those who have 'the earnest of the Spirit'[18] who will receive 'a house not made with hands, eternal in the heaven'. In several passages the apostle links the believer's resurrection with the supernatural activity of the Spirit. Our mortal bodies will be made alive by the indwelling Spirit, that Spirit which raised up Jesus Christ from the dead.[19] It is by the Holy Spirit we are sealed unto the day of redemption.[20]

It is, of course, in 1 Corinthians 15 that Paul deals with the believer's resurrection at length. Vv. 1-11 state the fundamental position which Christ's resurrection holds. In vv. 12-19 it is argued that if there is no resurrection then Christ could not have risen. In this case our faith is a vain thing. But since it is a well confirmed fact that Christ was raised from the dead, then the fact of a resurrection is assured. In vv. 20-34 it is shown that the resurrection of the dead is necessary for the establishing of the divine order and the subjection of all things to Christ. At this point Paul goes on to confirm the resurrection of the dead by analogies (vv. 35-44) and then by Scripture (vv. 45-49). Christ's resurrection is, for the apostle, the crowning proof that God will bring from the dead all those who have fallen asleep in Jesus. Union with Him is the pledge of a continued life beyond in the realm of the blessed. And if it is asked what sort of body shall be ours at the resurrection, Paul answers by rebuking our obtuseness, and perhaps our over-curiosity. Yet he does not leave us without some statement. He argues that all things have a body adapted to their needs and environment. There is a higher and a lower; a more glorious and a less glorious. So we can know that we shall have a body befitting our future state. It will be a future embodiment of our spirit suited to the conditions of the spiritual world to come. As the 'natural body' is conditioned for this present life there will be a 'spiritual body' adapted to the state of existence in the new heaven and new earth. It will be a house not made with hands, and a fit tabernacle for the redeemed spirit. It will be in the image of the glorified Christ,[21] a body conformed to His body of glory.[22] It will nevertheless be this body we now have and yet not it. As the grain comes out of the seed sown having a connection with it and a difference; so will it be in the resurrection. 'Thou sowest not a body that shall be', declares Paul in 1 Corinthians 15:37. The resurrection body will not be just this body resuscitated just as it is, and yet the resurrection body is not this body fully discarded.

4 Judgement

In considering the subject of judgement it is again necessary to keep in mind that the apostle is mainly concerned with believers, although, as we shall see, he is explicit regarding the judgement of the wicked. While for the believing man there is 'no condemnation', 'no sentence of death' as Karl Barth states it, there is still for the believer a judgement. In an admonition to the Christians in Rome not to pass judgement one on another Paul reminds them that 'we shall all stand before the judgement seat of Christ'.[23] In the thought of Paul there is no contradiction between his doctrine of justification by faith and judgement by works. For the Christian's 'works' are not conceived of as having legal merit. They are deeds and services flowing from a life renewed by the indwelling Spirit of God. Yet even so, such works shall be judged. Some people's deeds look impressive and loom large before the eyes of others but like wood and hay they will not stand the test of fire.[24] And although such believers will be saved from the everlasting fire, they themselves will be saved so as by fire. In the passage in 2 Corinthians in which the apostle is dealing with the subject of the new body which believers will possess when their mortal part is absorbed into immortal life, he calls upon his readers to make it their ambition to be well-pleasing to God. For, he declares, 'we must all appear before the judgement seat of Christ, so that each one may receive good or evil, according to what he has done in the body'.[25] There was no doubt in the apostle's mind that, saved everlastingly as he was sure he was, he was still answerable to God for his life's service. But he was himself confident before his Lord as the 'righteous judge', and awaited the verdict with joyful assurance because he knew that he had laboured more abundantly for his Saviour than the rest, and yet not he but the grace of God in him.[26] None more than Paul gloried in his freedom in Christ as the Epistle to the Galatians testifies; and still none more than he lived his life in the awareness that his whole living lay open before Him with whom he had to do. Paul carried on his work in the light of the final judgement of God upon all that he sought to accomplish. He virtually lived in the awesome reality of the throne of God, and the thought of his accountability kept his conscience quick, his mind alert and his heart sensitive, knowing that he would stand 'before our Lord Jesus, at his coming'. That is the judgement by which he is to be judged, the searching light in which his life is to be reviewed. And it needs no lesser faith and fact than this to keep character and conduct at that height of purity and faithfulness of which he is so noble a pattern. With his assurance that the Lord is a 'true judge' we can have confidence in 'that day', for herein we are being told that there is a rainbow around the throne.

But Paul does extend the reality of judgement to all men. Even in the section in 2 Corinthians (cf.vv.6-21) he seems to go beyond the judgement of believers. True he uses the word *bēma* here as he does in Romans 14:10, which some seek to restrict to the tribunal for the saved. But the apostle in 2 Corinthians goes on to declare that in view of Christ's coming judgement and the 'terror' of the Lord, he seeks to persuade men to be reconciled to God (cf.vv.11,18). One there is who at His coming will judge both the living and the dead.[27] For the world of men, God will act aright; and there is no respect of persons with Him.[28] He who knows the hearts of all will judge according to what a man is before Him.[29] For the wicked and the unbelieving the day will be one of 'wrath', of 'vengeance', of the 'manifestation of the righteous judgement of God'.[30] As clear as our Lord's own statement is that of the apostle's that those who obey not the gospel shall 'be punished with everlasting destruction from the presence of the Lord, and the glory of his power'.[31]

The question arises as to whether there are two judgements, one for the believer and another for the unbeliever separated by a period of time, or whether there is one general judgement. Certainly Paul has no reference to a Millennium. Yet some argue that the idea of a separate judgement is clearly implied. He tells the Corinthians that the saints shall judge the world and angels; they are to be assessors in the judgement day. It is then concluded that before this final judgement they themselves have been already judged. And attention is drawn to 1 Thessalonians 3:13 which speaks of the coming of the Lord *with* His saints as distinguished from a prior coming *for* them. Others do not find these conclusive. They make the point that at the judgement day the saints are on Christ's side and inevitably share with Him in the judging act. Thus His coming with the saints refers to those who as 'dead in Christ' are awakened to the breaking glory of the great day of Christ's final triumph and thus coming with Him unite with the believers then living to hail the dawn of the eternal kingdom of righteousness. Many are, therefore, satisfied with the idea of one general judgement, when all shall bow the knee to Christ in recognition of His right if not in obedience to His gospel.[32] Then shall Christ's mediatorial mission be accomplished and His kingdom be established and God become all in all.[33]

5   The Second Coming

The fact of Christ's return in power and great glory was part of Paul's gospel throughout. It is found in almost every epistle, in the latest as well as in the earliest. There is no evidence that the apostle changed his mind regarding the subject. His emphasis may have changed according to the need of the situation. Thus his earlier letters to the Thessalonians were specially concerned with the subject of Christ's return but because some later letters did not give an extended reference to it this must not be taken to mean that the hope burned less brightly with the passing of the years. The Epistle to the Galatians dealt with the necessity of faith without the works of the law for man's salvation. It would be absurd to say that Paul changed his mind regarding this because it figures in some later letters but little. The fact of the matter is that he wrote his second letter to the Thessalonians to warn them against abandoning their duty in the expectation of Christ's immediate return. It is clear from it that Paul regarded certain happenings to take place before this climatic event. Not every epistle occasioned reference to the subject in the same detailed manner. In the later pastoral epistles the apostle is found still speaking of Christ's second advent and that at a time when it was all the more natural for him to think of his own departure.[34]

While, then, the fact of the return of Christ is a dominating theme of the apostle's,[35] the idea of it is variously stated by him. Specifically it is the 'day of the Lord',[36] 'the day of Jesus Christ',[37] 'the day of our Lord Jesus',[38] 'the day of our Lord Jesus Christ'.[39] It is 'that day',[40] It is God's time; Christ's occasion. It is the moment of God's triumph in Christ and Christ's final victory for God. As such it is represented by Paul as a *parousia*, a presence or an arrival.[41] In Paul's use it refers particularly to a visible return of Christ from glory to raise the dead, to judge the world, and set up fully and finally God's everlasting kingdom.[42] This return will, therefore, be in the nature of an *apocalypsis*, an unveiling, an appearance, a manifestation.[43] Then will the glory which is now His in heaven be openly revealed to the world.[44] The unhidden nature of His coming again is expressed in Paul's use of the term *epiphaneia*, 'appearing'. Here stress is put upon the visibility of His coming.[45] By Christ's return again is, then, to be understood His personal forthcoming from His present invisible estate to receive His Bride, the Church, to judge the wicked and begin His eternal reign.[46]

Bright as shone the hope of this event for the apostle he himself was not precise as to the time. There was nothing wrong in his expectation of the happening in his own day. He had himself learned the truth as integral to Christ's own message; it was part of the revelation which was given to him.[47] But it was under the teaching of the Spirit that the fuller details were made known to him. There was revealed to him the necessary precursors of the event, things which were to take place before 'the day' came.[48] Yet Paul, like us, knew not the day nor the hour; but he sought to live himself, as he would have all believers do likewise, in the full expectation of Christ's certain manifestation.

It is for this reason that Paul, again and again, stresses the ethical importance of Christ's advent. It is the assurance that Christ shall come in power and great glory which gives hope to Christian faith, which demands faithfulness in Christian service, and which calls for consistency in Christian conduct.[49]

There is a word needing to be added about the cosmic significance of Christ's redemptive work. In Romans 8 the apostle tells us that the whole creation groans, waiting for the manifestation of the sons of light. In Colossians, we have noted that Christ's redemptive work extends to the very material universe. Christ, for Paul, is the first and the last in the universe. It is God's purpose to gather up in the dispensation of the fulness of time, all things in Christ.[50] The world, as the apostle sees it, is destined to become new in Him. Creation is centred in Christ and His redeeming grace reaches to the hidden depths of the universe. There is, therefore, something about the world which is on the side of the gospel; and the ultimate fact which provides the key to the riddle of the universe is in His hands. It is this sure faith which explains Paul's unshakeable confidence and deathless hope which shines through every page of his writings. Hell cannot prevail. The groans of creation will cease one day, the day of Christ's coming, the day of the manifestation of the sons of light. Nothing in earth or hell shall prevail to break the divine determination. And a Christ whom they once hustled up the green hill is marching from the green hill where He died to the throne of all the world. And the world will grow new at His coming; and the gates of the universe will be lifted up and the King of Glory will come in.

SCRIPTURE REFERENCES

1. 2 Tim. 1:10
2. 1 Cor. 15:5; cf. Hos. 13:14
3. 1 Cor. 15:26
4. Rom. 8:28
5. 1 Cor. 3:22
6. 1 Cor. 15:20, 51; 1 Thess. 4:14; 5:10
7. Cf. e.g. Mk. 12:23f.; Lk. 16:19f; 22:49; etc.
8. Phil. 1:23

9. 2 Cor. 5:6-8
10. Cf. Rom. 1:32; 6:2, 7, 8, 16, 21; 7:4, 6, 10; etc.; Gal. 2:19; Eph. 2:1, 5; Col. 2:13, 20; 3:3; 1 Tim. 5:6; 2 Tim. 2:11
11. 1 Cor. 15:56
12. Cf. 1 Cor. 3:14-15; 2 Cor. 5:10
13. 2 Cor. 5:4
14. Cf. 2 Cor. 5:1-8; 1 Thess. 4:14f.
15. Rom. 8:23
16. Phil. 3:21
17. Cf. verses 12, 13, 21
18. 2 Cor. 1:22; cf. 5:5; Eph. 1:14
19. Rom. 8:11; cf. 1 Cor. 6:19; 2 Cor. 6:16
20. Eph. 4:30
21. Rom. 8:29
22. Phil. 3:20
23. Cf. Rom. 14:10f.
24. 1 Cor. 3:13f.
25. 2 Cor. 5:10
26. 1 Cor. 15:10; 2 Tim. 4:8
27. 2 Tim. 4:1
28. Cf. Rom. 2:11-13
29. Rom. 2:1f.
30. Rom. 1:18; 2:5; 2 Thess. 1:8
31. 2 Thess. 1:8, 9
32. Phil. 2:10
33. Cf. 1 Cor. 15:24-28; Phil. 2:10, 11; Col. 1:20
34. Cf. 1 Tim. 6:14; 2 Tim. 4:1, 8
35. 1 Thess. 4:13f.; etc.; etc.
36. 1 Thess. 5:2; 2 Thess. 2:2, RV, RSV
37. Phil. 1:6
38. 1 Cor. 5:5; 2 Cor. 1:14
39. 1 Cor. 1:8
40. 2 Thess. 1:10; 2 Tim. 1:18; etc.
41. Cf. 1 Cor. 1:7; 2 Thess. 1:7
42. Cf. 1 Thess. 2:19; 3:13; 4:15; 2 Thess. 2:1, 8
43. Cf. Eph. 1:20-23; Phil. 2:9, 10
44. 1 Cor. 1:7, 8; 2 Thess. 1:7, 8
45. Cf. 2 Thess. 2:8; 1 Tim. 6:14; 2 Tim. 4:1, 8; Tit. 2:13
46. Cf. Eph. 5:27; 1 Thess 2:12; 2 Thess. 1:8
47. Cf. Gal. 1:12
48. 2 Thess. 2:3
49. Cf. e.g. 1 Cor. 15:58; 2 Cor. 4:16-18; 5:9f.; 1 Thess. 1:10; 2 Thess. 2:1f.; 1 Tim. 6:13f.; Tit. 2:11, 12
50. Eph. 1:10

THE
EPISTLE
TO
THE
HEBREWS

18

The Supremacy of the New Way

1 The New Way

Whoever it was that wrote the Epistle to the Hebrews, it was certainly someone well acquainted with the Old Testament. Indeed the purpose of the writing was to show the superiority of the new covenant to the old. In a sense Hebrews is not an epistle, a letter. It has no introduction; no opening words of address. It is, as the author calls it, 'a word of exhortation'.[1] That the writing is impregnated with Pauline ideas is obvious. Nevertheless the special purpose that was in the mind of the composer necessitated his own characteristic emphasis. Thus, for example, Hebrews does not state a connection between sin and law. In Hebrews faith is an assurance; in the Pauline letters it is a venture. In Hebrews it is a grand certainty of things hoped for: in Paul it is a glowing discovery of things present. Paul illustrates from the moral law to show that all have sinned: Hebrews illustrates from the ritual law to show that Christ is the perfect Saviour. Hebrews sets out to make good the superiority of the Christian faith and the sufficiency of the Christian gospel. The writer contrasts the Old Testament rituals and shows how and why Christ did what they were unable to do. They were shadows; but Christ is the reality: and it is absurd to live in the shadow when you could live

227

in the substance.

Yet the writer had a pastoral concern throughout. The believers were being urged to steadfastness. It was a day of 'shaking': but they are reminded that there are things which cannot be shaken.[2] In A.D. 63 the high priest Ananias and the Sadducees banished the Jewish Christians from the temple and all its privileges. They were treated as unclean apostates and cut off from even the outer court of the Gentiles. So they were compelled to go without the gates bearing the Master's reproach. They had to choose between steadfastly believing in spite of all the hot persecution 'to the gaining of their soul', or 'in shrinking back into perdition'.[3] True, they had not as yet resisted unto blood striving against sin,[4] but evidently the possibility was real. So they are reminded of the cloud of witnesses who 'through faith' sought 'a better country'. They are told to 'consider him' who endured the cross and despised the shame. For He, Son though He was and sinless though He remained, was not exempt from suffering. God has one Son without sin; but no sons without suffering.

From the expressions of the epistle there seems to have been another tack used to try and undermine the faith of the believing community. Cut off from the ritual of the temple, efforts were made to urge them to return again to their Jewish heritage. Their new religion, it was argued, is inferior by far to the long established faith of Israel. The old has the stamp of God upon it, being given through the ministry of angels and initiated by God's faithful servant Moses. 'Ours is a religion!' they would exclaim. 'We have our ancient order of priests, our smoking altars, our repeated sacrifices. But what have you people got? No priests, no altars, no sacrifices! You have really lost all: you have nothing; nothing but the Nazarene!'

The method of the writer is then to establish the faith of the believers against persecution and to fortify the faith of the believers against persuasion. In the first context there is the recurrence of the counsel to 'Hold fast'.[5] In the second context there comes the expression 'we have'. These Christians were being told that they had lost everything. The writer rings back an emphatic, 'Not so! in Jesus Christ we have everything!' Their enemies said, 'You have no priests'; he replies, 'We have a great high priest'.[6] They contend, 'You have no altar'; he retorts, 'We have an altar'.[7] They sneer, 'You are cast out and without the sanctuary'; he answers, 'We have liberty to enter the holiest by the blood of Jesus'.[8]

Thus to go back to Judaism, whether under the pressure of persecution or persuasion, would be to return to the shadows. It would be to leave what is the 'better' for all time, for what was 'good' at one time. For by his use of the term 'better' the writer shows the supremacy of the new way of Christ to the old way of Moses. On thirteen occasions this word occurs and is the keynote of the argument. Christ is 'better than the angels'.[9] And the writer is 'persuaded better things' of his readers than that they should fail.[10] In the case of Abraham paying tithes to Melchizedek, king of Salem, and Levi not yet born, paying tithes in him, 'the less is blessed of the better'.[11] But in contrast with those of old, those of the new covenant have 'a better hope',[12] 'a better testament',[13] 'a better covenant established upon better promises',[14] 'better sacrifices',[15] 'a better possession',[16] 'a better country'.[17] Some 'better things "are" for us'.[18] And the blood of Christ, 'speaketh better things than that of Abel'.[19] Throughout, then, Hebrews is a reasoned document in which the argument, though sometimes broken by long digressions, is instinct with a holy passion for Christ as the perfect author of salvation and an appeal for whole-hearted devotion to Him as worthy.

In his argument the writer makes constant backward glances to the old ritual. It is important, therefore, to see in what way he regarded it. In broad terms it can be said that while the apostle Paul looked upon Mosaism, for the man in Christ, as a broken fetter; this author sees it, for the man in Christ, as a vanished shadow. But it is possible to indicate more particularly his attitude to the old ritual. It was certainly valid for its time. It had its place. In the 'bits and pieces' of the old economy God spoke. The law was confirmed by angels and every transgression received its due recompense of reward. Thus the Old Testament ritual was valid in the context of its history. Yet it was imperfect. In contrast with the full and final revelation in the Son it was hesitant and fragmentary. The old may have been confirmed by angels but the new by One to whom all the angels ministered.[20] The old came by Moses who was a servant of the house; the new by the Son over the house.[21] The old had its priests who had for sins of their own to offer sacrifices, and who pass on one by one. The new had as Priest One who was 'without sin' and 'ever liveth'. The old had sacrifices which had to be repeated, the new a sacrifice made once for all.

In the light, therefore, of the new, the old is seen to be but a passing phase in God's unfolding purpose of redemption. The law was but a shadow of better things to come. The whole Levitical ritual was but a sketch in outline, a rough drawing, a sort of quivering shadow of the things in heaven. The new has the true realities which are immoveable and eternal. The old is then an illustration of the new by contrast with which the new is shown to be the genuine thing. The comparison between the old and the new is that between the shadow and the reality. The Mosaic system was centred in the tabernacle, the priesthood and the sacrifice. But for the author of Hebrews, now that God has spoken in these last days by His Son, these are to be seen as no more than 'a copy',[22] 'a preamble',[23] 'a pre-figuration',[24] 'a shadow',[25] in contrast with which the new covenant has 'the genuine'[26] and 'the very image'.[27] Thus, in broad terms, if Paul felt the 'law' as a tyranny; this writer saw the 'law' as a type.

230

2 The Full Redemption

The Epistle to the Hebrews has much to say about the subject of the atonement wrought for us by the Mediator of the new covenant. For this writer, as for Paul, the relation of Christ's death to man's salvation is central. But what the apostle to the Gentiles refers to as the 'justifying' of those who believe in Christ, this author describes as their 'perfecting'. The significant ideas are that of 'purging',[28] 'access by the blood of Jesus',[29] 'sanctified'.[30]

Beginning with the ritual of the Day of Atonement, Christ is seen to inaugurate a new covenant. By His own blood He entered the heavenly sanctuary and those who have been cleansed from an evil conscience have access into the holiest of all. The more closely the epistle is studied the clearer does it become that men are not saved by observing a ritual, by following an example, by imbibing a moral influence: they are saved by faith in Christ's sacrifice of Himself. The ringing challenge of the message of Hebrews is, 'Without shedding of blood there is no remission of sin'.[31]

Throughout the whole argument of the epistle, the writer seeks to exhibit a doctrine of atonement based on Christ's sacrifice of Himself. He is at special pains to show how the Mediator is by nature and experience fitted for such a divine work. Salvation is through sacrifice; but Jesus can give Himself in sacrifice for us because He is so deeply related in sympathy to us. He saves because He became fully 'one with' men. He who was in eternity came into time in the form and fashion of man. He took a place in our common life and shared in the difficulties and dangers of our human way. He took His stand with us in the arena of life. No angel ever felt our condition as He came to do. They were but messengers of the divine purpose: He was our Companion on the road. Because He was 'one with' man, He could become the 'one for' man. He saves because His is our great

231

high priest. This thought leads on to a consideration of His high priesthood—and with this we will be concerned in the next chapter. The dominating thought of the epistle, it must be noted here, is that 'He that sanctifieth and they that are sanctified belong together'.[32] It is because He shared our life and we shared His that He acted for us as Mediator. Yet He is such a Mediator who not only stood in the midst between God and man, but died in the midst between two robbers. Thus in the thought of the writer the shedding of Christ's blood is compared to that of the victim on the altar. There Christ was offered 'to bear the sins of many'.[33] Animal sacrifices could not atone for sin; such could not come voluntary out of obedience to God. But He delighted to do the Father's will and in His obedience unto death rendered an acceptable sacrifice thereby procuring for man a full and a perfect atonement.[34] Christ's sacrifice consecrates and purifies those who are His. Throughout the epistle the effect of Christ's work in human experience is underscored. God pardons in Christ a people who are made holy by Christ. Taking, then, from the ritual system of the ancient Leviticalism the two great truths it dimly shadowed, that the 'real' Mediator must 'sum up' mankind in Himself, and that the remission of sins can only come by death, the writer makes clear that the old still did this 'with the ineluctable inadequacy of a "shadow"'. But he adds that there were two other truths that it did not and could not pre-figure, namely that the 'real' Mediator must be Son of God, and that He must die and rise again to become the great high priest on the throne of God.

3   The Sure Faith

Although Hebrews has much to say about faith, the idea of trust is not prominent in his use of the word. Broadly we may say that while Paul stresses the abandonment of faith, this writer stresses the attitude of faith. The reason why he should do so is, of course, found in the context of the purpose for which he sent his word of exhortation. The flock, probably somewhere in Italy, for which he was concerned was not in danger of falling back from faith to works as the Galatians were; but they were in danger of falling from faith to despair. On the one hand, as we have seen, they were facing persecution. In such a condition faith is regarded as endurance; and a looking unto Jesus. They are to hold fast, for by faith and patience they obtain the promise.[35] On the other hand, they were being persuaded. They were being chided about the emptiness of their religion. But they are reminded that by faith they possess the world to come.

The writer then seeks to emphasize not the object of faith, so much as its duty. He has in mind the 'perfecting' of faith. In the midst of suffering, faith's attitude is patience. In the midst of disappointment faith's attitude is hope. Faith is, then, attachment to the promises of God, in confidence, in endurance and in boldness.

The writer's thought for his flock was that of Christ's for Peter, that their faith should not fail.[36] He re-inforces his message by issuing a warning about faith. In chapters 3 and 4 there is the well-known section about the 'rest of faith'. The Israelites failed to enter Canaan because of their unbelief. But all who would enter into His 'rest' must have faith.[37] All who hear the word of God must do so in faith.[38] A faith that fades cannot realize God's promises. The writer, then, gives an encouragement to faith. At the end of chapter 10 where the argument about the great high priest concludes, there comes an exhortation to the readers 'to draw near with a true heart in full assurance of faith'.[39] Thus is the record of Israel a warning for faith, and the section about the great high priest is an encouragement to faith. The great passage on the heroes of the faith, chapter 10:36 to 12:2, begins with a quotation from Habakkuk 2:4, but it is used by the writer of Hebrews as an exhortation not to 'draw back'.[40]

Faith is defined as the conviction of a reality we do not

yet see and of an anticipation of a perfection we do not yet know (cf. ch. 11). 'Faith is the substance (*upostasis*) of things hoped for and the evidence (*elenchos*) of things not seen'.[41] The man of faith has the conviction of a reality which transcends the present order and the anticipation of a perfection beyond the passing world. The believer must then keep on in the race with his eyes on Jesus. For although it is made clear by the author that He is finally the true object of faith his concern for the people to whom he writes is such that in his wish to urge them on to faith's endurance, he presents Jesus as the supreme example of faith. In this one verse all he has to say about faith is gathered up, Christ is 'the pioneer and perfector of our faith'.[42]

4 The True Grace

In Hebrews the idea of grace is set forth characteristically as a moral incentive and security for the forgiven. The term *charis* is found eight times in the epistle and the concept is basic to the teaching of the letter about the covenant. The Alexandrian Jewish philosopher, Philo, whose views seem to have been congenial to the writer of Hebrews comments on Genesis 17:2 in these words, 'Covenants are drawn up for the benefit of those who deserve the free gift, so that a covenant is a symbol of grace, which God sets up between Himself and the Bestower and man as the receiver'. Such is the idea of the writer of Hebrews about the new covenant which Christ initiated and sealed by His own blood. It is to be seen as a gift of grace. It is not man's doing. The new covenant is all of grace; and yet it offers grace for all; for He who instituted it tasted death for all men.

In particular, however, the author's grace-words are found in the context in which he is encouraging his readers to steadfastness under insults and injuries and warning them against the danger of falling away from faith. He sees grace exhibited in the sufferings of Christ. It was by the grace

THE SUPREMACY OF THE NEW WAY

of God that He tasted death for every man.[43] The readers
were suffering and the prospect of an increase in its intensity
was real. But they were being taught from the supreme
example of Christ's suffering, that such is not incompatible
with God's saving purpose. He was made perfect through
suffering and crowned His suffering life with obedience unto
death. In and through His life God's grace was working.
More specifically, however, the words mean that in the sufferings of Christ God's grace is revealed. The action is God's.
The words do not mean that Christ was allowed to suffer as
a signal favour of God, but rather the signal favour of God
is shown in the suffering of Christ.

There are a couple of references to grace as divine aid.[44]
It is at the 'throne of grace' where royal bounty can be
received by those who will come in the boldness of faith.

In chapter 10 there is a warning against apostasy and in
it grace is referred to the judgements of God. Those convicted
of disobedience to the law of Moses suffered punishment. A
severer punishment must surely come to those who trample
under foot the Son of God, and count the blood of the
covenant, which He has sanctified, an unholy thing, and
'outrage the Spirit of grace'.[45] The phrase 'the Spirit of grace'
is an unusual one. It is probably derived from the prophecy
of Zechariah 12:10. In the last days, according to the
prophet, God will pour out the spirit of grace and supplica-
tion upon His people. In the thought of the writer of
Hebrews the present dispensation is the 'last days'.[46] He
regards then the outraging of the Spirit of grace as tanta-
mount to a repudiation of the grace of God. In all prob-
ability the term 'Spirit of grace' was in the mind of the
author, the Holy Spirit, although there are few references to
the Holy Spirit as such in the epistle.[47]

While grace is seen as divine aid received at the throne
of God it is also used in the sense of thankfulness to God.
It is a grace to be grateful. In view of God's gracious initiative, His act of mercy revealed in the Christ of the covenant,

235

the believing man cannot be other than thankful. In spite of the fact that all shall be shaken, faith sees a kingdom which cannot be moved. The only response worthy is one of adoring gratitude: therefore 'let us have grace' (12:28, AV), or 'give thanks to God' (NEB). The RSV has, 'let us offer to God acceptable worship'; while Phillips translates, 'let us serve God with thankfulness in the ways which please Him'. In chapter 12:14f. the writer calls upon his readers to take care lest they fall away from the grace of God. There is a holiness without which no man can see God. But it is a holiness, not only as a demand of grace, but as a possibility by grace. There is a gracious goodwill which shows itself as a timely gift and provision. There is grace available so that none may fail of the grace of God. To outrage the 'Spirit of grace' is to outreach the grace of God. In chapter 13:9 grace is contrasted with the inadequacy of ritual. 'It is well that the heart be established with grace, not by foods.' The 'heart' here is the inner life, while 'grace' is the revelation of God's gracious power therein. 'Meats' or 'foods' seem to have reference to the sacrificial ritual.[48] Sacrificial meats cannot establish the heart. And there are not needed—for once again it is stated that all the old ritual has lost its effect now that the new way has been opened up. We 'have an altar' at which to eat[49] and we have 'blood' by which we are sanctified.[50] It is a coming city for which we look.[51] Meanwhile there is a 'sacrifice' to be offered—a 'sacrifice of praise', that is, 'the tribute of lips which acknowledge his name'.[52]

SCRIPTURE REFERENCES

1. Heb. 13:22
2. Heb. 12:27, 28
3. Heb. 10:29
4. Heb. 12:4
5. Cf. Heb. 3:6, 14; 4:14; 10:23
6. Heb. 4:14; 8:1; 10:21
7. Heb. 13:10
8. Heb. 10:19

9. Heb. 1:14
10. Heb. 6:9
11. Heb. 7:7
12. Heb. 7:19
13. Heb. 7:22
14. Heb. 8:6
15. Heb. 9:23
16. Heb. 10:34
17. Heb. 11:35
18. Heb. 11:40
19. Heb. 12:24
20. Cf. Heb. 2:2; 1:7
21. Heb. 3:5, 6
22. Heb. 8:5
23. Heb. 9:9
24. Heb. 9:24
25. Heb. 10:1
26. Heb. 8:2
27. Heb. 10:1
28. Heb. 9:14, 22; cf. vv. 13, 23
29. Heb. 10:19
30. Heb. 13:12; cf. 2:11; 9:13; 10:10, 14, 29
31. Heb. 9:22
32. Heb. 2:11
33. Heb. 9:28
34. Cf. Heb. 10:9, 10
35. Heb. 6:12; cf. 10:36; 12:1
36. Cf. Lk. 22:32
37. Cf. Heb. 2:18ff.
38. Heb. 4:2
39. Heb. 10:22
40. Heb. 10:38, 39
41. Heb. 11:1
42. Heb. 12:2; RSV
43. Heb. 2:9
44. Cf. Heb. 4:16
45. Heb. 10:29
46. Heb. 1:2
47. Cf. Heb. 2:4; 3:7; 6:4-8; 9:8; 10:15, 29
48. Cf. Heb. 13:10, 11
49. Heb. 13:10
50. Heb. 13:12
51. Heb. 13:13
52. Heb. 13:14; NEB

19

The Priest Who Abides

At chapter 4:14 the writer begins his exposition of the high priesthood of Christ. He has, of course, already alluded to the subject by presenting Christ as 'a merciful and faithful high priest' who being made like His brethren in every respect, has made expiation for the sins of the people.[1] And having suffered being tempted He is to be considered as 'the apostle and high priest of our confession'.[2] But at this point in chapter four all the threads of the foregoing argument are gathered up to become the thought elaborated in the following sections. The one glorious fact is here confidently stated, 'Having a great high priest'. All that was thought lost is here shown as greater gain. The high priest still remains. And having Him, all that is of lasting worth in the old economy is found. When all is lost, all is regained, in fuller and finer measure, if we 'have' the high priest.

In seeking to express what the high priesthood means the writer sets himself to answer the question, In what ways is a Jewish high priest like and unlike our high priest? He does not pose the question the other way round; he does not, that is, ask, In what ways is Jesus like the high priest of the old covenant? That way would be like asking how is a man like his shadow, when it is more fitting to ask in what ways is the shadow like the man?

The conception of Christ as high priest while not entirely absent from other New Testament writings[3] finds a large place in the Epistle to the Hebrews. The idea would, of course, be well understood by his readers; and in declaring his particular purpose to be the unfolding of the 'better' way of the new covenant a full reference to that which was central in the old, the high priesthood, was virtually demanded. In broad perspective the writer begins first with a discussion of the personality of the high priest.

The very first requisite of a priest is sympathy. Without this there is no true priesthood. The writer delineates this requirement and shows how it belonged supremely to Him whom we 'have' as high priest. He is 'not a high priest who is unable to sympathize with our weaknesses'.[4] Essential to the calling of a priest was a sense of vocation. No man taketh this honour to himself.[5] And He did not 'exalt' (*edoxazen*) Himself to be made such. He was 'appointed'—was authenticated a high priest by Him who declared, Thou art my Son.[6] For Aaron it was indeed an 'honour' (*timē*) to be made a high priest.[7] Aaron was authorized to act for God. But Christ's priesthood is not derived, for no external authorities could confer it. It is part of the glory inseparable from His Sonship. His office sprang from His personality, and was not, as in the case of Aaron, a prerogative superadded. His high priesthood is not 'from man', not of the will of the flesh; and not even a gift of God's. He was not giving Himself importance—as is the literal meaning of the word glorified (*edoxazen*), used in 5:5 by taking on the office of priesthood. It was His place by eternal right.

Under the symbol of the historic figure of Melchizedek the writer emphasizes the distinctive thing about Christ's priesthood, it's 'foreverness'. He ever liveth as high priest. Whence Melchizedek came and whither he went none could say. There is no record of his birth or death. He just stood forth as priest; Abraham's encounter with him was with one who was a priest. Abraham never knew him as other than a priest-king. Jesus likewise is no priest by physical descent or legal enactments. He was not made a priest—made to carry out priestly functions. He is a priest who is at the same time everlasting, Son of God; a priest of whom it is said, 'Thy throne, O God, is for ever and ever'. He thus abides in the glory of His sympathy, and in the greatness of His vocation; a priest forever. From a consideration of the personality of the high priest, the writer turns to consider the work of the high priest. He thus interprets the work of Christ through the symbolism of the Jewish sacrifices.

He starts with the ritual of the Day of Atonement, but his main emphasis falls upon the sin-offering. Here the high priest was the sole officiant; he alone had the right to enter through the veil. And he could not enter that holy of holiest without blood, which was sprinkled on the mercy-seat. All the symbolism of the occasion was fulfilled by Jesus. He, for our salvation, entered a 'more perfect tabernacle', and with 'his own blood'.[8] Being both officiant and victim He has 'obtained eternal redemption for us'. The central passage, however, comes in 9: 15-19. Throughout a series of contrasts is implied. The high priest of olden times came with the blood of bulls and goats. But He 'offered himself'. This phrase ought to be well underscored for in it the whole theology of Hebrews is contained. The cross is effective just because it is His cross. Not any death could finally avail. It is because He was among us as man, yet as the Lord of glory, that there is power in His blood. He 'offered himself'—here is 'Sacrifice at its Fullest'! And He was 'without spot'. In not a few places the writer stresses Christ's freedom from sin's stain. He is emphatically declared to have been 'without sin'.[9] 'Here is the High Priest we need. A Man who is holy, faultless, unstained, beyond the very reach of sin and lifted above the highest heavens'.[10] Here is 'Sacrifice at its Holiest'! 'How much more shall the blood of Christ . . . purge?' The phrase 'the blood of Christ' is a recurrent one and contrasts the superlative glory of the new with that of the old. To the ancients the blood spoke of life; and significantly Hebrews never refers to 'the death of Christ', although it is stated that He came 'that by the grace of God he might taste death

for every man'.[11] The phrase 'the blood of Christ' is eloquent
with life. 'The blood is the life.' In the blood of Christ is that
which is living and life-giving. This is a sacrifice of nobler
name, and richer blood. Here is the life of God poured forth
for man. Here is 'Sacrifice at its Costliest'! Christ's offering,
the writer adds, was made 'through the eternal Spirit'. Most
commentators take this to refer to the Holy Spirit, following
the AV and RSV which have a capital S for Spirit. Phillips
has a small 's' and the NEB translates as 'spiritual'. If the
small 's' is preferred then it specifies either the spirit in which
His offering was made or His own Spirit as the offerer. Some
would regard the term as indicating the voluntary nature of
Christ's sacrifice. In the Levitical sacrifices involuntary
victims bled; but His sacrifice was offered by the will of His
own eternal nature.[12] Others, however, take the words as a
description not of the impulse under which the Son offered
Himself, but as referring to His own personal nature. In
this case the term 'spirit' describes the being of the Son and
'eternal' is an attribute of that nature.[13] The phrase then
describes the divine nature which was His, and which proved
itself to be inextinguishable by death, thus enabling Him
to carry on forever His priestly work in the higher sanctuary.
'Spirit' puts His 'offering' in the sphere of 'absolute reality'
and 'eternal' puts it in the sphere of 'absolute validity'. Yet
whichever way the term is used, either as referring to the
Holy Spirit or to Christ's own spirit, here is 'Sacrifice at its
Highest'!

The question has still to be answered how, in the judgement of the author of Hebrews, is the Jewish high priest like
and unlike Jesus? The Jewish high priest is like to our great
high priest in that he was more than a delegate and representative of his people. In some sense he was both of the
people and was the people. Thus is Christ. He partook of
flesh and blood and in Him we are brought into the inner
sanctuary. The high priest of the Jewish economy had to
do with 'things pertaining to God'. This was indeed his main

function. The whole epistle to the Hebrews insists upon and is inspired by this one thought, that He deals with God on behalf of men. In this He fulfils with glorious competency the priest's unique function. The high priest of olden days dealt with God on behalf of men's sins. In this respect he was like our high priest. Atonement for sin was the grand accomplishment of Jesus. Thus the writer throughout links Christ's atoning work to His priesthood. The high priest and the blood went together. Every high priest was 'appointed' by God. His priesthood, as we have seen, was not the result of a divine gift but was consequent upon His being who He is. In early days every high priest was 'taken from among men' and thus 'appointed for men'. It is for this reason stress is put throughout the epistle upon the humanity of Jesus. He is one among many brethren who took not upon Himself the nature of angels, but the seed of Abraham.

In what specific ways is the Jewish high priest unlike Jesus? It is in the context of the Aaronic priesthood that the writer discusses the likeness between the Jewish high priest and Jesus. The differences are brought out in two contexts, the first in reference to Melchizedek and the second in reference to the new covenant.

With regard to the first the main passages for reference are, chapter 4:14 to 5:10 and 6:13 to 7:28. There we learn that the priesthood of Jesus is 'immutable'. The Aaronic priesthood on the other hand and by implication is both 'mutable' and 'transient'. There is nothing imperfect about His priesthood, but the old was imperfect. What is perfect needs no repetition, generation after generation, by priest after priest, year after year. In the old ritual the atonement had to be oft repeated. Besides, the character of the ancient priests was defective. They were men needing to offer sacrifice for their own sins, because they were men 'having infirmities'. But He was without sin: and even when it is said that He was made perfect through suffering, this is not to be taken as meaning that He overcame faults and defects, but that He came to full stature by realizing what He had it in Him always to be. Thus He is 'Named of God a high priest after the order of Melchizedek'.[14] And 'having become a high priest for ever after the order of Melchizedek'. He has entered 'within the veil' as 'a forerunner' 'for us'.[15]

The other chief difference between the Jewish high priest and Jesus occurs in the context of the writer's discussion of the new covenant centring on chapters 9 and 10. Here stress is given to Christ's work as 'the mediator of a new covenant',[16] by the offering up of Himself.[17] There is no need for His sacrifice to be repeated.[18] Once at the end of the ages hath he been made manifest to put away sin by the sacrifice of Himself.[19] Death comes to man but once,[20] 'so Christ also, having been once offered to bear the sins of many, shall appear, a second time apart from sin, to them that wait for him, unto salvation'.[21] Meanwhile we may have boldness to enter the holy place by the blood of Jesus, and to draw near with a true heart in full assurance of faith, because we have a great high priest over the house of God.[22]

By reason, then, of the first difference Christ is able to save to the uttermost all that come unto God by Him;[23] and by reason of the second He is able to succour them that are tempted.[24]

His ministry above as our great high priest abides, He is a priest forever. His interest in His brethren is not a thing of the past. Now and always at the throne of God we are understood. He cares for us because He bears with us. It is by reason of who He is, the Son beloved, that His high priestly work is of such value and virtue. His intercession as the ascended Lord is not only a prayer but a life; a life that is a prayer and a prayer that is a life. As the throned Priest-King He has rights above. Having been made like unto His brethren, and taking His place as their File-leader, He knows our need and therefore what to ask for us. As the Father's Well-beloved He is assured of a hearing and an answer. He

LIVING DOCTRINES OF THE NEW TESTAMENT

is the Father's 'Amen' to our request through Him, and He
is our 'Amen' to our request to the Father.

SCRIPTURE REFERENCES

1. Heb. 2:17
2. Heb. 3:1
3. Cf. Rom. 8:34; Rev. 1:3; see the high priestly prayer of Jn. 17
4. Heb. 4:15
5. Heb. 5:4
6. Heb. 5:5
7. Heb. 5:4
8. Heb. 9:11, 12
9. Heb. 4:15; cf. 9:28
10. Heb. 7:23, Phillips
11. Heb. 2:9
12. Heb. 10:7, 9
13. Cf. He. 7:3
14. Heb. 5:10
15. Heb. 6:19, 20
16. Heb. 9:15
17. Heb. 9:14
18. Heb. 9:25
19. Heb. 9:26
20. Heb. 9:27
21. Heb. 9:28, RV
22. Heb. 10:19-22
23. Heb. 7:25
24. Heb. 2:18

20

The Son Who Remains

The Epistle to the Hebrews is concerned supremely with the redeeming work of Christ. It is for this reason, as we have seen, the dominant thought of the writer is that of salvation through Jesus, the great high priest, who offered Himself for us and now lives to intercede on our behalf. Almost incidentally does the author introduce his conception of the person of Christ. But for that very reason what he has to say is the more valuable, as it is the more fundamental to all the writer has to declare about the Redeemer's work. In a variety of terms is this work of Christ portrayed; He is High Priest, Apostle, Mediator, Pioneer, Shepherd, Forerunner, Surety. But there is one term which designates Him as He is in His essential nature and inmost personality, and that is 'the Son'. Jesus is Son of God, or more absolutely and simply, the Son. These other titles describe His office; but that of Son is expressive of being. They reveal what He does; this reveals what He is. They set forth His relation to men; this sets forth His relation to God. In the thought of the writer the Sonship of Jesus is a presupposition of all that Jesus did and does for men.

As with the apostle Paul, the Epistle to the Hebrews regards Christianity as the unfolding of all the Christ is and does. All that is true and eternal find their centre and goal in Him. Describing the person of Christ, the writer unites in the most emphatic manner His divinity with the most tender and touching traits of His real humanity more than

meets us anywhere else in the New Testament. He makes
inescapable the fact that no Christian faith is possible which
fails to discern a two-fold significance in the person of Christ.
He is our brother man, who inspires our hope and confidence
because of His oneness with us in our life's experiences. But
He is also other than we are, having a power to impart new
life and bring us to God. In this regard He was 'separated
from sinners and made higher than the heavens'. The Epistle
to the Hebrews, more than any other New Testament writing, seeks to do justice to these two separate and necessary
elements in our faith. Of course we must not look for any
attempt on the writer's part to reconcile these two facts.
There is consequently no speculative Christology in
Hebrews. Jesus is set forth as our Brother and our Lord—
as made less than the angels, and as more than they. The
fundamental fact of Christ's unique divine Sonship is certainly for this writer decisive for Christian faith; for only
if He can be so spoken of can He be the true Object of faith.
The Sonship of Jesus is then the basic thought of the epistle.
And this Sonship can be considered in certain broad contexts.

1 The Pre-existent Son

The opening chapter presents us with the Son in whom
God has spoken. God has in these last days spoken in One
who is Son by nature. The absence of the article in the
Greek—in Son, *en uiō*—is meant to direct attention to His
nature rather than His personality. The writer almost
immediately goes on to expound more fully what this means.
It is as Son, and because He is Son, that Jesus is the brightness of God's glory and the express image of His person. The
word for 'brightness' is *apaugasma* and is best translated as
'outshining' or 'effulgence'. The writer of Hebrews cannot
have been unacquainted with the phrase in the Book of
Wisdom in which Wisdom is regarded as 'reflecting the
invisible light'. This is precisely what Jesus does. He is the
246

effulgence of God's bright glory. By the 'glory of God' is to be understood all that God is; His essential nature. Thus is the Son, God's final Word, and as such He is 'the express image of His person'. The word translated in the King James' version 'express image' is in the original *charakter*— our word 'character'—and the word for 'person' is *hupostasis* which really means 'nature' or 'essence'. Thus the Son is the character of God's own essence. He bears the stamp of God's nature. He is the One in whom God's glory is fully expressed and on whom God's character is perfectly impressed.

For the writer of Hebrews, Jesus is God thrown on the screen of human life. He comes among men 'in essence all divine'. In Him, to echo some words of John Milton whose mind was on the Greek text with which we have been concerned, in Him all His Father shone, substantially expressed. Without equivocation what is being claimed for Christ is this; He belongs to the divine side of reality, having essential unity with God, and exact likeness to Him. So convinced, indeed, is the writer of the absolute divineness of Christ that he does not hesitate to refer to Him words from the Old Testament which were written in the first place of God. The Lord who in the beginning laid the foundations of the earth, is in Hebrews identified with the Son of God.[1] He finds no incongruity in interchanging the title Lord with God and Christ. In a further passage, if read in the only way that the Greek text demands, the writer, once again, takes words addressed to God, and applies them to Christ. Of Him, it may be rightly stated 'Thy throne, O God, is for ever and ever'.[2] Throughout there is no suggestion of the personification of an idea. The reference is to One who is Son; to a Divine Person.

This view of Christ, as Son, having essential unity with God and exact likeness to God, and in whom God can be fully seen and known, necessarily presupposes His pre-existence. This fact is brought out in many ways.

There is the Son's position of eminence in the universe.

247

He is set forth as the agent of creation and the channel of providence. By Him the worlds were made and the universe upheld. As the epistle unfolds we are made aware that to create is but a small matter to Him who can save.[3] There is again the Son's pre-eminence over the angels. To no angel did God ever give the title Son. The Son could be made a little lower than the angels because in the eternal realm He was greatly above them. The idea involves a descent from a higher to a lower. Such a phrase as 'in the days of His flesh'[4] hints at other days when flesh was not His native sphere. Once again there is the Son's position as providential director of all things. He is the chain band of all existence; or in Pauline language He is the One by whom all things hold together.[5] Creation is centred in Christ as Christ is its origin and goal. Without doubt then, the Epistle to the Hebrews presents Christ as a pre-existent divine being. He is shown as coming into humanity not as growing out of it. The Son's native sphere is the heavenly and the eternal. And He who comes to fill the soul's horizon, has already filled the Father's home and heart. Such a One cannot ever be understood as a mere incident of human history. He is only rightly conceived, as our author conceives Him, as Son by nature having the roots of His being in unbeginning Deity. Moses was but a servant in the house; but He is the Son over the house. Thus His person assures His pre-eminence; and His pre-eminence His pre-existence.

2 The Incarnate Son

Little is said in the epistle about the coming of the Son into human life. The fact is asserted, but not the mode. 'Our Lord sprang out of Judah',[6] taking 'the seed of Abraham'.[7] But much is said about the reason for His coming. He came to purge our sins and to obtain eternal redemption for us. Beyond all He accomplished for man is the deeper fact that He came to do the will of His Father.[8] And the Father's will clearly involved the 'offering of Himself'. It is inexact then to say, as Moffatt does, that there is no definite suggestion that He made a sacrifice in becoming incarnate. True, the writer does not put the idea as emphatically as Paul. But by implication it is there. Son though He was, He did not glorify Himself, but learned obedience to the Father's will during His life in the flesh by the things that He suffered. In His pre-existent state He shared in the Father's purpose and thus knew what was involved in His taking the form of a servant.

The epistle dwells much upon the Son in the days of His flesh. 'This man,' says the writer thrice over.[9] He is evidently well acquainted with the experiences of the historic person who lived, sorrowed and died.[10] There is a sense in which Hebrews is like Mark's gospel. Hebrews, too, presents us with 'The gospel of Jesus Christ the Son of God'. The Son has come, and as man partakes of flesh and blood.[11] He is thus 'the brother', who like His brethren depends upon God.[12] Jesus did not come upon earth a fully-fashioned Saviour. He had, so to speak, to make experiment of our human ways and to work Himself into His place in fulfilment of the Father's will in the redemption of mankind. It is for this reason that so much is made of His inner life and His earthly experiences. He grew and He learned. We have, therefore, reference to His faith,[13] His fear,[14] His obedience and suffering,[15] His temptations and sympathy,[16] His humility.[17] What the Epistle shows us is then, a personality creating its own form by a series of acts, by surmounting moral crises. He faced life's tests and temptations, and overcame. He exposed Himself to all the stresses and strains of our human ways and through all was more than conqueror. Thus was His enlarging life more and more offered as an adequate medium of the self-revealing Godhead. In Him the perfect revelation of God found embodiment. All of God that can be expressed in human personality found in the Man Jesus Christ its one uninhibited organ. As He stooped to save so He grew in the

LIVING DOCTRINES OF THE NEW TESTAMENT

stature of divine humanity.

The writer's interest in the human life of Jesus is, then, of the profoundest theological interest. It was no mere afterthought consequent upon the necessity of rescuing the doctrine of Christ's high priesthood from the mist of obscurity. Indeed the very opposite is the case. The writer's valuation of Christ's high priestly ministry is due to the fact that He was in all points tempted like as we are. His sympathy above depends upon His stay below. It almost seems that the writer's conception of Christ's continuing intercession was in no small measure consequent upon his meditation upon the life of Jesus in the flesh.

3 The Exalted Son

Several times in the epistle the word 'heir' occurs; and in each reference it is to the Son's final glory as Redeemer. There is an emphasis throughout on the ascension and exaltation of the Son. The idea is often presented under the figure of a priest returning from his sacrifice or as a warrior from the field of victory. In solemn procession He passes from the scene of sacrifice and conquest, up through the heavens, and behind the veil, and into the innermost sanctuary. He comes again to the place which is His by right, to the seat of power and authority at the right hand of the majesty on high. He re-enters the eternal realms in the power of His indestructible life, and there He appears in the presence of God on our behalf. In the reality of the victory which He has won through the power of His outpoured life, He ever lives to make intercession for us. By His ascension He has been re-instated to the status of Son of God which was His by nature. And so, too, has He become the forerunner within the veil.

There is, however, throughout a futuristic note, as, for example when reference is made to 'the world to come whereof we speak'.[18] A new and divine order is coming when

Christ shall appear the second time without sin unto salvation.[19] So the whole epistle is as it were, thrown into a series of vivid contrasts. There are things that shall pass, and things that abide: things that shall perish, but He remains, a Priest forever, a Son forever. Here we have no abiding place, we seek one to come. The world to come is the eternal order, the kingdom which cannot be shaken, the rest that remaineth, the city that abides. Everything connected with it shares its eternity. It is the sphere of eternal salvation,[20] eternal judgement,[21] eternal redemption,[22] eternal spirit,[23] eternal inheritance,[24] eternal covenant.[25] But the word eternal means more than timelessness; it includes time and yet transcends it. The eternal is the absolute, the final, the ultimate, in contrast with the earthly things which are but shadows of the true. The true things themselves are eternal in the heavens. For these things men of faith have looked and endured. And in so doing they declare plainly that they seek a better country. They would come to Mount Zion, and to the heavenly Jerusalem.[26]

But while the Son, as now exalted, is our great high priest within the veil, the writer is sure that He shall not remain forever hidden. He is to be manifested once again. Thus there is associated with this coming event the advent, the judgement, and the unveiling of the eternal kingdom.

There is to be a breaking in of the eternal world in all its fullness which involves a taking up into the life of heaven.[27] Then Christ's coming will be 'apart from sin unto salvation'. Here salvation is to be read in its final act. At present we stand outside the veil, but then we shall pass beyond, the veil indeed being taken away in the manifestation of Christ. Anything less than that would be for Hebrews a salvation that is incomplete. We cannot have the true and the eternal until we are raised by Christ to the heavenlies. And this is the purport of the Second advent of Christ; the manifestation of the kingdom within which just men are made perfect.

There is no mention of the resurrection in Hebrews. But

the fact of it is presupposed; for in the togetherness of the eternal kingdom they without us cannot be made perfect.[28] And those who in an earlier dispensation greeted from afar the better land sought in faith a better resurrection.[29] But in general the idea of resurrection is taken up into the idea of the second advent, as the resurrection of our Lord is taken up into that of His ascension. With the coming is associated the judgement.[30] Thus the advent is the consummation of the age and the manifestation of the King.

Meanwhile we do not see all things put in subjection to Him, but we see Jesus crowned. And having such a high priest as Jesus, the Son of God,[31] who has passed into the heavens, we are to hold fast the profession of our faith without wavering. This is the word of exhortation.

Yet all through the epistle the writer distinguished Christ from God. It is God who appointed Him heir of all things,[32] and who subjects all things to Him,[33] and by whom He is raised from the dead.[34] At the same time the closeness of the relation between God and Christ is everywhere maintained. Christ as Son of God comes to us from God's side. He is more to God than the host of sinless angels. It is with Him that God conferred in the creation of the world. The Christology of this epistle is the same 'higher Christology' that is found in Paul and John. Chapter 1 : 18 speaks of Him as God, and 1 : 10 as Lord. Thus must the writer have held a view of Christ's person which made it natural for him to apply to Him the titles 'God' and 'Lord'; titles with which he was perfectly familiar as designations for the supreme deity.

SCRIPTURE REFERENCES

1. Heb. 1 : 10
2. Heb. 1 : 8
3. Cf. Heb. 1 : 3, 10
4. Heb. 5 : 7
5. Cf. Col. 1 : 16, 17
6. Heb. 7 : 14

7. Heb. 2:16
8. Heb. 10:7f.
9. Heb. 3:3; 7:24; 10:12
10. Cf. Heb. 2:3, 4; 5:7; 12:2, 3; 13:12
11. Heb. 2:14, 17
12. Heb. 2:11-13
13. Cf. Heb. 12:2, 3
14. Heb. 5:7; 12:28
15. Heb. 5:8; 10:5
16. Heb. 2:18; 4:15
17. Heb. 5:5
18. Heb. 2:5
19. Heb. 9:28
20. Heb. 5:9
21. Heb. 6:2
22. Heb. 9:12
23. Heb. 9:14
24. Heb. 9:15
25. Heb. 13:20
26. Heb. 12:22f.
27. Heb. 9:26f.
28. Heb. 11:40
29. Heb. 11:35
30. Heb. 9:27
31. Heb. 4:14
32. Heb. 1:2
33. Heb. 2:8
34. Heb. 13:20

THE
LETTERS
OF
JAMES
AND
JUDE

21

The Letters of James and Jude

THE LETTER OF JAMES

Although we are not concerned in these chapters with questions of authorship and dates we may take it as fairly certain that the James by whom this letter was composed was none other than James, the Lord's brother, mentioned in Galatians 1:9 and 1 Corinthians 15:7 and known to us as head of the Church in Jerusalem, or James the Just. The absence of controversy concerning the law suggests that it was written prior to the Council of Jerusalem of Acts 15. It seems that the Church had not yet broken away from the synagogue,[1] and that there is no evident conflict between the two. The Judaistic form of Christianity with which we are presented is witness to the fact that salvation was to the Jew first. But as yet the new wine had not burst the old wineskins. Evidently the message James had to give was for those Jewish Christians of 'the poorer sort' scattered abroad at the time of the Dispersion.[2] They were for the most part a servant-class who suffered not a little at the hands of their wealthy non-Christian employers. But they are reminded that their position is not on that account unenviable. For the greatest wealth is to be rich in faith. It will be best for those so tried to remember that a genuine faith does not go untried.[3] And

257

if the devil tempts man to bring out the evil, God tests to draw out the good. Riches are, after all, perishable stuff; and the rich man shall fade away in the midst of his pursuits.⁴ The one who stands the test shall have great gain—'the crown of life which God has promised to them that love him'.⁵ James would have those who are scattered abroad remember that God is the judge of all. The 'plutocrats' may have their good time now, but it will be short-lived. In the present, they will not learn that their stored wealth is stained wealth, and that what is stolen is short-lived. They hold up the wages of those who slave for them; they defraud; they fatten themselves like cattle. But vengeance cries, and the Lord of Hosts shall certainly hear.

This does not mean that the Christian is to take matters into his own hands. The right to judge is God's alone. Resentment and hatred on the part of the Christian towards those who hold sway over him is unbecoming in those who are to obey the royal law of love.⁶ The wrath of God against evil men is sure to come; let the Christian, then, learn to be patient as the farmer awaits the harvest time.⁷ But the Christian must be slow to anger, for his anger is not unmixed and unclouded, 'the wrath of man worketh not the righteousness of God'.⁸ Such in broad outline is the purport of the epistle.

Yet while James is Jewish in its appeal it is no less Christian in outlook. Most of the Old Testament books are alluded to in it, yet no other New Testament epistle reflects so truly the teaching of the Sermon on the Mount. James is not a theological but an ethical treatise. It has not to do with the content of the faith as with the conduct of the faith. It is 'the agenda of faith'. It is for this reason that there are some fifty-four imperatives in its one hundred and eight verses. It would, however, be unjust to regard James as essentially a Jewish homily. There is certainly no mention of the 'gospel', but throughout there is the evangelical faith. It is too much leavened with the new spirit of Christianity to conceive of it as having meaning outside the community of Christian believers. And even in his reference to 'the law' James has the more specific teaching of Jesus in mind. He sees the law as the 'perfect law of liberty'; as that which is fulfilled in Christ. For him the law is inward and spiritual; not that of external compulsion and constraint. It may perhaps be false to conclude from this letter that its writer knew no more of the gospel than is here presented. The practical aim of his message must never be lost sight of. Nor can we think that James was less informed as to the essentials of the gospel than were any other of the writers of the New Testament; what we know of his life and contacts, apart from the promise of the Holy Spirit to teach him as well as others, would not lead us to such a conclusion. James will warn against misuse of wealth, denounce injustice, urge to patience and steadfastness, and counsel against evil-speaking, lying and slandering. But that precisely was the message those suffering at the hands of cruel masters needed most.

None the less his theology is not as meagre as some have suggested. Writing with the Old Testament very much in mind his favourite name for God is Lord. And this Lord is 'the God of Sabaoth'—'the God of armies'.[9] Yet He is Father; and this in the most intimate and general sense. He is 'our God and Father',[10] and the Lord and Father'.[11] He is also 'the Father of lights',[12] which seems to mean that He is the creator of the heavenly bodies; and thus the source of light and life. Such a God is good both in the absolute sense and in His relationship with men. He cannot be tempted of evil. He is forever true to His own nature. His light never suffers eclipse, and His life never ebbs away. In Him is no variableness, neither shadow cast by turning. And being what He is, to be in His will is life's highest good.[13] His goodness extends to His children, for every good and every perfect gift is from above;[14] and it is He who gives 'more grace'.[15] But the worldly and the proud are the enemies of God and their end is destruction. To the penitent and the humble, 'the Lord is full of pity and merciful'.[16] Here is the Old Testament picture of God enriched by the conception of Jesus as the Father which is in heaven.

In the likeness of God man was made.[17] And as such he must seek security and satisfaction outside himself; either in the things of the world, or in God. James is keenly aware that the world is too much with us. Its pomp and its pleasures call for immediate test. The world is evidently that wherein moral evil has its operation. It is without in the sense that it provides the stimuli for our evil passions; yet it is within, for there is the *locus* of our evil desires.[18] It is this evil nature which enters into competition and conflict with God. It is this which draws us away from God. Thus, declares James, 'friendship with the world is enmity against God'.[19] True religion on the other hand is to 'keep oneself unstained from the world'.[20]

It is in relation to God and the world, then, that, according to James, determines what is good and what is sinful. Chapter 1:14,15 contains James's philosophy of sin. Evil desire is its causative principle; sin is the offspring of one's own will. Its final outcome is death,[21] and by death James would have us understand something more than the dissolution of the body. The death which results from man's wilful transgression is moral and ethical, the separation of the soul from God. Sin, therefore, for James, is man's fault, not his misfortune. It arises out of his yielding to self-gratification. Here is the inner principle which gives birth to that vile catalogue of evil things that James specifies, anger, pride, evil-speaking and so forth. But fundamentally it is a false and fatal show of wisdom which is 'earthly, unspiritual, devilish'.[22] It is a boasted knowledge which therefore belongs to the passing age, the lower nature, the demonic realm. This spurious wisdom is the pregnant source of 'every evil practice'.[23] Although James is not concerned to trace back the origin of evil beyond man's own evil desire and will, he has one reference to Satan.[24] And without doubt he regarded the 'Evil One' as the ultimate cause of all human woe. He, therefore, calls upon his readers to 'resist' the devil, recalling, perhaps, as he does so, the victory of Christ over Satan in the wilderness. James, too, was sure that, in the last, man's fight was against spiritual hosts of wickedness. The reality of God is terror to the demonic agents of Satan.[25] They shudder in His presence as they did in the presence of Jesus in the days of His earthly ministry.[26]

We have seen that James has something to say about God's absolute goodness but this involves the necessity of goodness on the part of man made in the image of God. The blueprint of this required righteousness is the divine law; but not just obedience to a formal code. It is for James the law as taught by Christ, the obedience to the will of God out of a loving heart. James, therefore, can speak of it as 'the law of liberty',[27] 'the perfect law',[28] 'the royal law'.[29] This is the law of the Lord which converts and comforts the soul. It is something inward and spiritual and freely chosen. It is not a yoke of bondage, but a principle of freedom. Yet it is such a law that stands against us when its terms are unheeded and its provisions are disobeyed.[30] By emphasizing in the way he does the inner principle of the law, James is showing, in his way, what Paul came to discover so dramatically in his own experience, that the law is not the way of salvation. It is patient love which recovers the erring sinner and covers a multitude of sins. And James's message in its ultimate is that 'the Lord is compassionate and merciful'.[31]

Certainly James does not intend to teach that salvation is of the law. The ultimate cause is not in anything in man or of man. It is in the will of God.[32] The procuring cause is 'the word of truth'.[33] That word 'implanted' in the heart[34] is the creative source of new life in the believer. A passage like this shows how close is the teaching of the earlier epistle of James to the later and maturer doctrine of John[35] and Peter.[36] For James, too, salvation has a present,[37] and a future aspect.[38]

Although not so much is stated about Christ as such, there is very much implied. His whole spirit permeates all that James has to teach. Jesus is Christ, the 'Messiah',[39] and James is His 'bondservant'.[40] He is the true object of faith as 'the Lord of Glory'[41] and He bears 'the honourable name'. To James, the Lord Jesus is supremely great and is at an immeasurable distance from himself. Elijah was 'a man of like passions with us',[42] but Jesus was different and distinctive. On a number of occasions James has referred to God as Lord[43] and he also refers to Jesus as such. Indeed in some passages we are left to put in our own preference so apparently sure is James that the title can be rightly used interchangeably of God or Christ.[44] There are also some passages where the reference is unmistakably to Jesus in which He fulfils a Godlike function. It is surely His coming James has in mind in chapter 5:8; and He is the judge standing at the door in chapter 5:9. Yet there is but one lawgiver and judge.[45] James then presents us with a view of Christ's person in which He is exalted Messiah, the author of salvation and the coming judge. His faith in Jesus as divine is evident, breaking through in a letter in which it was not within his purpose to give an outline of his Christology.

The issue in the epistle of James which has given rise to the most comment concerns the relation between faith and works. There are fewer today who take the view that Paul's Romans and Galatians are a downright contradiction of James. It is in fact quite incorrect to regard James as minimising faith in the interest of works. James has a high doctrine of faith. The gospel is for him 'the faith of our Lord Jesus Christ'.[46] The epistle is specially concerned to give comfort to the troubled poor; so he commends those who are scarce in this world's goods and yet who are 'rich in faith'.[47] True prayer must be in faith.[48] About fifteen times in all James speaks about faith: and he is specially anxious to show that works must go with faith if faith itself is to be seen as authentic.

James is not without a specific doctrine of grace either. In one place the term (*charis*) comes with its original connotation of 'charm' or 'glory'.[49] But again, however, he quotes from Proverbs 3:34, the only Old Testament passage where *charis* is used in anything like its 'Pauline' sense. God gives 'more grace'; for He is such a God who resists the proud and gives grace to the humble.[50]

With grace must ever go faith. And in two passages this relationship is worked out. In 2:14-26 there is that between faith and works: and in 5:14f. that between faith and healing.

It is the first of these which needs comment. As we have seen James is far from preaching a Pharisaic doctrine of works. Salvation is of God and by His word. What then does he mean by saying that 'by works a man is justified and not by faith alone'? Broadly we may say that James is concerned to stress the sort of faith that saves. A faith that does not issue in works 'is barren'.[51] There is present no evident fertilizing principle of life; no proof that the 'implanted' word has germinated. He almost seems to say that while it is faith which justifies a man before God ('He giveth grace to the humble'), it is works which justify a man before men ('I by my works will *show* thee my faith'). James's antithesis is, then, between two sorts of faith: faith as a mere intellectual ascent and faith as a living fruit-bearing principle. The devils have the first sort; Abraham had the second. In Romans 4 Paul takes Abraham as an illustration of the fact that faith apart from works justifies. But the faith that justifies according to Paul is that which lays hold of the promises of God. Without contradicting each other both rightly take hold of the story of Abraham to illustrate their point. Paul has in mind the view of works as supposed to possess some meritorious efficacy. He shows from the life of God's dealing with Abraham that meritorious works cannot justify. James has in mind a static intellectual faith and he takes the life of Abraham to show that inactive faith cannot justify. Thus while Paul is speaking of the necessity of a living faith, James is denouncing a tragedy of a dead faith. Paul is describing the instrument of justification; and James is describing the nature of faith. They are like two men beset by a couple of robbers. Back to back, each strikes out against the robber opposite him; each has his eye on a different enemy. James's antithesis is between two sorts of faith, the genuine and the spurious; Paul's is between faith and works. Paul's 'works' are legalistic; the works of a slave who thinks that by doing good deeds he will be elevated into a son of the house. James's 'works' are of those who claim to be believers. About works which do not show faith, works which might conceivably be done apart from faith, James has nothing to say. In the final analysis, however, there is no fundamental difference between Paul and James. In 1 Thessalonians, Paul speaks of the works of faith and the labour of love exhibited by the believers in that city. And in Romans he refutes the charge that his teaching on justification leads to a neglect of good works. In Ephesians 2, after his emphatic declaration that man is saved by grace without works, he goes on to state that the believer is created anew in Christ unto good works. Thus if in broad terms Paul says that 'faith must work by love'; James is simply declaring that faith must work. Faith alone justifies, but not the faith that is alone.

THE LETTER OF JUDE

Jude, the author of this short letter, was, like James, a natural brother of Jesus. The poetic strain in the letter certainly suggests one of the same family: and we do know that Jude, our Lord's brother, did become a Christian.[52] Short though the epistle is it combines the most eloquent and rhythmical Greek with the Hebrew intensity of expression. After encouraging his readers to defend the faith once and for all delivered to the saints, Jude continues with examples of disobedience, the exposure of disbelief, and the explanation of doom. In a few verses he elaborates Christian duties and closes with a stirring benediction. Naturally explicit theological declarations must be meagre in such a short practical letter.

But there are nevertheless very strong theological presuppositions throughout. God is presented as Father,[53] who saves through Jesus Christ.[54] The over-arching idea is that of the Lordship of Christ. Faith is stressed;[55] it is God's gift and the basis of Christian character. The Holy Spirit is revealed as the divine principle of the Christian life.[56] Christ is the judge. Salvation has an echatological reference,[57] giving the believer hope for mercy and eternal life at the last day. Faith is presented in the main as an objective body of revealed truth which is to be believed and which becomes the motive force of Christian living.[58] These are the truths basic to those who share in 'our common salvation'.[59] Yet faith is not just assent to a body of Christian doctrine; those in other days who withheld or withdrew trust in God were doomed through disbelief. Antinomianism is rebuked by reference to those who turn 'the grace of our God into licentiousness'.[60] The message stated and implied in the letter of Jude is then this: Salvation is through Christ out of grace and by faith; and the Christian, through the Holy Spirit, is to live a life which assures him in hope of salvation in the judgement day. The believer is to keep himself in the love of God,[61] and yet he is being kept by One who is able so to do.[62] A doxology fitting for such a mighty work which presents the believer faultless before the presence of the divine glory with exceeding joy is added: 'To the only wise God, our Saviour, be glory and majesty, dominion and power, both now and ever. Amen'.[63]

1. See Jas. 2:2
2. Jas. 1:1
3. Jas. 1:1-15
4. Jas. 1:9f.
5. Jas. 1:12
6. Jas. 2:8
7. Jas. 5:7f.
8. Jas. 1:19, 20
9. Jas. 5:4; cf. 2 Kings 3:14
10. Jas. 1:27
11. Jas. 3:9
12. Jas. 1:17
13. Jas. 4:15
14. Jas. 1:17
15. Jas. 4:6
16. Jas. 5:11
17. Jas. 3:9
18. Cf. Jas. 1:14; 4:1f.
19. Jas. 4:4
20. Jas. 1:27
21. Jas. 1:15; cf. 5:20
22. Jas. 3:14
23. Jas. 3:16
24. Jas. 4:7
25. Jas. 2:19
26. Cf. Mt. 8:28; Lk. 4:41
27. Jas. 1:25
28. Jas. 1:25
29. Jas. 2:8
30. Cf. Jas. 2:10
31. Jas. 5:11
32. Jas. 1:18; cf. Jn. 1:13

33. Jas. 1:18
34. Jas. 1:21
35. Cf. 1 Jn. 5
36. Cf. 1 Pet. 1:23
37. Cf. Jas. 1:22f.; 2:14f.
38. Jas. 2:5; cf. 1:12
39. Jas. 1:1; 2:1
40. Jas. 1:1
41. Jas. 2:1
42. Jas. 5:17
43. Cf. e.g. Jas. 5:10, 11
44. Cf. e.g. Jas. 5:14, 15
45. Jas. 4:12
46. Jas. 2:1
47. Jas. 2:5
48. Cf. Jas. 1:6; 5:15
49. Jas. 1:11
50. Jas. 4:6
51. Jas. 2:20
52. Ac. 1:14; 1 Cor. 15:7
53. Jude 1
54. Jude 25
55. Jude 25
56. Jude 19-21
57. Jude 21
58. Cf. Jude 3, 20
59. Jude 3
60. Jude 4
61. Jude 21
62. Jude 24
63. Jude 25

THE
LETTERS
OF
JOHN

22

The Letters of John

The Christology of the Johannine letters is in essential harmony with the teaching of the Fourth Gospel. The first three verses of the first epistle are almost an implicit commentary on the prologue with which the gospel opens. The gospel, as we have seen, insists upon the humanness of Jesus as the Word made flesh. Both the personality and the historic actuality of the Word incarnate are insisted upon in the gospel. But even so, it almost seems that some enthusiastic students of the Alexandrian philosophy were intent upon interpreting John's Logos doctrine in terms of docetic idealism. Such a view would leave us with a mystical figure who could not be touched with a feeling of our infirmities. Against any notion of a Christ-idea floating about in an unreal body John set himself in his first epistle.

He begins by identifying again the Son of God with the Word of Life: and he then goes on to refute the error of an unreal Jesus by an appeal to personal experience.[1] The presence of the Life among men was audible, visible and tangible. Thus to deny that Jesus Christ is come in the flesh is of antichrist.[2] Not only does John insist on identifying the Christ with the human Jesus,[3] but he equally insists upon relating this Jesus Christ with God.[4] So complete indeed is this identification of Christ with God that in several references it is hard to be sure of which John speaks.[5]

The Johannine letters have a very spiritual understanding

of God. He is love;[6] and light;[7] and life;[8] and Father;[9] and truth.[10]

In a series of vivid contrasts, especially in his first letter, John sets forth certain vital realities of his message. There are the antitheses of 'love' and 'hate';[11] 'life' and 'death';[12] 'sons of God' and 'children of the devil';[13] 'light' and 'darkness';[14] 'truth' and 'lies'.[15] Those who are of God follow the ways of the Son. Believing in the Son of God they have eternal life.[16] Such walk even as He walked, in light, in love, in truth, as sons of God.

God is love; but John has no definition of God's love. It is rather a love displayed in action. It is a love which seeks fellowship and enters into relationships. Hate isolates and destroys. In love God came to enter into fellowship with man.[17] And in response to this greater love our love finds fulfilment. Such a love dispels fear and is shown in a love-filled life.[18] Love therefore sacrifices; it has a self-giving and self-imparting quality. This is supremely exemplified in Him whose very nature is love.[19] Yet it is God's indwelling love in us which becomes the source and spring of our love for Him,[20] and for others.[21]

God is light.[22] Here John is referring to God's essential being. There is nothing in Him doubtful, uncertain, equivocal. He is the absolutely pure and holy; the one perfect being that there is. It is the nature of light to shine forth, thus the passage 2:8 refers to God in His expression. His light shone into the world's darkness and the darkness is now passing, more and more unto the perfect day. It is as one walks in the light, that is, lives in the presence of God, that fellowship is maintained and sustained, and there is constant experience of cleansing from sin.[23] The evidence of being in and abiding in the light is love of the brethren.[24] Thus in His light our darkness is passed.

God is life. This idea which is so prominent in the gospel clearly underlies many of the concepts of the epistles.[25] God is the very reality and actuality of life which belongs to the

Son in like manner. So the Son is the Word of Life, and as the Word of Life He is manifested to us as the eternal life. Consequently eternal life is not merely life of duration, but of quality. It is divine life given to us in the Son.[26]

God is Father. Jesus's favourite designation for God, that of Father, came naturally to the thought of John who had heard so often and learned so well his Master's words. It appears however, that John had in mind the spiritual relationship of the believer to God when he writes of the divine Fatherhood. It is by the love bestowed on us by the Father that we become children of God—*tekne*, children, is John's word, not *uioi*, sons, which is characteristically Paul's. Consistent with this idea of spiritual relationship is the constant recurrence of the phrase 'born of God'. 'Everyone that doeth righteousness is born of God' says the last verse of chapter 2 and this is immediately followed in 3:1 by the declaration that it is in the bestowed love of the Father that this new relationship becomes a fact of experience. So again in 3:9, 10, the juxtaposition of the two phrases is important. Verse 9 'whosoever is born of God . . .' is followed immediately by 'in this the children of God are manifested . . .'[27]

God is truth. The idea of 'truth' pervades the three epistles. There would seem indeed to be throughout an identification of 'truth' with God. In 4:2 and 4:6 there is an equation of the Spirit of God with the Spirit of Truth, an idea which need not sound strange in view of our Lord's own words in the Upper Room concerning the coming of the Spirit as the Spirit of Truth.[28] In 5:20 John qualifies his reference to God by declaring that this is the true God. The word for true (*alēthinos*) should be rendered 'genuine'. He is the genuine God in contrast to the idols from which we are to keep ourselves free.[29] Such images are empty things, mere nothings. But He alone is worthy of the name God; He alone corresponds to what is meant by God. Thus all God's revelations are revelations of divine truth, because it is His self-disclosure. And thus, too, is the Son, as God's final revelation, ultimate truth. He is the true way and the living way.

Man is, according to the Johannine epistles, in need of such a revelation. For the world in which men live, is a world in which evil reigns.[30] In a sense the devil's power is real in the world and shows itself in that spirit of antichrist which denies Christ, and which reveals itself in the world as falsehood, denial and death. This spirit does not merely lie outside man as the atmosphere in which he passes his life. It is within becoming the lust of the flesh, the lust of the eyes and the pride of life.[31] John certainly thinks of sin as originating in a personal devil. Those who commit sin are of the devil,[32] and the devil originated sin.[33] To be enslaved by sin is to be a child of the devil.

But about such a state of affairs Jesus has done something. 'He was manifested to take away our sins, and in Him was no sin',[34] and 'He was manifested to destroy the works of the devil'.[35] Christ's manifestation is His total act from the moment of His becoming flesh until the day He was taken up. And that manifestation of Christ was related to human sin and the devil's power. He came to take away our sins and in doing so released the hold that Satan had upon men. So Christ is our 'propitiation'.[36] To propitiate means both to cover and to conciliate. And this is what Christ came and did. In Him God and man were reconciled and man's sin covered by being taken away. Christ is also our means of cleansing.[37] From any defilement, which the light in which one walks shows up, there is cleansing available in the blood of Christ. The emphasis here is on the continual efficacy of Christ's work in the believer's heart and conscience. He is no less our Advocate.[38] The word *Paraclete* is a sort of active noun. Christ is the one who can be called along side in any time of need. In the gospel the Holy Spirit is presented as the Advocate within. Here we are assured of an Advocate above. There is the present and perpetual help of a Sinless Saviour who has Himself been through our way and who never hesitates or fails to state our case and plead our cause.

John views the saving act of Christ in experience from the human and the divine side. On man's side there must be faith. And this faith is a 'believing',[39] a 'receiving',[40] a 'confessing'.[41] On God's side there is the divine begetting, the imparting of a spiritual life from God. We have thus, as we noted above, the recurrence of the phrase 'born of God'. The reality of possessing this new life in Christ is not overlooked by John. In various ways is it evidenced, as in the doing of righteousness,[42] loving the brethren,[43] confessing Jesus as the Christ,[44] overcoming the world,[45] forsaking the life of sin for the life of holiness.[46]

SCRIPTURE REFERENCES

1. 1 Jn. 1:1
2. 1 Jn. 4:2, 3; 5:6
3. 1 Jn. 2:22
4. 1 Jn. 5:5
5. Cf. 1 Jn. 5:10, 20
6. 1 Jn. 4:8, 16
7. 1 Jn. 1:5
8. 1 Jn. 5:20
9. 1 Jn. 2:1; 3:1; 2 Jn. 3, 4
10. 1 Jn. 5:20; cf. 3 Jn. 12, where the 'truth' which bears witness to Demetrius seems to be personified.
11. Cf. e.g. 1 Jn. 4:20
12. Cf. e.g. 1 Jn. 3:14, 15
13. Cf. e.g. 1 Jn. 2:1-10
14. Cf. e.g. 1 Jn. 1:7-2:11
15. Cf. e.g. 1 Jn. 2:21, 22
16. 1 Jn. 5:12
17. 1 Jn. 3:1
18. 1 Jn. 4:7
19. 1 Jn. 4:9
20. 1 Jn. 4:19
21. 1 Jn. 4:7, 16
22. 1 Jn. 1:5
23. 1 Jn. 1:7f.
24. 1 Jn. 2:9, 10
25. Cf. e.g. 1 Jn. 5:20
26. 1 Jn. 5:11, 12
27. Cf. also 1 Jn. 5:1, 4, 18, where the phrase 'born of God' is also found.
28. Cf. Jn. 16:15

29. 1 Jn. 5:21
30. 1 Jn. 5:19
31. 1 Jn. 2:16
32. 1 Jn. 3:8
33. 1 Jn. 3:8
34. 1 Jn. 3:5
35. 1 Jn. 3:8
36. 1 Jn. 2:2; 4:10
37. 1 Jn. 1:7
38. 1 Jn. 2:1
39. 1 Jn. 5:1
40. 1 Jn. 5:12
41. 1 Jn. 4:2, 15
42. 1 Jn. 2:29
43. 1 Jn. 4:7
44. 1 Jn. 5:1
45. 1 Jn. 5:4
46. 1 Jn. 5:18

THE
LETTERS
OF
PETER

23

The Letters of Peter

THE FIRST LETTER OF PETER

Although Peter wrote his first letter to the exiles of the Dispersion[1] spread over Asia Minor, he had also Gentiles in mind as well.[2] His main concern is with the Christian's experience of salvation,[3] and the Christian's endurance of suffering.[4] From a doctrinal point of view salvation is given a trinitarian context.[5] From a practical point of view it has both an individual and a social reference.[6] For the Christian in suffering there is the great example[7] and the great expectation.[8] Evidently, then, the purpose of the epistle is to comfort Christians in trial. This is the dark background against which 'the result of their faith' in 'the salvation of their souls' is assured. The believing community are heirs of the promises made to God's ancient people. The blessings of the Messianic age belongs to them. In his speeches in Acts, Peter has contended that Jesus is the true Messiah in spite of His crucifixion; in this epistle he contends that Christians are the true people of God in spite of their sufferings. Therefore they are God's elect race, royal priesthood, holy nation, a people for His own possession.[9] Peter would set the eyes of his readers, tried and tormented as they were, upon the glorious future and encourage them in their 'living hope'.[10] The keywords of the epistle are then suffering and hope. This means that the emphasis throughout will be practical rather than doctrinal. Only incidentally does Peter touch upon great dogmatic issues; and then always with a practical end in view. Yet while he regarded himself as very much the apostle to the old Israel he has learned that no special privilege was now theirs. Gentiles who 'were no people' are 'now' 'the people of God'.[11] They, too, are among those 'elect according to the foreknowledge of God',[12] and 'called' by Him.[13]

Throughout his letter Peter makes use of the Old Testament both as pattern and as proof. He sees Christ as fulfilling the prophetic hope of Israel. He has several allusions to Old Testament forms of expression; Christ is the lamb without blemish;[14] believers are called to holiness, for it is declared that God is holy;[15] all flesh is as grass;[16] and so on. In this way Peter is able to interpret the Old Testament from a Christian angle.

In a most suggestive way Peter refers to the Fatherhood of God; a message which must have meant much to a people persecuted. He is 'God the Father',[17] but intimately and tenderly 'the Father of our Lord Jesus Christ';[18] the same one whom Christians may address as their Father.[19] The Father is 'the faithful Creator'.[20] As such He is judge.[21] He is a God of holiness[22] and grace.[23] It is of His abundant mercy that men are brought to salvation.[24]

In his first letter Peter re-echoes the thought of his speeches in Acts of Jesus being delivered to death by the determined council and foreknowledge of God.[25] The prophecy from Psalm 118:22 of Christ as the Stone set at nought of the builders is quoted.[26] Only once, however, in the epistle is He designated the Christ. The title has now become a proper name. His pre-existence is stated;[27] and that this cannot be explained away in any ideal sense is evident from the added statement that He was manifested at the chosen time. He was foreknown because He was there to be known before. With a certain solemnity Peter often gives the full title the Lord Jesus Christ. He is the medium of spiritual worship,[28] the chief corner-stone,[29] the Shepherd and Bishop of souls,[30] and the chief Shepherd yet to be manifested.[31] In Him we are called to eternal glory,[32] and through Him God is glorified,[33] while the believing man is called to sanctify in his heart Jesus as Lord.[34] The deed of our salvation involves God in His triune nature; while in some passages it is difficult to be sure whether the term God is used of the Father or Christ.

While the sufferings of Christ are considered in the context of the suffering of his readers they are not regarded merely as our pattern. The exemplary nature of His sufferings are of course presented. To suffer because a Christian one must suffer as a Christian; as Christ's man whose example is supreme.[35] Christ's sufferings are the final grounds upon which a man is redeemed.[36] This last reference unites the person and work of Christ in the divine act of man's salvation. 'For Christ also died for sins once for all, the righteous for the unrighteous, that he might bring us to God.' He the righteous for us the unrighteous; here is the paradox of the cross. He died for sin 'once for all'; here is the perfection of the cross. He dies that He might bring us to God; here is the purpose of the cross.[37]

Peter has much to say about the Holy Spirit. He is 'the Spirit of glory'.[38] He is 'sent forth from heaven',[39] and rests upon believers.[40] Our sanctification is the work of the Spirit.[41] Although he does not say in so many words that the Spirit is sent by Christ, he does link both, while clearly distinguishing between the two. The Spirit which moved the prophets of old is thus 'the Spirit of Christ'.[42]

When he treats of sin, Peter has the pre-Christian condition of Gentiles mainly in view. His concern is with the sins of the sinner rather than with the sins of the saint. He regards the flesh (sarx) as the source and seat of human evil. Their former manner of life is described as a living in the flesh.[43] And it is the evil outgrowth of these which war against the soul that his readers are to guard against.[44] In 4:2 and 2:11 Peter used the term 'flesh' (sarx) in an ethical sense. But in other places, for example, 1:24; 3:18,21; 4:1,6, there is the physical sense where the term denotes the material of the body. Peter is not, however, unmindful of the fact that sin is not eradicated from the believer. There are clinging evils, malice, deceit, envy and the like, which those who have experienced the salvation of God must avoid.

Peter sees salvation as a real and radical thing, affecting the whole life of the believer in his personal and social relationships. The eternal purpose of God the Father lies behind man's salvation.[45] It is connected with the work of Christ, with His death[46] and with His blood.[47] It comes by faith.[48] Yet it is in the main eschatologically conceived—a salvation to be revealed at the last day. It has, however, a present outworking in praise, in hope, in holiness, in love, in spiritual growth. Of salvation then God the Father is the source, the Son the procurer, and the Spirit the one by whom its sanctifying effects are applied. The 'word of God' is the efficient cause of our salvation. A regenerating power resides in the word; it 'liveth and abideth' for ever.[49] It is like the inheritance into which it introduces us and like the blood of Christ which redeems us, the 'incorruptible word'.[50]

And in the end, for Peter as for Paul, all is of grace. The grace of God in the heart of man is a tender plant in a strange and unkindly soil. It is Peter's purpose to tend this plant. He thus refers 'grace' (*charis*) broadly to the Christian's power and privilege in the present and to his hope for the future. There are six references to grace in the epistle. But in keeping with his set purpose it has a practical reference.

Peter speaks of the 'grace of life'.[51] This does not mean grace for living. Life is used in the passage in an eschatological sense. Peter is the first to use grace to include the final blessings of life. Thus husbands are to honour their wives as sharers with them in the grace of life to come.

Peter speaks of the grace of the divine security. This rests upon the divine call. It is based on the foreknowledge of God, through the Spirit's sanctification, and unto the obedience and sprinkling of the blood of Christ. From this triune God, grace is multiplied. This 'divine security' is the motive power of good behaviour. Being called out of darkness and into His marvellous light we are to endure hardness in the guarantee of ultimate victory. Such blessings come to us through the God of all grace and are seen in and secured through the sufferings of Christ and the glory which followed.

Peter speaks of grace in the context of the final destiny of life. The God of all grace has called us to His eternal glory after this brief time of suffering.[52] Therefore the readers are to put their hope 'for good and all' in the grace that is coming to them at the revelation of Jesus Christ.

Peter speaks of suffering in terms of grace. He tells his readers that such suffering is temporary (awhile), and has a use (more precious than of gold which perishes). But still they must suffer as those who are themselves innocent. It is no cause for commendation to suffer for wrongdoing. But it is a grace (*charis*), a merit, to suffer wrongfully as did Christ. It is not, of course, a 'salvation-merit', yet it is a grace which is more than a mark of grace. It is something which inspires grace and which in its turn is inspired by grace. It is therefore, something which is not only God's work but His delight.

Peter refers to stewardship as grace. Each has received a *charisma*, which is to be used to the help and blessing of others. In this sense we are stewards of the manifold grace of God.

Peter conceives of humility as a special evidence of grace. Humility is set forth as the gem of the Christian life. Believers are to put on the apron of humility and serve one another. In this context Peter quotes, like James, from Proverbs 3:24, the only passage in the book of Proverbs where grace has anything like a religious sense.

Two special emphases of Peter's understanding of grace are these. He regards 'grace' as the subject of Old Testament prophecy. The prophets spoke of 'the grace that should come'; and this grace Peter sees in the person and sufferings of Christ. And Peter considers grace in the context of eschatological blessings. Here is the reason for the inheritance which is ours at the end of the road.

Strong emphasis is given throughout 1 Peter to the resurrection of Christ. It gives the believer confidence that the coming salvation will be realized. It is presented, too, as a motive for faith.[53] It assures Christ's continued life and attests His mission and implies His ascension.[54]

It is here we come to one of the most discussed passages in the whole of the New Testament writings, that concerning the 'spirits in prison' in 3:18ff. Before we set down the five main interpretations we should note that the phrase 'in spirit' (*pneumati*) is contrasted with 'in flesh' (*sarki*) and must not be taken as personal. 'In which' (*en ō*) means 'in which spirit' not 'in the flesh'. The difference among commentators arise from (a) the force of, He proclaimed (*ekēruxen*), (b) the identity of the spirits, and (c) the meaning of 'in prison'. Interpretations are as follows:

i. He went and preached repentance to those angels who sinned in the antediluvian times and had since been in prison in Hades (Gunkel).

ii. He went and preached repentance to those spirits who had no chance to repent when the flood came (Alford, Plumtre, Bernard, Dorner, Selywn, etc.).

iii. He went and proclaimed deliverance to the souls of the righteous patriarchs imprisoned till then in Hades (Irenaeus Tertullian, Zwingli, etc.).

The question left begging here is why the restriction to the patriarchs of Noah's time only?

iv. He went and preached deliverance to those who were in Noah's time disobedient (Luther, Bengel, etc.). The only wonder here is why did not Peter just say so.

v. He went and proclaimed—not to preach the gospel,

what is proclaimed is not stated—to those who were in Noah's time disobedient, and to lead into paradise the souls of the Old Testament saints, though this is not stated.

Some commentators have refused to admit a reference here at all to Christ's descent into Hades. They interpret that He went in the Spirit and preached through the Spirit by Noah to those disobedient in Noah's time, who were in the prison of ignorance or the body or who are now in prison in Hades (Augustine, Aquinas, Lightfoot, Hodge, etc.). The sufficient objection to this is that it disassociates the words completely from their context, in which the death of Christ is the important thing.

Each one of the five theories has spawned its own multitude of variants and in the end the number of possible interpretations runs into a vast multitude. The exegetical problems of the passage are certainly considerable and are beyond the expert, much less the ordinary reader, to fathom with any convincing assurance. It is for this reason that so many commentaries pass over the section without comment. They seem unable to discover the precise significance of what was evidently quite clear to the apostle. The fact is, that we just do not have the key to unlock the meaning of the passage. At the same time, of the numerous suggested interpretations some are less likely than others on linguistic and some on theological grounds.

Yet we may take from the section some secure theological truth for faith's inspiration and comfort. Although it is certain that none of the immediate post-apostolic writers ever quote this Petrine passage in support of the credal declaration of Christ's Descent into Hades, yet, in view of Peter's own quotation from Psalm 16:8-11 in his sermon at Pentecost the thought may well have been in his mind. The idea that Christ should enter the realm of the departed in victory is suggested elsewhere.[55]

From first to last Christ's conflict was with the hosts of evil powers and principalities. In the days of His flesh He cast out demons, and made it clear that He had come to bind the 'strong man', and despoil His house.[56] Throughout His ministry He did 'before the time', what His cross, resurrection and ascension was to accomplish in full effectiveness. It is thus He saw Satan as lightning fall from heaven.[57] From the cross His quickened human spirit went to the abode of the dead, before His body was raised from the tomb, and there He displayed Himself as Victor over the grave, and Conqueror of him who had the power of death, that is, the devil. But connected with the judgement upon the devil, there went in Peter's mind the glorious reality of the divine mercy in the midst of judgement, of which the cross was the supreme manifestation. And these two came together for him in the story of Noah.[58] The story of Noah was for Peter something akin to what that of Abraham was for Paul. For the Flood was a signal display of divine judgement and mercy. So Christ's death upon the tree and His rising from the dead to reign are the realities in which judgement and mercy unite, and from which they both flow. Thus in Christ seen as leading a host of captives in triumphal procession and thereby declaring His victory over death and Hades and the evil forces which are typified by the rebellious of Noah's day and contrasted with those of Noah and his family saved by the divine intervention. That which destroyed the rebellious was the means of salvation for those who heeded God's warning and accepted the divine provision.

Whatever the interpretation preferred this at least is clear, that the work of Christ has wide range and reach. His resurrection was a necessary prelude to His enthronement. And it is the enthroned Christ who is 'on the right hand of God; angels and authorities being made subject unto him'.

THE SECOND LETTER OF PETER

The differences between the style and outlook of first and second Peter have often been noted; and the hesitancy over the reception of second Peter into the canon of the New Testament has been a matter of considerable comment. But such questions are not our concern here. Suffice it to note in passing that while the differences are there, there are also an impressive list of words, otherwise unfamiliar, common to both epistles, for example, 'precious',[59] 'grace and peace be multiplied',[60] 'add'.[61] There is undoubted reference to Christ's transfiguration experience in 2 Peter 1:16-18, and allusion to it in the first epistle.[62] And if point has to be made of the contrast of style and outlook between the two epistles, equal stress ought to be put on the same spirit and teaching which pervade both.

The three chapters into which the epistle is divided happen to set out the main ideas of the letter. Chapter 1 calls for progress in the Christian life; chapter 2 warns against perils in Christian doctrine; and chapter 3 states the Christian's position in Christ. The epistle shows evident indebtedness to that of Jude and it makes use of Jude's language to describe the false teachers. The dominant thought of 2 Peter is that the kingdom will be revealed at the second advent.[63] The kingdom may seem to tarry, but it will come at God's right time;[64] and it will have cataclastic results, for although 'the day of the Lord will come like a thief',[65] it will bring about the judgement and overthrow of the old order, and bring in the new realm—the 'new heavens and a new earth, wherein dwelleth righteousness'.[66]

Basic to all the blessings for the Christian now and in the future is knowledge of God. The idea of knowledge (*gnosis*) is indeed the keynote of the whole letter.[67] Those who have made their 'calling and election sure' will not fall, but will have an 'abundant entrance' into 'the everlasting kingdom'. Because of their 'precious faith' they have entered 'the common salvation' which is in 'the righteousness of God and our Saviour Jesus Christ'. This is the true knowledge of God which calls for advance and assures its consummation at the Lord's coming.

The Lordship of Christ is stressed,[68] and He is the Saviour.[69] He is God's beloved Son, whose majestic glory was attested by the Voice from heaven.[70] Only on one occasion does the letter refer to redemption through Christ,[71] but throughout the principle of redemption through the Saviour, Jesus Christ the Lord, is assumed. The Christian life is founded upon grace,[72] through a God-given faith.[73] The believer through the precious and great promises of God is made a sharer of God's very nature.[74] The Holy Spirit is mentioned specially in connection with the inspiration of the prophetic Scriptures.[75] Being therefore the result of the Spirit's action, no prophecy of Scripture is of any private interpretation. There is discussion as to the precise meaning of this passage. Some suggest that it should be read in conjunction with 1 Peter 1:10-12 and thus as re-echoing the idea that the significance of his message was beyond the prophet's own grasp. Others suggest that what is being said is that no prophecy can be interpreted out of the context of the whole. There is an inherent harmony between the prophetic utterances, so that any one interpretation can only be true if it is supported by that of others. More would prefer to find in the words a warning against eccentric individualism. No individual interpretation can be regarded as final, for since prophecy is of the Holy Spirit its significance can only be found in the general support of the informed consciousness of the Church of God. It would seem, however, that the passage intends us to understand that prophecy given through the operation of the Holy Spirit can only be understood by the illumination of the same Spirit. The words translated 'one's own interpretation'[76] link up with what follows rather than with what has gone before. We should then read, 'We have also a sure word of prophecy: whereunto you do well to take heed (as a light that shineth in a dark place until the day dawn and the day star arise) in your hearts. Knowing this first that no prophecy of Scripture is of *one's own unfolding*, because no prophecy ever came by the impulse of men, but, impelled by the Holy Spirit they spoke the words of God'. It is then the Holy Spirit who has inspired the word who can illuminate the mind. In this way He takes the things of Christ and reveals them unto us. But why do some disbelieve and scoff at the prophetic word, and ask sceptically where is the promise of His coming? Why? Because they have not the Spirit in their hearts.

Peter is then a letter of hope. It is this which underlies the futuristic outlook of the epistle. If in a short time the writer 'must put off this tabernacle',[77] he is not dismayed. His readers are exhorted to wait for and hasten the coming of the day of the Lord.[78] Second Peter is almost an Apocalypse in miniature and it bears a Petrine stamp by its threefold use of the genuinely Petrine word *spoudazein* (the word occurs only seven times in all the epistles of Paul), with its ringing call to holiness of life with which the hope of life forever more is brought into immediate connection.

SCRIPTURE REFERENCES

1. 1 Pet. 1:1
2. See 1 Pet. 1:14, 18; 2:10; 4:3
3. 1 Pet. 1:2-3:13
4. 1 Pet. 3:13-5:11
5. 1 Pet. 1:3-12
6. 1 Pet. 1:13-3:13
7. 1 Pet. 3:13-4:9
8. 1 Pet. 5
9. 1 Pet. 2:9
10. 1 Pet. 1:3
11. 1 Pet. 2:10
12. 1 Pet. 1:2
13. 1 Pet. 1:15
14. 1 Pet. 1:19
15. 1 Pet. 1:16
16. 1 Pet. 1:24f.
17. 1 Pet. 1:2
18. 1 Pet. 1:3
19. 1 Pet. 1:17
20. 1 Pet. 4:19
21. 1 Pet. 1:17

22. 1 Pet 1:15
23. 1 Pet. 4:10
24. 1 Pet. 1:3
25. Cf. Ac. 2:23; 4:28; 10:42; 1 Pet. 1:2, 20
26. Ac. 4:11; 1 Pet. 2:6
27. 1 Pet. 1:11, 20
28. 1 Pet. 2:5
29. 1 Pet. 2:6
30. 1 Pet. 2:25
31. 1 Pet. 5:4
32. 1 Pet. 5:10
33. 1 Pet. 4:11
34. 1 Pet. 3:15, RV.
35. 1 Pet. 2:21, 22; 4:1, 13; 5:9
36. 1 Pet. 1:19; 2:24; 3:18
37. Cf. 1 Pet. 2:23-25
38. 1 Pet. 4:14
39. 1 Pet. 1:12
40. 1 Pet. 1:12
41. 1 Pet. 1:2
42. 1 Pet. 1:11
43. 1 Pet 4:2
44. 1 Pet. 2:11
45. 1 Pet. 1:3
46. 1 Pet. 1:11
47. 1 Pet. 1:19
48. 1 Pet. 1:9, 21
49. 1 Pet. 1:23
50. Cf. 1 Pet. 1:4, 23; 1:18
51. 1 Pet. 3:7
52. 1 Pet. 5:10
53. 1 Pet. 1:21
54. 1 Pet. 3:21
55. Cf. Rom. 10:6-8; Eph. 4:8-10; 1 Tim. 3:16
56. Mt. 12:29
57. Lk. 10:18
58. Cf. Mt. 24:37, 38; 2 Pet. 2:5
59. 1 Pet. 1:7, 7, 10; 2 Pet. 2:1
60. 1 Pet. 1:1, 2; 2 Pet. 2:2
61. 1 Pet. 1:1, 14; 2 Pet. 2:5
62. 1 Pet. 3:1
63. 2 Pet. 1:11, 16; 3:13
64. 2 Pet. 3:1ff.
65. 2 Pet. 3:10
66. 2 Pet. 3:13
67. 2 Pet. 1:2, 3, 5, 6, 8, 16, 20; 2:20, 21; 3:3, 17, 18
68. 2 Pet. 1:2; etc.
69. 2 Pet 1:1, 11; 2:20; 3:2, 18

70. 2 Pet. 1:17
71. 2 Pet. 2:1
72. 2 Pet. 3:18
73. 2 Pet. 1:1
74. 2 Pet. 1:4
75. 2 Pet. 1:19f.
76. 2 Pet. 1:20
77. 2 Pet. 1:14
78. 2 Pet. 3:14

THE
BOOK
OF
REVELATION

24

The Victory of God

An apocalypse is a product of 'bad times'. It is a sort of tract designed to bring encouragement and hope to the people of God suffering under the burden of oppression. The writer's object is to steel them to patient endurance with the assurance that in spite of the seeming evidence to the contrary, the Lord still reigns. In the most vivid way the apocalyptic type of literature seeks to portray God's interest in world affairs. The events of history are not outside His control. Tribulation may be the present lot of the people of God but the last word is not with the evil rulers of the existing order. A glorious future, breaking suddenly by God's own act, awaits those who suffer for His sake. The time may seem long; but the truth which must be grasped is that God will come quickly; and then evil shall be done away with and the eternal kingdom will be ushered in. As apocalypse, the last book in the New Testament is certainly to be read as a tract for the bad times in which the early Christians found themselves. But no less, it seems to us, is it to be read as a tract for all times and for any time; as well as a tract for the last times. This means that we regard the book as too great to be pressed into one neat scheme of interpretation.

Undoubtedly they are right who say that the events with which Revelation deals had fulfilment in the Roman empire of the writer's lifetime. The figures referred to as 'the beast' and 'the false prophet' were identifiable to the early readers of the book. Some context for these allusions were present for those to whom the message of Revelation first came. In this sense it was certainly a tract for the first times. To limit the application of John's Apocalypse to this 'praeterist' canon of interpretation would, however, be to miss much of its richness. Revelation has a continuous message. There is then place to be given to the 'historicist' scheme; to the reading of the book, that is, as a prophetically given history of the Church from the age of the apostles until the 'end'. This way of looking at the book prevents us from taking the order of events which are pictorially given as arbitrary. There is an evident connectedness about the events in which the images of the vision are arranged. In so far as this view of Revelation can be followed it can be seen as a tract for all times. The idealist interpretation would see in the symbolism of the book a pictorial unfolding of the great principles of good and evil, of Christ and antichrist, which are in constant conflict throughout the ages until the final conquest of the good and the complete victory of God. In this sense Revelation can be taken as a tract for any time. According to the futurist thesis the greater part of the book remains to be fulfilled. Chapters 1-3 are said to belong to the Church, and beginning with chapter 4:1, with the door opening in heaven, there is the prophetic unfolding of events which follow the taking away of the Church into heaven. Those who take this line exclusively see Revelation as a tract for the last times.

The truth seems to be that the book of Revelation is too great to be crushed into any one mould, or to be interpreted according to any one method. There are sincere and devout men who advocate each view. It almost appears that the full message of the Revelation will only yield itself to those who recognize that it is not to be restricted to a limited period. Blessings are for those at all times who read and understand and keep its words.[1] It is a word for the first times, the middle times and the last times. Its early readers, as we believe, could identify its beast and false prophet; but history has had throughout like figures in whom all that is beastly and all

294

that is false have found incarnation. This does not preclude us from believing, which seems so obvious, that there will be a last beast and a last false prophet who will embody in awful finality all that was worst in those who preceded them.

History itself is in some real sense a judgement of God; and yet history will end in judgement. Thus there ever is the abiding significance of the Apocalypse. And thus, too, does apocalypse merge into eschatology. In every judgement of God in history God makes Himself felt in world-shaking events. In the final judging act of God all the foes of good-ness and truth will gather in force and come in like a flood. All the more dramatic therefore will be the final victory of God over those same enemies which have opposed Him in every stage of the way.

Revelation depicts the struggle between God and Satan, between good and evil, between Christ and antichrist to the final victory of God and good and Christ. The hostile powers which array themselves against God, and good, and Christ are sometimes depicted as of Jewish and sometimes of Roman origin. We may characterize these two broadly then as apostate religionism and antagonistic paganism. The opposition from apostate religionism is confined to the early chapters in which the thought of the Church is uppermost. The evil world power is more directly described in the middle chapters of the book. But both seem to be brought together under the figures of the beast and the false prophet. Both political power and pagan fanaticism unite to make war against the Lamb and to seek to destroy the saints of the Most High. And back of all stands the sinister figure of the Dragon of the bottomless pit, even Satan himself.

Chapter 6 begins the series of conflicts between God and Satan, good and evil, Christ and antichrist, which reaches its climax in the world-shaking holocaust described in chapters 16-18. Under various figures this idea of conflict is set forth. There is, for example, the unnumbered army of 9:16f. There is the battle between the two witnesses and the beast that ascends out of the bottomless pit.[2] There is the war between the dragon and the seed of the woman.[3] The climax is reached in the battle of Armageddon[4] and the consequent fall of mystic Babylon. That these chapters had reference to historic Rome is certain. Under the figure of a woman drunk with the blood of saints, the great city, the pride of all the earth, is pictured. The woman is revealed as sitting upon many waters and carried by a beast with seven heads and ten horns. The Christians of A.D. 100 read and understood the words of this prophecy which is indeed explained to them. The woman imaged the great city itself;[5] the waters represented her multitude of people;[6] the ten horns are the ten kingships into which the Roman empire was eventually split.[7] And the seven heads are the seven mountains upon which Rome rested.[8]

Here was depicted the mighty struggle between pagan Rome, urged on by apostasy, and the people of God; between the forces of Satan and the followers of the Lamb. Chapter 18 describes the impending doom and destruction of the great Babylon; and contains a heartening message for the persecuted saints. But its message is no less a warning word to every nation which exalts itself above all that is called God. The message of these chapters so graphically and pictorially given has been continuously re-enacted in the pages of human history. In that first titanic conflict between evil and good, John records the victory of God. And in all ages and stages of world history ever since, when seen in their eternal context, God has remembered the iniquity of nations and rewarded them accordingly.[9] No less overwhelming shall be God's triumph in the last struggle which lies yet in the future when the beast and the kings of the earth and their armies are gathered together to make war against the Unnameable One who is known as the Word of God.[10]

Every victory of God is in itself a judgement. The Book of Revelation depicts the judgings of God as a series and in its consummation. The judgement as a series of acts is given in what is undoubtedly the kernel of the Apocalypse which begins with the opening of the sealed book in chapter 6 and ends with the outpouring of the bowls in chapter 16. Before the writer approaches the unfolding of impending judgement, he unveils the heavenly and eternal background in front of which these coming events are to be transacted. This is the significance of chapters 4 and 5.

Against this background he discloses three series of judging acts under the symbols of the Seals, the Trumpets, and the Bowls. These series are clearly neither contemporary nor entirely consecutive. The last of one series overlaps the beginning of another. Theologically the important point of the section is that the writer sets out to depict the judgement of God upon mankind in its certainty, its nearness and the stages of its process. He gets behind the web of nature and history and lets us see the Hand which sets these and all such phenomena in the fabric of human experience. God has pledged Himself to make an end of evil; and that cannot be done without cataclastic happenings in the world which lies in the Evil one. The cycle of judgements lead on to the 'last judgement'. In all great crises men who have been caught up in the maelstrom of catastrophe have felt that there must be an end to it all; a final settling of accounts. Thus as the Revelation unfolds there is depicted, in the most impressive way, judgement in continuous execution and its indubitable future.

In Revelation, therefore, apocalypse passes into eschatology. Every stage of history has its own act of divine judgement, and consequently there is no incongruity in reading chapters 17 and 18 as having reference to historic Rome. But it is still to be insisted that this is only a partial reading of the story: here is pictured that judgement which brings history itself to a close. For there is a similarity between every previous act and the final one. There shall be a last mystic Babylon to fall in a final conflict. These chapters have, therefore, an ultimate reference which cannot be over-looked. Following the fall of the mystic Babylon and the defeat of the false prophet,[11] a strong angel appears to bind Satan. This is the prelude to the utter and ultimate destruction of Satan and his hosts. This is the last expiring effort of antichrist. This is the final victory of God, after which appears the new heaven and the new earth, the holy city descending out of heaven from God.[12]

Revelation is a book dark with the clouds of judgement. Yet its pessimism is not its last word. The mystic Babylon which bartered with the souls of men[13] is finally obliterated, and in its place comes the New Jerusalem. This is the city eternal in which the redeemed of all ages shall dwell forever. The details of this heavenly city are given in striking symbolism. But what stands out in its description is the absence of everything corresponding to the experience of enjoyment on earth. Revelation assures us that the words of the Epistle to the Hebrews will be fulfilled, that those who have gone before will be perfected together with those who follow after. The judgement which issues in the reign of righteousness will also call forth from the triumphant and rejoicing Church the everlasting song of victory.

Now and forever death and hades are destroyed,[14] and the head of the old serpent crushed finally and for ever.[15] Christ has thus performed His cosmic service. He who through His death has conquered the 'world'[16] now sees of the travail of His soul in full satisfaction. In His cross He brought to nought him that had the power of death, that is, the Devil; now is that victory made final. The whole creation is wrested from the power of the Evil One and so the Saviour of the world becomes the eternal Victor.[17]

In every drama of judgement as Revelation unfolds, the one name which stands supreme is He who is the Word of God, King of kings, and Lord of lords. And in the glory that follows the final judgement it is the person of Christ, the first and the last, which shines as the sun forever. His praises are sung there and the Head which on earth had no resting place is now crowned with 'many diadems'.

SCRIPTURE REFERENCES

1. Rev. 1:3
2. Rev. 11
3. Rev. 12
4. Rev. 16:16
5. Rev. 17:18
6. Rev. 17:15
7. Rev. 17:12
8. Rev. 17:9
9. Rev. 18:6
10. Rev. 19:11f.
11. Rev. 19:20
12. Rev. 21:1, 2
13. Rev. 18:13
14. Rev. 20:14; 21:4
15. Rev. 12:7ff.; 20:2f.
16. Jn. 16:33
17. Rev. 6:2; 17:14; etc.

25
The Lamb of God

This chapter is concerned mainly with the Christology of the Apocalypse. What sort of Christ is here presented? What is the writer's estimation of Him? The author has one phrase which occurs frequently—some twenty-nine times in all—in reference to Jesus. It is the phrase 'the Lamb of God'. This is his characteristic designation for the Saviour. The word used in Revelation is not the same as that in the gospel of John.[1] The word used in the Apocalypse does, however, occur in the Gospel[2] although it is not there used of Christ. Yet it is only in Revelation and the Fourth Gospel that He is *called* Lamb: in First Peter He is *likened to* a Lamb. It is around this phrase 'the Lamb of God' in Revelation that we propose to gather its significance for Christological doctrine.

There is a Logos doctrine in the Book of Revelation. It is in the Johannine writings only that the name 'The Word' is ascribed to the Lord Jesus. The coincidence is not however entire. In Revelation He is called 'the Word of God'; in the First Epistle[3] He is 'the Word of Life'; and in the Gospel He is 'the Word' absolutely, but the contexts suggest that if the ellipsis were filled out it could only be in the same fashion as in the Revelation. In the mind of the writer of the Apocalypse there is the same conception of Christ, the Word, as that expressed in the prologue to the Gospel and the preface to the First Epistle.

But the Revelation is not so much concerned with Christ's Sonship in the eternal past as with His Kingship in the future and His Redeemership in the present. Thus the great conception is that of Christ as the Royal-Redeemer, the Sovereign-

300

Saviour. Such a conception of course presupposes His earthly
life. It was in the days of His flesh that He wrought out that
salvation that redeems us to God by His own blood. There
is, therefore, frequent reference to His earthly life as the
sphere in which the redeeming act was performed and the
basis upon which His Kingly authority rests. The Christ of
the Revelation is then no ethereal ministral pilgrim of the
sky. John grounds the person of Christ firmly in history.
He makes constant use of the personal human name Jesus.
And in stressing His glory the author does not remove Him
from the earth. John definitely underlines the humanity of
the Christ whom he saw in vision moving amid the celestial
realms. This One is of the tribe of Judah and the family of
David.[4] His death in Jerusalem is specially mentioned.[5] We
feel all through that although such mystical terms as Word,
Lamb and Lion are frequently applied to the central figure
of the Revelation, He is none the less of our nature.[6] The
book that most exalts Him to the throne does not in the least
detach Him from the world. Throughout the Revelation the
historic Jesus breaks through and thus sets aside as worthless
all theologies which deny or discount the unique significance
of His appearance in history. Only the historic Jesus can
account for the historical Jesus, whose advent has affected
all history. John does not relegate Jesus to a faith-history,
He centres Him in a fact history. Revelation makes clear,
in a manner harmonious with the Fourth Gospel, that it is
the historical Jesus, the Logos made flesh, who must ever
be an object of faith. Those whose hearts are opened to give
voice to the adoring cry, 'My Lord and my God', with which
the Gospel closes, must be assured that the living centre of
that believing affirmation is the actual Jesus of factual
history. And on that score the book of Revelation leaves us
in no doubt.

John, however, does see Christ in the super-sensuous world,
above and beyond history and yet the moving power and
the guiding presence in all things. And it is in this context

that His specific description of Jesus as the Lamb finds its significance. An examination of the passages where the phrase occurs will reveal that in this designation is united the two ideas of Redemption and Kingship. On the one side there are such texts as these—'a Lamb as it hath been slain';[7] those 'who have washed their robes and made them white in the blood of the Lamb';[8] 'they overcame him by the blood of the Lamb, and by the word of their testimony';[9] 'they which are written in the Lamb's book of life'.[10] The stress here falls upon the redeeming work of Christ as the Lamb of God. On the other side there is connected with the title Lamb the idea of sovereignty. It is the Lamb that was slain who has the power to take the book and loose the seals thereof.[11] As such He is worthy to receive power, riches, wisdom, strength, honour, glory and blessing.[12] There is then reference to the wrath of the Lamb;[13] and the Lamb is seen in the midst of the throne.[14] The throne in heaven is the throne of God and of the Lamb.[15] The wicked make war against the Lamb but the Lamb is victorious.[16]

In the general term Lamb, then, two ideas are united: vicarious suffering and victorious power. At the heart of God's sovereignty there is sacrificial love.

Under the figure of the suffering Lamb can be considered the redemptive aspect of Christ's work as seen in the Revelation. The Apocalypse depicts the suffering of Christ in its eternal significance.[17] Thus for John the Cross has a reach beyond the limited period of Golgotha and Calvary. What became a fact of half a day is the truth for every day. The cross was a revelation in time of an eternal event. John was clear that the One who wrought a sacrificial work for men is One most intimately related to God. He is of such a nature that what He has done carries with it the impress of timelessness. The crucifixion was what men did to Jesus, the shame, the scoff, the spear-wounds. But the cross was what God did in Jesus. Calvary is from the perspective of grace an eternal fact and from the perspective of Christ's life in the flesh an historic fact. But no less is Calvary a divine fact. The mystery, the awe, the terror of the cross is this: that where Christ hung God hung, that His heart, too, was there broken by man's huge folly and sin.

The Apocalypse also sees the suffering of Christ in its experimental efficacy. The cross gives liberty.[18] He who loves us has loosed us from our sins. The cross brings redemption.[19] We have been purchased unto God by the blood of Christ. The cross assures cleansing.[20] Songs of praise are for Him whose blood sweeps away sin's defilement. The cross proclaims victory.[21] It is then the blood of the Lamb which is the ground of our liberty, redemption, cleansing and victory. The fact is proclaimed but the method is not disclosed.

The figure of the Lamb carries with it, as we have seen, the idea of sovereignty. This sovereignty relates to the Churches.[22] Here Christ is presented as the A and the Z, and all the colourful description of Him goes to accentuate this idea of Lordship. In the most striking imagery His dignity and authority are stated. Both the vision of 1:12-15a and the voice of 1:15b-18 alike serve to reveal this sovereignty. He has the clothes of royalty, the head of glory, the eyes of brilliancy, the feet of victory, the voice of majesty, the hand of authority.

His sovereignty relates to the world. The world-shaking events which accompany the opening of the seals of the book are due to the 'wrath of the Lamb';[23] and this authority extends to the nations.[24] His sovereignty relates to the ultimate victory of God. It is by the blood of the Lamb that the word of testimony becomes triumphant. In the Epistle to the Hebrews the writer sees not all things put in subjection to Him although he sees Jesus crowned. But in the prophetic vision of the Revelation all things are at last brought under the sway of that crowned Christ. The devil that deceived is cast out forever; and the creation that groaneth and travaileth waiting for the manifestation of the sons of God is, in the Apocalypse, made again a new heaven and new earth. In the judging act of God, Christ is the supreme actor. It is He who comes with great power and glory to judge the world and to save the people.[25] So the Morning Star will arise and the Lamb shall be the light of the city foursquare. For He is the Faithful Witness and the First begotten of the dead and the Ruler of the Kings of the earth.[26] He is the King of kings and the Lord of lords.[27] Such a presentation of Christ must of necessity involve His essential deity. He is the object of divine honours. To Him both worship and praise are given in the same way as God.[28] He is ministered to by the angelic hosts as to God Himself.[29] He sits with God in His throne having the keys of hades and death. He is the redeemer of man giving liberty, cleansing and power through His blood.

Throughout Revelation the greatest emphasis is put upon the divine nature of Christ. There is no single passage which can be given an Arian interpretation. Quite evidently for John, as for Paul, the whole creation is centred in Christ; and what it took a whole God to create cannot be redeemed by a half God. The statements made about Jesus in the Revelation defy explanation in terms of a post-Calvary deification of a man greatly beloved. In the Apocalypse Christ is elevated to the plane of Deity, a place which is His by eternal rights.

The One whom John worships and adores is, then, not the product of human history, although, as we have seen His real humanity is clearly asserted. The Christ of the Revelation is One who came into history. Thus the thought of His pre-existence is implied in the most natural manner. He is the one that liveth and 'became' dead and is alive forever more.[30] He is the Alpha and the Omega, the First and the Last, the Beginning and the End.[31] The words 'I am the first and the last' are a quotation from Isaiah 44:6 in which context they function as a description of the absolute eternity of God. In Revelation they are referred again to the Lord

God,[32] but, significantly, our Saviour takes them to Himself,[33] and speaks in His own name as 'the Alpha and the Omega, the first and the last, the beginning and the end'.[34] He is also the Amen, a witness faithful and true, authenticating the promises of God in His own nature.[35] It is therefore, impossible to take the phrase 'the beginning of the creation of God',[36] as including Him within the order of created beings. The very opposite is indeed the case. He is the 'first' of all things, the beginning of creation; the One, that is, who began creation, as He is the same who will bring about the end. He was prior to creation and not included in it. John, in this way, seeks to stress the fullness of Christ. He is the fullness of space, for in Him and through Him and unto Him are all thing. He is the fullness of time, for He fills eternity, as the One who was and is to come. Here is the finality of Christ. There is nothing beyond Him—nothing before, nothing after, nothing more. He has no 'before' and no 'after'. In this 'title of eternity' we have a solemn affirmation of Christ's eternal deity. He is the Ultimate One. There is none before Him, nought beyond Him and nothing without Him. Other than Jesus will not do; less than Jesus will not suit; more than Jesus is not possible. Everything of God is found in Him; and little of God is to be found apart from Him.

Christ refers to God as Father in a way which suggests a unique relationship;[37] and the designation 'our Father' does not appear. He is the One to whom the sevenfold perfection of God is ascribed.[38] He possesses as a clear right the secret of Jehovah, and writes His own mysterious Name upon the foreheads of the saints.[39] Sovereignly He disposes of the angelic hosts as their Ruler and Lord;[40] and He gathers to Himself the incense of adoration kindled by lives redeemed.[41] The Lamb of God is the Lion of the tribe of Judah. The verdict of Thomas in the Gospel of John concerning Him as 'my Lord and my God', is the affirmation of John in the Book of Revelation.

305

SCRIPTURE REFERENCES

1. Jn. 1:29, 36
2. Jn. 21:15
3. 1 Jn. 1:1
4. Rev. 5:6; 22:16
5. Rev. 11:8
6. Rev. 1:13
7. Rev. 5:8, 12
8. Rev. 7:14
9. Rev. 12:11
10. Rev. 22:27
11. Rev. 5:6, 7
12. Rev. 5:12
13. Rev. 6:16
14. Rev. 7:17
15. Rev. 21:1, 3
16. Rev. 17:14
17. Rev. 5:9; 13:8
18. Rev. 1:5
19. Rev. 5:9; 14:3, 4
20. Rev. 7:14; 22:14
21. Rev. 12:11
22. Cf. Rev. 1:11-18
23. Rev. 6:16
24. Rev. 12:5
25. Rev. 1:7; 14:14-16; 22:20
26. Rev. 1:5
27. Rev. 17:14; 19:16
28. Rev. 5:11, 12; 7:10; 22:8, 9
29. Rev. 20:6
30. Rev. 1:18
31. Rev. 1:8, 17; 21:6; 22:13
32. Rev. 1:8
33. Rev. 1:18; 2:8
34. Rev. 22:13
35. Rev. 3:14; cf. 2 Cor. 1:20
36. Rev. 3:14; cf. Col. 1:15, 18
37. Rev. 1:6; 2:27; 3:5, 21; 14:1
38. Rev. 3:1; 5:6; cf. 1:4; 4:5
39. Rev. 2:17; 3:12; 14:1
40. Rev. 22:16
41. Rev. 5:8f.

For Further Reading

Books specially recommended marked *

General Works on New Testament Theology

Bultmann, R., *Theology of the New Testament* (2 vols, London, 1952-5).

Conzelmann, H., *An Outline of the Theology of the New Testament* (London, 1969).

Fuller, R. H., *The Foundations of New Testament Christology* (London, 1965).

Hunter, A. M., *Introducing New Testament Theology* (London, 1957).

Jeremias, J., *The Central Message of the New Testament* (London, 1965).

Jessop, T. E., *An Introduction to Christian Theology* (London, 1926).

Rawlinson, A. E. J., *The New Testament Doctrine of Christ* (London, 1926).

Richardson, A., *An Introduction to the Theology of the New Testament* (London, 1958).

Rust, E. C., *Salvation History* (Richmond, Virginia, U.S.A., 1961).

Smith, D., *The Days of His Flesh* (London, 1906).

Stauffer, E., *New Testament Theology* (London, 1955).

*Stewart J. S., *The Life and Teaching of Jesus Christ* (London, 1953).

Stevens, G. B., *Theology of the New Testament* (Edinburgh, 1906).

*Vos, G., *Biblical Theology, Old and New Testaments* (Grand Rapids, U.S.A., 1948).

Wright, G. E., *Biblical Theology as Recital* (London, 1952).

The Gospels

Conzelmann, H., *The Theology of St Luke* (London, 1960).

*Denney, J., *Jesus and the Gospels* (London, 1908).

Dodd, C. H., *The Interpretation of the Fourth Gospel* (Cambridge, 1953).

Gardner-Smith, P., *The Christ of the Gospels* (Cambridge, 1938).

Flender, H., *St Luke, The Theologian of Redemptive History* (London, 1967).

Moffatt, J., *The Theology of the Gospels* (London, 1948).

Lynch, W. E., *Jesus and the Synoptic Gospels* (Milwaukee, 1967).

Rohde, J. (Editor), *Rediscovering the Teaching of the Evangelists* (London, 1968).

Rawlinson, A. E. J., *Christ in the Gospels* (London, 1944).

*Stonehouse, N. B., *The Witness of Matthew and Mark to Christ* (London, 1958).

*Shepherd, J. W., *The Christ of the Gospels* (Grand Rapids, U.S.A., 1939).

Sidebottom, E. M., *The Christ of the Fourth Gospel* (London, 1961).

The Pauline Letters

Andrews, E. M., *The Meaning of Christ for Paul* (New York, 1922).

Barclay, W., *The Mind of St. Paul* (London, 1958).

Cerfaux, L., *Christ in the Theology of Paul* (New York, 1959).

Hunter, A. M., *Interpreting St Paul's Gospel* (London, 1954).

Kennedy, H. A. A., *The Theology of the Epistles,* (London, 1917).

Morgan, W., *The Religion and Theology of Paul* (Edinburgh, 1917).

Scott, C. A. A., *Christianity According to St Paul* (Cambridge, 1927).

*Stewart, J. S., *A Man in Christ* (London, 1935).

Whiteley, D. E. H., *The Theology of St Paul* (Oxford, 1959).

Wand, J. C., *What St Paul Really Said* (London, 1968).

General Epistles and Revelation

*Alexander, J. P., *A Priest Forever* (London, 1937).

DuBose, W. P., *High Priest and Sacrifice* (London, 1908).

Kennedy, H. A. A., *The Theology of the Epistles* (London, 1934).

Rissi, M., *Time and History* (London, 1966).

*Tenney, M. C., *Interpreting Revelation* (Grand Rapids, Michigan, U.S.A., 1958).

Special Subjects
God

Argyle, A. W., *God in the New Testament* (London, 1965).

*Berkouwer, G. C., *The Providence of God* (Grand Rapids, 1952).

Brunner, E., *The Christian Doctrine of God*, Dogmatics, Vol. i (London, 1952).

Barth, K., *The Doctrine of God*, Church Dogmatics, Vol. ii (Edinburgh, 1957).

*Candlish, J. S., *The Christian Doctrine of God* (Edinburgh, n.d.).

Clarke, W. N., *The Christian Doctrine of God* (Edinburgh, 1909).

Ferré, N. F. S., *The Christian Understanding of God* (London, 1951).

Forsyth, P. T., *God the Holy Father* (London).

Franks, R. S., *The Doctrine of the Trinity* (London, 1953).

Hughes, H. M., *The Christian Idea of God* (London, 1936).

Hanson, R. P. C., *God: Creator, Saviour, Spirit* (London, 1960).

Hodgson, L., *The Doctrine of the Trinity* (London, 1955).

Mackintosh, H. R., *The Christian Apprehension of God* (London, 1934).

Lidgett, J. S., *The Fatherhood of God* (Edinburgh, 1902).

Matthews, W. R., *God in Christian Thought and Experience* (London, 1942).

Wainwright, A. M., *The Trinity in the New Testament* (London, 1952).

*Ward, R. A., *Royal Theology: Our Lord's Teaching about God* (London, 1964).

Smith, R. G., *The Doctrine of God* (London, 1970).

Christ

Argyle, A. W., *Christ in the New Testament* (London, 1952).

Adam, Karl, *The Son of God* (London, 1937).

Andrews, H. T., *The Christ of the Apostolic Faith* (London, 1922).

Baillie, D. M., *God was in Christ* (London, 1947).

Boettner, L., *The Person of Christ* (Grand Rapids, 1943).

*Berkoüwer, G. C., *The Person of Christ* (Grand Rapids, 1954).

Bornkamm, Günther, *Jesus of Nazareth* (London, 1959).

*Borchert, O., *The Original Jesus* (London, 1933, Reprint, 1969).

Bosc, Jean, *The Kingly Office of the Lord Jesus Christ* (London, 1959).

Boslooper, T., *The Virgin Birth* (London, 1962).

*Craig, S. G., *Jesus of Yesterday and Today* (Philadelphia, 1956).

Creed, J. M., *The Divinity of Jesus Christ* (Cambridge, 1938).

Curtis, W. A., *Jesus the Teacher* (Oxford, 1943).

Davies, J. G., *He Ascended into Heaven* (London, 1958).

Dibelius, M., *Jesus* (London, 1963).

Duncan, G. S., *Jesus, Son of Man* (London, 1947).

Edwards, D., *The Virgin Birth in History and Faith* (London, 1941).

Ferré, N. F. S., *Christ and the Christian* (London, 1958).

Filson, F. V., *Jesus Christ the Risen Lord* (Abingdon, 1956).

*Forsyth, P. T., *The Person and Place of Jesus Christ* (London, 1909).

*Henry, C. F. H., *Jesus of Nazareth: Saviour and Lord* (Grand Rapids, U.S.A., 1966).

Heim, K., *Jesus the World's Perfector* (Edinburgh and London, 1959).

Higgins, A. J. B., *Jesus and the Son of Man* (London, 1964).

Hodgson, L., *And Was Made Flesh* (London 1928).

Hooker, M. D., *Jesus and the Servant* (London, 1959).

Jay, E. G., *Son of Man, Son of God* (London, 1962).

Johnson, H., *The Humanity of the Saviour* (London, 1962).

Knight, H. J. C., *The Temptation of Our Lord* (London, 1922).

Künneth, W., *The Theology of the Resurrection* (London, 1965).

Knox, J., *Jesus, Lord and Christ* (New York, 1958).

Loos, vanDer, H., *The Miracles of Jesus* (Leiden, 1965).

*Machen, J. Gresham, *The Virgin Birth of Christ* (London, 1930).

Manson, W., *The Messiah* (London, 1943).

Manson, T. W., *The Servant-Messiah* (Cambridge, 1912).

*McDonald, H. D., *Jesus—Human and Divine* (London, 1968, Grand Rapids, U.S.A., 1969).

Milligan, W., *The Ascension of our Lord* (London, 1898).

*Morris, L., *The Lord from Heaven* (London, 1958).

*Orr, J., *The Resurrection of Jesus* (London, 1908).

*Orr, J., *The Virgin Birth of Jesus* (London, 1914).

*Owen, J., *The Glory of Christ* (London, 1933).

Pannenberg, W., *Jesus-God and Man* (London, 1968).

Ramsey, A. M., *The Glory of God and the Transfiguration of Christ* (London, 1949).

——, *The Resurrection of Jesus Christ* (London, 1946).

Stalker, J., *The Christology of Jesus* (London, 1899).

*Speer, R. E., *The Finality of Jesus Christ* (New York, 1933).

Strong, E. L., *The Incarnation of God* (London, 1920).

Swete, H. B., *The Ascended Christ* (London, 1916).

*Tait A. J., *The Heavenly Session of our Lord* (London, 1908).

Taylor, V., *The Names of Jesus* (London, 1959).

*Tenney, M. C., *The Reality of the Resurrection* (New York, 1963).

Thorburn, T. J., *The Doctrine of the Virgin Birth* (London, 1908).

Turner, H. E. W., *Jesus, Master and Lord* (London, 1953).

Ulmann, C., *The Sinlessness of Jesus* (Edinburgh, 1901).

Venn, G. and Meagher, P. K., *The Temptation of Christ* (London, 1957).

*Vos, G., *The Self-Disclosure of Jesus* (Grand Rapids, U.S.A., 1905).

*Warfield, B. B., *The Glory of Christ* (London, 1907).

*——, *The Person and Work of Jesus Christ* (Philadelphia, 1950).

Wright, C. J., *Jesus the Revelation of God* (London, 1950).

The Holy Spirit

Barrett, C. K., *The Holy Spirit and the Gospel Tradition* (London, 1965).

Barth, K., *The Holy Ghost and the Christian Life* (London, 1938).

*Berkhof, H., *The Doctrine of the Holy Spirit* (London, 1965).

Cumming, J. Elder, *Through the Eternal Spirit* (London, n.d.).

Downer, A. C., *The Mission and Ministration of the Holy Spirit* (Edinburgh, 1909).

Gordon, A. J., *The Ministry of the Spirit* (Philadelphia, 1869).

Hendry, G. S., *The Holy Spirit in Christian Theology* (London, 1957).

Hull, J. H. E., *The Holy Spirit in the Acts of the Apostles* (London, 1967).

*Kuyper, A., *The Work of the Holy Spirit* (New York, 1900, Grand Rapids, 1964).

*Morris, L., *Spirit of the Living God* (London, 1960).

Moule, H. C. G., Veni Creator (London, 1890).

*Morgan, G. Campbell, *The Spirit of God* (London, 1909).

Owen, J., *The Holy Spirit* (Grand Rapids, 1954).

*Pache, René, *The Person and Work of the Holy Spirit* (London, 1956).

Reece, T., *The Holy Spirit* (London, 1914).

Robinson, H. W., *The Christian Experience of the Holy Spirit* (London, 1928).

Schweizer, E., *Spirit of God* (London, 1960).

*Thomas, W. H. G., *The Holy Spirit of God* (London, 1913).

*Winslow, O., *The Work of the Holy Spirit* (London, 1843 reprint, 1961).

Yates, J. E., *The Spirit and the Kingdom* (London, 1963).

Man

Brunner, E., *Man in Revolt* (London, 1939).

*Berkoüwer, G. C., *Man in the Image of God* (Grand Rapids, 1962).

Bonhoeffer, D., *Creation and Fall* (London, 1959).

Cairns, D., *The Image of God in Man* (London, 1953).

Cave, S., *The Christian Estimate of Man* (London, 1944).

deChardin, P. T., *The Phenomenon of Man* (London, 1959).

Kümmel, W. G., *Man in the New Testament* (London, 1963).

*Laidlaw, J., *The Bible Doctrine of Man* (Edinburgh, 1895).

*Machen, J. G., *The Christian View of Man* (New York, 1937).

Mascall, E. L., *The Importance of Being Human* (London, 1959).

Niebuhr, R., *The Nature and Destiny of Man* (London, 1953).

*Orr, J., *God's Image in Man* (London, 1905).

Pittenger, N., *The Christian Understanding of Human Nature* (London, 1964).

Robinson, E. H., *Man's Estimate of Man* (London, 1964).

Robinson, H. W., *The Christian Doctrine of Man* (Edinburgh, 1926).

Scott, E. F., *Man and Society in the New Testament* (New York, 1947).

Smith, C. R., *The Bible Doctrine of Man* (London, 1951).

Stacey, W. D., *The Pauline View of Man* (London, 1956).

Wright, J. S., *What is Man?* (Exeter, 1955).

Sin

*Candlish, J., *The Biblical Doctrine of Sin* (Edinburgh, n.d.).

Greeves, F., *The Meaning of Sin* (London, 1956).

*Murray, J., *The Imputation of Adam's Sin* (Grand Rapids, U.S.A., 1959).

Müller, J., *The Christian Doctrine of Sin* 2 Vols. (Edinburgh, 1852-3).

*Orr, J., *Sin as a Problem of Today* (London, 1910).

Orchard, W. E., *Modern Theories of Sin* (London, 1909).

Tennant, F. R., *The Sources of the Doctrine of the Fall and Original Sin* (Cambridge, 1903).

——, *The Concept of Sin* (Cambridge, 1912).

——, *The Origin and Propagation of Sin* (Cambridge, 1902).

Williams, N. P., *The Ideas of the Fall and Original Sin* (London, 1927).
Robinson, N. H. G., *Faith and Duty* (London, 1950).
Smith, C. R., *The Bible Doctrine of Sin* (London, 1953).
Quell, G. et al., *Sin* (London, 1951).

Grace

*Berkoüwer, G. C., *Divine Election* (Grand Rapids, U.S.A., 1960).
*——, *Faith and Justification* (Grand Rapids, U.S.A., 1954).
*——, *Faith and Sanctification* (Grand Rapids, U.S.A., 1952).
*Buis, H., *Historic Protestantism and Predestination* (Philadelphia, U.S.A., 1958).
Chafer, L. S., *Grace* (Philadelphia, U.S.A., 1926).
Jauncey, *The Doctrine of Grace* (London, 1925).
Marshall, I. H., *Kept By the Power of God* (London, 1969).
*McDonald, H. D., *I and He* (London, 1966), chs. 5 and 6.
Moffatt, J., *Grace in the New Testament* (London, 1931).
Hardiman, O., *The Christian Doctrine of Grace* (London, 1947).
Oman, J., *Grace and Personality* (Cambridge, 1917).
Rowley, H. H., *The Biblical Doctrine of Election* (London, 1950).
Smith, C. R., *The Bible Doctrine of Grace* (London, 1956).
Taylor, V., *Forgiveness and Reconciliation* (London, 1946).
Townsend, H., *The Doctrine of Grace in the Synoptic Gospels* (London, 1919).
Whitley, W. T. (Editor), *The Doctrine of Grace* (London, 1932).
Williams, D. D., *The Spirit and the Forms of Love* (London, 1968).
Yates, A. S., *The Doctrine of Assurance* (London, 1952).

Salvation

Barclay, W., *Turning to God* (London, 1963).

*Berkoüwer, G. C., *The Work of Christ* (Grand Rapids, U.S.A., 1965).

Citron, B., *New Birth* (Edinburgh, 1951).

Crabtree, A. B., *The Restored Fellowship* (London, 1963).

*Denney, J., *The Death of Christ* (London, 1905).

*——, *The Christian Doctrine of Reconciliation* (London, 1917).

*Forsyth, P. T., *The Work of Christ* (London, 1938).

Flew, R. N., *The Idea of Perfection in Christian Theology* (Oxford, 1934).

*Green, E. M. B., *The Meaning of Salvation* (London, 1965).

*Hammond, T. C., *The New Creation* (London, 1953).

*Kevan, E. F., *Salvation* (Grand Rapids, U.S.A., 1963).

Mackintosh, H. R., *The Christian Experience of Forgiveness* (London, 1934).

*Micklem, N., *The Doctrine of our Redemption* (Oxford, 1960).

*Morris, L., *The Apostolic Preaching of the Cross* (London, 1955).

*——, *The Cross in the New Testament* (London, n.d.).

Munck, J., *Paul and the Salvation of Mankind* (London, 1959).

*Murray, J., *Redemption Accomplished and Applied* (Grand Rapids, U.S.A., 1958).

Smith, C. R., *The Bible Doctrine of Salvation* (London, 1941).

Taylor, V., *The Atonement in the New Testament* (London, 1958).

Telfer, W., *The Forgiveness of Sins* (London, 1959).

*Warfield, B. B., *The Plan of Salvation* (Grand Rapids, U.S.A., 1942).

The Kingdom of God

Bright, J., *The Kingdom of God* (New York, 1953).

Bruce, A. B., *The Kingdom of God* (Edinburgh, 1909).

Cadoux, C. J., *The Historic Mission of Jesus* (London, 1941).

Chafer, L. S., *The Kingdom in History and Prophecy* (Philadelphia, 1922).

Candlish, J., *The Kingdom of God* (Edinburgh, 1884).

Dodd, C. H., *The Parables of the Kingdom* (London, 1936).

Grant, F. C., *The Gospel of the Kingdom* (New York, 1940).

*Hodges, J. W., *Christ's Kingdom and Coming* (Grand Rapids, U.S.A., 1957).

Kümmel, W. G., *Promise and Fulfilment* (London, 1957).

*Ladd, G. E., *Crucial Questions about the Kingdom of God* (Grand Rapids, U.S.A., 1952).

*——, *The Gospel of the Kingdom* (London, 1959).

*——, *Jesus and the Kingdom* (London, 1964).

Manson, W., *Christ's View of the Kingdom of God* (London, 1918).

Mowinckel, S., *He That Cometh* (Oxford, 1956).

Otto, R., *The Kingdom of God and the Son of Man* (London, 1938).

Pannenberg, W., *Theology and the Kingdom of God* (Philadelphia, U.S.A., 1969).

Perrin, N., *The Kingdom of God in the Teaching of Jesus* (London, 1963).

*Ridderbos, H., *The Coming of the Kingdom* (Philadelphia, 1962).

Roberts, H., *Jesus and the Kingdom of God* (London, 1955).

Robertson, J. A. T., *Jesus and His Coming* (London, 1957).

Schmidt, K. L. et al., *Basileia* (London, 1958).

Schnackenburg, R., *God's Rule and Kingdom* (London, 1963).

Schweizer, E., *Lordship and Discipleship* (London, 1960).

Scott, E. F., *The Kingdom of God in the New Testament* (London, 1931).

Final Things

Adams-Brown, W., *The Christian Hope* (London, 1912).
*Anderson, R., *Human Destiny* (London, 1890).
*Baillie, J., *And the Life Everlasting* (Oxford, 1934).
Beet, Agar, J., *The Immortality of the Soul* (London, 1901).
Beasley-Murray, G. R., *Jesus and the Future* (London, 1954).
Boettner, L., *Immortality* (Philadelphia, U.S.A., 1956).
Brunner, E., *The Eternal Hope* (London, 1954).
*Buis, H., *The Doctrine of Eternal Punishment* (Grand Rapids, U.S.A., 1957).
*Brown, H. D., *Our Happy Dead* (London, 1917).
Bultmann, R., *Life and Death* (London, 1965).
Cullmann, O., *Immortality of the Soul or Resurrection of the Dead?* (London, 1956).
Dahl, M. E., *The Resurrection of the Body* (London, 1962).
Deane, A. C., *The Valley and Beyond* (London, 1936).
Dodd, C. H., *The Coming of Christ* (Cambridge, 1951).
*Forsyth, P. T., *This Life and the Next* (London, 1918).
Fyfe, J., *The Hereafter* (Edinburgh, 1890).
Glasson, T. E., *The Second Advent* (London, 1945).
Guy, H. A., *The New Testament of 'Last Things'* (Oxford, 1948).
Guinness, H. G., *Light for the Last Days* (London, 1887).
Hamilton, F. E., *The Basis of Millennial Faith* (Grand Rapids, U.S.A., 1955).
*Hodges, J. W., *Christ's Kingdom and Coming* (Grand Rapids, U.S.A., 1957).
Hughes, A., *A New Heaven and a New Earth* (London, 1958).
Kennedy, H. A. A., *St Paul's Conception of Last Things* (London, 1904).
Künneth, W., *The Theology of the Resurrection* (London, 1951).

*Ladd, G. E., *The Blessed Hope* (Grand Rapids, U.S.A., 1956).

*Lang, G. H., *World Chaos* (London, 1948).

*Manley, G. T., *The Return of Jesus Christ* (London, 1960).

*Minear, P. S., *Christian Hope and the Second Coming* (Philadelphia, 1954).

Moore, A. J., *The Parousia in the New Testament* (Leiden, 1966).

Moltmann, J., *The Theology of Hope* (London, 1967).

Müller, J. J., *When Christ Comes Again* (London, 1956).

Neville, G., *The Advent Hope* (London, 1961).

Rahner, K., *On the Theology of Death* (Edinburgh, 1961).

*Ridderbos, H., *The Coming of the Kingdom* (Philadelphia, 1962).

Robinson, J. A. T., *In the End God* (London, 1950).

Smith, C. R., *The Bible Doctrine of the Hereafter* (London, 1958).

Salmond, S. W. F., *The Christian Doctrine of Immortality* (Edinburgh, 1897).

Simon, U., *Heaven in the Christian Tradition* (London, 1958).

——, *The End is Not Yet* (London, 1964).

Staudinger, J., *Life Everlasting* (Dublin, 1964).

Scroggie, W. G., *The Lord's Return* (London, 1938).

Strawson, W., *Jesus and the Future Life* (London, 1959).

Swete, H. B., *The Life of the World to Come* (London, 1917).

*Vos, G., *The Pauline Eschatology* (Grand Rapids, U.S.A., 1953).

*Walvoord, J. F., *The Millennial Kingdom* (Findlay, Ohio, U.S.A., 1963).

Winklhofer, A., *The Coming of the Kingdom* (London, 1953).

Young, L., *What Happens After Death?* (London, n.d.).